BIG BOOK OF
HOLIDAY COOKING

Grandmother's
Pound Cake
(page 100)

BIG BOOK OF
HOLIDAY COOKING

Celebrate year-round with favorite family recipes

Oxmoor House®

BIG BOOK OF
HOLIDAY COOKING

©2012 by Gooseberry Patch
2500 Farmers Dr., #110, Columbus, Ohio 43235
1-800-854-6673, **gooseberrypatch.com**

©2012 by Time Home Entertainment Inc.
135 West 50th Street, New York, NY 10020

ISBN-13: 978-0-8487-3715-3
ISBN-10: 0-8487-3715-6
Library of Congress Control Number: 2012937205
Printed in the United States of America
First Printing 2012

Oxmoor House
VP, Publishing Director: Jim Childs
Editorial Director: Leah McLaughlin
Creative Director: Felicity Keane
Brand Manager: Vanessa Tiongson
Senior Editor: Rebecca Brennan
Managing Editor: Rebecca Benton

Gooseberry Patch Big Book of Holiday Cooking
Editor: Ashley T. Strickland
Project Editor: Sarah H. Doss
Assistant Designer: Allison Sperando Potter
Director, Test Kitchen: Elizabeth Tyler Austin
Assistant Directors, Test Kitchen: Julie Christopher,
    Julie Gunter
Test Kitchen Professionals: Wendy Ball, R.D.; Victoria E.
    Cox; Margaret Monroe Dickey; Stefanie Maloney;
    Callie Nash; Catherine Crowell Steele; Leah Van Deren
Photography Director: Jim Bathie
Senior Photo Stylist: Kay E. Clarke
Photo Stylist: Katherine Eckert Coyne
Assistant Photo Stylist: Mary Louise Menendez
Assistant Production Manager: Diane Rose

Contributors
Copy Editors: Kate Johnson, Rhonda Lee Lother
Proofreader: Polly Linthicum
Indexer: Mary Ann Laurens
Interns: Erin Bishop; Maribeth Browning; Mackenzie Cogle;
    Jessica Cox, R.D.; Laura Hoxworth; Alicia Lavender; Anna
    Pollock; Ashley White
Food Stylist: Ana Price Kelly
Test Kitchen Professionals: Tamara Goldis, Erica Hopper,
    Kathleen Royal Phillips
Photographers: Beau Gustafson, Mary Britton Senseney
Photo Stylists: Anna Pollock, Lydia Pursell

Time Home Entertainment Inc.
Publisher: Richard Fraiman
VP, Strategy & Business Development: Steven Sandonato
Executive Director, Marketing Services: Carol Pittard
Executive Director, Retail & Special Sales: Tom Mifsud
Director, Bookazine Development & Marketing: Laura Adam
Publishing Director: Joy Butts
Finance Director: Glenn Buonocore
Associate General Counsel: Helen Wan

To order additional publications, call 1-800-765-6400 or 1-800-491-0551.

For more books to enrich your life, visit **oxmoorhouse.com**
To search, savor, and share thousands of recipes, visit **myrecipes.com**

Front Cover (from left to right, top to bottom): Spinach & Clementine Salad *(page 95)*, Patriotic Cupcakes *(page 305)*,
Turtle Pumpkin Pie *(page 211)*, Two Herb-Roasted Turkey with Bourbon Gravy *(page 235)*

Page 1: Cranberry-Glazed Ham *(page 242)*

Back Cover (from left to right, top to bottom): Speedy Chicken Cordon Bleu *(page 183)*, Easiest-Ever Cheescake *(page 98)*,
Minestrone Soup *(page 230)*

Dear Friend,

Special occasions and holidays are meant to be spent with family & friends. What better way to celebrate than over a wonderful meal? This book is chock-full of scrumptious dishes from your friends at Gooseberry Patch. Whether you're hoping to add some cheer to your Christmas table, honor a graduate for his success in school, or tote along the perfect dish for a summertime picnic, this brand-new recipe collection will be your go-to source for years to come.

Warm up tummies with Creamy Wild Rice Soup (page 179) after a day of playing in the snow. Or serve up Sweet Strawberry Bread (page 73) to celebrate spring. Need a recipe for Sunday dinner at Grandma's? Zesty Roasted Chicken & Potatoes (page 183) is just the ticket. Start the first day of school off with a surprise breakfast of Rise & Shine Bacon Waffles (page 121) or French Toast Berry Bake (page 275).

If you're short on time during the hustle and bustle of the holiday season, whip up Easy Cheesy Lasagna (page 286) or Shepherd's Pie (page 190)… they'll please the whole family and are so easy to prepare! Friends will delight in a gift of Double Chocolate Mint Brownies (page 332), and knowing that they were made from the heart makes them even more special.

So join us as we celebrate all year-round…you'll find lots of homestyle recipes as well as clever tips, helpful menu suggestions and heartfelt memories. No matter the occasion, we hope *Big Book of Holiday Cooking* will inspire you.

From our kitchen to yours,

JoAnn & Vickie

Garlicky Chicken &
Redskin Potatoes (page 30)

Herbed Shrimp Tacos
(page 132)

30-Minute Chili
(page 180)

Patchwork Bean Soup
Mix (page 345)

contents

Spiced Oranges (page 51)

Company Breakfast Casserole (page 17)

Saucy Meatloaf (page 36)
Loaded Baked Potato Casserole
(page 49)

Chocolate-Cappuccino Brownies (page 57)

FIRESIDE FAVORITES

Cozy wintertime dishes that warm heart & soul

Cheese Bread Bites

Cheese Bread Bites

Make up a double batch of these yummy bites to have on hand for unexpected company...or for yourself for snacking! They're a handy snack because you can bake just a few at a time when you want them.

12-oz. loaf French bread, crusts trimmed
1 c. butter
½ lb. sharp Cheddar cheese, cubed
2 3-oz. pkgs. cream cheese, softened
4 egg whites, stiffly beaten
Optional: marinara sauce

    Cut bread into one-inch cubes; set aside. Melt butter and cheeses in a double boiler over low heat, stirring often. Remove from heat; fold in egg whites. Dip bread cubes into cheese mixture; set on greased baking sheets. Place in freezer until frozen; remove from baking sheets and store in plastic zipping bags in the freezer up to one month.
    To serve, bake frozen bites at 400 degrees for 12 minutes on greased baking sheets. Serve with marinara sauce for dipping, if desired. Serves 8 to 10.

Nola Laflin
Coral Springs, FL

I like simple and easy make-ahead recipes. This is a favorite of my grandchildren and family. When they tell me when they're flying into Florida, I start making and storing these right away! —Nola

Cheesy Pizza Fondue

My mom would make this recipe for very special occasions when we had guests over to visit...a taste takes me right back to my childhood! My sister and I got to help out by toasting the muffins.

½ lb. ground beef
1 onion, chopped
2 8-oz. cans pizza sauce
1 T. cornstarch
1½ t. dried oregano
¼ t. garlic powder
1¼ c. shredded Cheddar cheese
1 c. shredded mozzarella cheese
6 English muffins, toasted and cubed

    Brown beef with onion in a skillet over medium heat; drain. Stir in pizza sauce, cornstarch and seasonings. Add cheeses, one-third at a time, stirring until melted. Pour mixture into a fondue pot to keep warm. Serve with toasted English muffin cubes for dipping. Serves 6.

Tara Reiter-Marolf
Granger, IA

kitchen express
When chopping onions or celery, it only takes a moment to chop a little extra. Tuck them away in the freezer for a quick start to dinner another day.

Baked Jalapeño Poppers

Baked Jalapeño Poppers

We host a biweekly Bible study in our home and serve a variety of snacks to go with the study. Here's a spicy favorite!

8-oz. pkg. cream cheese, softened
1 c. shredded Cheddar cheese
1 c. shredded Monterey Jack cheese
6 slices bacon, crisply cooked and crumbled
¼ t. chili powder
¼ t. garlic powder
¼ t. salt
1 lb. jalapeño peppers, halved lengthwise and
    seeded
½ c. dry bread crumbs
Garnish: sour cream, onion dip, ranch salad
    dressing

Combine cheeses, bacon and seasonings; mix well. Spoon about 2 tablespoons of cheese mixture into each pepper half. Roll in bread crumbs to coat. Place on a greased baking sheet. Bake, uncovered, at 300 degrees for 20 minutes for spicy flavor; 30 minutes for medium flavor; 40 minutes for mild flavor. Garnish as desired. Serves 8 to 10.

Ann Aucelli
Painesville, OH

Nana's Slow-Cooker Meatballs

These meatballs have been famous for generations and begged for at parties by young & old alike.

2½ c. catsup
1 c. brown sugar, packed
2 T. Worcestershire sauce
2 lbs. ground beef
1.35-oz. pkg. onion soup mix
5-oz. can evaporated milk

Stir together catsup, brown sugar and Worcestershire sauce in a 3 to 4-quart slow cooker; cover. Turn slow cooker to high setting and allow mixture to warm while preparing meatballs. Combine remaining ingredients; mix well and form into one-inch balls. Place meatballs on an ungreased rimmed baking sheet. Bake at 325 degrees for 20 minutes; drain. Transfer meatballs to slow cooker. Turn slow cooker to low setting. Cover and cook for 2 to 3 hours, stirring gently halfway through. Makes 4 dozen.

Stephanie Norton
Saginaw, TX

Cranberry-Lime Cooler

A refreshing beverage for an autumn brunch.

6-oz. can frozen limeade concentrate, thawed
4 c. cold water
16-oz. bottle cranberry juice cocktail
¼ c. orange drink mix
ice cubes
Garnish: fresh mint sprigs

Prepare limeade with water in a large pitcher. Stir in cranberry juice and orange drink mix. Pour over ice cubes in tall mugs or glasses. Garnish each with a sprig of mint. Serves 8.

Ellie Brandel
Milwaukie, OR

old-timey fun
Serve beverages in old-fashioned Mason jars. Setting the jars inside wire drink carriers makes it easy to tote them from the kitchen to the table.

White Hot Chocolate

Serve in thick mugs with whipped cream, a dash of cinnamon or baking cocoa and a candy cane.

3 c. half-and-half, divided
⅔ c. white chocolate chips
3-inch cinnamon stick
⅛ t. nutmeg
1 t. vanilla extract
¼ t. almond extract
Garnish: whipped topping, cinnamon, candy canes

Combine ¼ cup half-and-half, white chocolate chips, cinnamon stick and nutmeg in a saucepan. Whisk over low heat until chips are melted. Remove cinnamon stick. Add remaining half-and-half. Whisk until heated throughout. Remove from heat; add extracts. Garnish with whipped topping, cinnamon and candy canes. Serves 4 to 6.

So-Simple Eggnog

When we were kids, we were allowed to drink this eggnog from the "special" glasses...that was always such a big deal to us!

½ gal. milk, divided
3.4-oz. pkg. instant vanilla pudding mix
¼ c. sugar
2 t. vanilla extract
½ t. cinnamon
½ t. nutmeg

In a large bowl or pitcher, whisk together ¾ cup milk and pudding mix until smooth. Whisk in sugar, vanilla and spices until sugar dissolves; stir in remaining milk. Chill before serving. Serves 16.

Denise Mainville
Huber Heights, OH

White Hot Chocolate

Warm Country Gingerbread Waffles

Serve with brown sugar, powdered sugar, hot maple syrup or raspberries.

2 c. all-purpose flour
1 t. cinnamon
½ t. ground ginger
½ t. salt
1 c. molasses
½ c. butter
1½ t. baking soda
1 c. buttermilk
1 egg, beaten

Combine flour, cinnamon, ginger and salt. Heat molasses and butter until butter melts. Remove from heat and stir in baking soda. Add buttermilk and egg; fold in flour mixture. Cook in a preheated, greased waffle iron according to manufacturer's instructions. Makes 9 (4-inch) waffles.

French Toast Croissants

When mornings beckon with so much to do, this breakfast is quick & easy!

⅓ c. milk
2 eggs, beaten
1 T. frozen orange juice concentrate, thawed
4 croissants, halved lengthwise
Garnish: powdered sugar

Stir together milk, eggs and orange juice in a shallow dish. Dip croissant halves into mixture, turning to coat both sides. Place in a greased skillet over medium heat; cook 2 to 3 minutes until golden on both sides. Dust with powdered sugar. Serves 4.

Kathy Grashoff
Fort Wayne, IN

Simmered Eggs in Tomatoes

Don't let the simplicity of this recipe fool you...it is delicious!

2 T. olive oil
1 c. stewed tomatoes, chopped
½ c. onion, chopped
4 eggs
salt and pepper to taste
buttered toast

Heat oil in a skillet over low heat. Place tomatoes and onion in oil; cook for 5 minutes. Drop eggs into skillet, one at a time; sprinkle with salt and pepper. Cover and simmer until eggs are cooked through as desired. Serve hot on buttered toast. Serves 2.

Janis Parr
Ontario, Canada

Company Breakfast Casserole

For a Southwestern flair, replace the mushrooms with a small can of sliced olives, use Monterey Jack cheese instead of Cheddar and serve with spicy salsa on the side. (Pictured on page 8)

16-oz. pkg. frozen shredded hashbrowns, thawed and divided
1 onion, chopped and divided
1 lb. ground pork sausage, browned and drained
1 green pepper, chopped
4-oz. can sliced mushrooms, drained
½ to 1 c. shredded Cheddar cheese, divided
1 doz. eggs, beaten
1½ c. milk
salt and pepper to taste
Optional: garlic salt to taste

Spread half of the hashbrowns in a lightly greased 13"x9" baking pan. Layer ingredients as follows: half the onion, sausage, remaining onion, green pepper, mushrooms and half the cheese. Whisk together eggs, milk and seasonings in a separate bowl. Pour egg mixture over casserole; top with remaining hashbrowns and remaining cheese. Cover with aluminum foil and refrigerate overnight.

Bake, covered, at 350 degrees for 45 to 60 minutes. Uncover and bake an additional 20 minutes, or until a knife inserted near center comes out clean. Serves 8 to 10.

Jena Buckler
Bloomington Springs, TN

time-saving trick
Make-ahead breakfast casseroles are super time-savers for busy mornings. Assemble the night before, cover and refrigerate overnight. In the morning, just pop in the oven...breakfast is served!

White Cheddar Cheese Grits

Here in Virginia, we just love grits! Try this recipe, and your family will love 'em, too.

2 c. chicken broth
2 T. butter
½ c. quick-cooking grits, uncooked
1 c. shredded white Cheddar cheese

Bring broth and butter to a boil in a saucepan over medium heat. Gradually whisk in grits and return to a boil. Reduce heat to medium-low. Simmer, stirring occasionally, for 5 minutes, or until thickened. Stir in cheese until melted. Serve immediately. Serves 4 to 6.

Tina Goodpasture
Meadowview, VA

this little light

Make some charming tealight jars...a terrific craft for kids. Brush slightly thinned craft glue over empty baby food jars and cover with small squares of tissue paper. Brush a little more thinned glue over the finished jars. When dry, pop a tealight inside. Shades of gold and yellow create a cozy glow for cold winter nights.

Rita's Turkey Hash

This is my favorite hearty breakfast to serve every Black Friday, before my sisters and I head to the mall to do some serious shopping. Add a side of leftover cranberry sauce...delish!

1 T. butter
1 T. oil
1 onion, chopped
1 red pepper, chopped
2 c. potatoes, peeled, cooked and diced
2 c. roast turkey, diced
1 t. fresh thyme
salt and pepper to taste

Melt butter with oil in a large, heavy skillet over medium heat. Add onion and pepper. Sauté until onion is tender, about 5 minutes. Add remaining ingredients. Spread out mixture in skillet, pressing lightly to form an even layer. Cook until golden on bottom. Using a spatula, turn over mixture (it doesn't need to stay in one piece). Cook until golden. Remove from heat. Spoon hash onto 4 plates. Top with Poached Eggs and serve immediately. Serves 4.

Poached Eggs:

1 T. white vinegar
4 eggs
salt and pepper to taste

Add several inches of water to a deep skillet or saucepan. Bring water to a simmer over medium-high heat. Stir in vinegar. One at a time, crack eggs into water. Cook just until whites are firm and yolks are still soft, about 3 to 4 minutes. Remove eggs with a slotted spoon. Sprinkle with salt and pepper.

Rita Morgan
Pueblo, CO

Rita's Turkey Hash

Red-Eye Gravy
& Biscuits

Brown Sugar-Glazed Bacon

1 lb. bacon
⅓ c. brown sugar, packed
1 t. all-purpose flour
½ c. pecans, finely chopped

Place a wire rack over a baking sheet. Arrange bacon slices on rack, close together but not over-lapping. Combine remaining ingredients in a bowl and sprinkle evenly over bacon. Bake at 350 degrees for about 30 minutes, until bacon is crisp and glazed. Drain on paper towels before serving. Serves 6 to 8.

Caitlin Hagy
West Chester, PA

Red-Eye Gravy & Biscuits

My grandma lived in Kentucky, and whenever we visited her, my dad would pick up a country ham to bring home. This was my favorite breakfast that my dad made for us on chilly mornings.

2 T. butter
12 slices country-style ham
1 T. all-purpose flour
1 c. strong brewed coffee
1½ T. brown sugar, packed
½ c. water
salt and pepper to taste
Optional: hot pepper sauce to taste
6 biscuits, split and buttered

Melt butter in a skillet over medium-high heat. Cook ham slices until lightly browned; remove from skillet. Add flour to drippings in skillet; cook and stir for one minute. Add coffee, brown sugar and water. Cook and stir for 3 minutes, or until thickened; return ham to skillet. Stir in seasonings. Serve ham and gravy over biscuits. Serves 6.

Stacie Avner
Delaware, OH

Angel Biscuits

There's nothing like a basket filled with tender biscuits baked from my grandmother's recipe! We've always called them biscuits, but they are really more like yeast rolls.

5 c. all-purpose flour
⅓ c. sugar
1 T. baking powder
2 t. baking soda
2 t. salt
½ c. corn oil
2½ c. buttermilk
½ c. water
2 envs. active dry yeast

Mix together flour, sugar, baking powder, baking soda and salt in a large bowl; set aside. Mix together oil and buttermilk in a separate bowl; add to flour mixture. Heat water until very warm, about 110 to 115 degrees. Dissolve yeast in warm water; add to flour mixture and mix thoroughly. Refrigerate overnight in a tightly closed container.

With floured hands, pinch off palm-size pieces of dough; tuck under sides and arrange rolls in a greased 13"x9" baking pan. Cover and let rise 40 minutes to an hour, until double in bulk. Bake at 450 degrees for 20 minutes, or until golden. Makes 2 to 3 dozen rolls.

Tara Geiger
Carrollton, TX

Butter Rum Muffins

Butter Rum Muffins

My grandson, Kanon, loves this breakfast treat...I think you will, too!

⅔ c. butter, softened
1⅓ c. sugar
3 eggs, beaten
2 T. baking powder
¼ t. salt
1 t. butter flavoring
1 t. rum extract
2 c. milk
4 c. all-purpose flour
11-oz. pkg. butterscotch chips

Blend together butter, sugar and eggs in a large bowl. Mix in baking powder, salt and flavorings. Alternately mix in milk and flour. Divide evenly into greased muffin cups, filling ⅔ full. Bake at 350 degrees for 15 to 20 minutes, until a toothpick inserted near center comes out clean. Place butterscotch chips in a small microwave-safe bowl; microwave on high 30 seconds, or until melted. Drizzle over warm muffins. Makes 2½ dozen.

Diana Krol
Nickerson, KS

Marcia's Pear Bread

You'll love this yummy bread...spread warm slices with butter or softened cream cheese.

½ c. butter
1 c. sugar
2 eggs, beaten
1 t. vanilla extract
½ t. salt
1 t. baking powder
⅛ t. nutmeg
2 c. all-purpose flour
¼ c. buttermilk or plain yogurt
1 c. pears, cored, peeled and coarsely chopped

Blend butter until smooth; stir in sugar until mixture is creamy. Add eggs and vanilla. Whisk together salt, baking powder, nutmeg and flour; stir into egg mixture alternately with buttermilk or yogurt, too. Stir in pears. Pour into a greased 9"x5" loaf pan. Bake at 350 degrees for one hour. Makes one loaf.

Marcia Marcoux
Charlton, MA

Broccoli-Cheese Cornbread

This recipe, given to me by my Aunt Ora Lee, is one I enjoy toting to potluck dinners at church and at work. (Pictured on page 24)

2 8½-oz. pkgs. cornbread mix
1½ c. cottage cheese
5 eggs, beaten
10-oz. pkg. frozen chopped broccoli, thawed
1 onion, chopped
½ c. butter or margarine, melted
1 c. shredded Cheddar cheese

Mix together all ingredients except Cheddar cheese; spread in a lightly greased 13"x9" baking pan. Bake, uncovered, at 350 degrees for 45 minutes. Sprinkle with Cheddar cheese and bake for an additional 3 minutes, or until cheese is melted. Serves about 12.

Jane Reynolds
Rowlett, TX

Snowy Day Chili
Broccoli-Cheese Cornbread
(page 23)

Snowy Day Chili

In Wisconsin, snow is inevitable, but shoveling sidewalks isn't so dreaded when there's a pot of chili simmering on the stove!

2 lbs. ground beef or venison
2 c. chopped onion
4 c. tomato sauce
4 c. water
15-oz. can kidney beans, drained and rinsed
6-oz. can tomato paste
¼ c. Worcestershire sauce
2 T. brown sugar, packed
1 T. seasoned salt
1 T. lemon juice
3 bay leaves
chili powder to taste
Optional: hot pepper sauce to taste
Garnish: shredded Cheddar cheese, chopped
    onion, sour cream, corn chips

Brown meat in a large stockpot over medium heat; drain. Stir in remaining ingredients except garnish. Reduce heat; simmer for 3 to 4 hours, stirring occasionally. Garnish as desired. Serves 8 to 10.

Kathie Poritz
Burlington, WI

serving suggestion
When serving soups and stews, stack two or three cake stands and then fill each tier with a different type of roll for guests to try.

Oven Beef Stew

This recipe is a lifesaver on busy days…just pop it in the oven and finish up your to-do list!

1½ lbs. stew beef, cubed
5 carrots, peeled and sliced
1 c. celery, chopped
2 onions, sliced
1 potato, peeled and chopped
2 14.5-oz. cans stewed tomatoes
½ c. soft bread crumbs
2 t. salt
3 T. instant tapioca, uncooked

Place beef, carrots, celery, onions and potato in a bowl. Combine remaining ingredients and add to beef mixture; blend well. Place in a greased 2½-quart Dutch oven. Cover and bake at 325 degrees for 4 hours. Serves 6.

Alice Monaghan
Saint Joseph, MO

Oven Beef Stew

Black-Eyed Pea Soup

Black-Eyed Pea Soup

Add bacon, garlic and chiles to a classic soup recipe and you get this delicious variation!

6 slices bacon
1 onion, finely chopped
1 clove garlic, minced
½ t. salt
½ t. pepper
4-oz. can chopped green chiles, drained
4 15½-oz. cans black-eyed peas, undrained
2 14½-oz. cans beef broth
10-oz. can diced tomatoes with green chiles
cornbread

Cook bacon in a Dutch oven until crisp; remove bacon, reserving drippings in pan. Crumble bacon and set aside. Add onion, garlic, salt, pepper and chiles to bacon drippings; sauté until onion is golden. Add bacon, peas, broth and tomatoes with green chiles. Increase heat to medium-high and bring to a boil; remove from heat. Serve with cornbread. Serves 12 to 14.

Down-Home Pea Soup

This slow-cooker soup is delicious year-round but is especially warming on winter days.

8 c. water
2 c. dried split peas
1½ c. celery, sliced
1½ c. carrots, peeled and sliced
1 onion, sliced
2 bay leaves
salt and pepper to taste
Optional: 1 to 2 c. cooked ham, cubed

Combine all ingredients in a 4 to 5-quart slow cooker. Cover and cook on low setting for 4 to 6 hours. Discard bay leaves before serving. Serves 8 to 10.

Jude Trimnal
Brevard, NC

Crockery Black Bean Soup

When last year's garden was full, I paired fresh veggies with pantry items in my slow cooker. This recipe was the result, and we absolutely love it!

1 T. olive oil
2 red onions, chopped
1 red pepper, chopped
1 green pepper, chopped
4 cloves garlic, minced
4 t. ground cumin
16-oz. pkg. dried black beans
1 T. canned chopped chipotle chiles
7 c. hot water
2 T. lime juice
2 t. kosher salt
¼ t. pepper
1 c. plain yogurt
½ c. plum tomatoes, seeded and chopped
Garnish: chopped fresh cilantro

Heat oil in a skillet over medium-high heat. Add onions and red and green peppers; sauté until tender. Stir in garlic and cumin; cook one minute. Use a slotted spoon to transfer mixture to a 4-quart slow cooker. Add beans, chiles and hot water. Cover and cook on high setting for 6 hours. Transfer 2 cups bean mixture to a blender. Purée bean mixture until smooth. Return mixture to slow cooker; stir in remaining ingredients except garnish. Garnish servings with cilantro. Serves 6.

Beth Kramer
Port Saint Lucie, FL

Irish Spud Soup

My kids can't wait for the weather to get colder so they can curl up with a steaming bowl of this scrumptious potato soup.

2 T. butter
2 c. onion, chopped
1 c. celery, chopped
1 t. garlic, minced
8 c. chicken broth
3½ lbs. potatoes, peeled and cubed
2 c. shredded Cheddar cheese
1 c. green onion, chopped
1½ t. salt
1 t. pepper
Garnish: shredded Cheddar cheese, sliced
    green onion

Melt butter in a stockpot over medium heat. Add onion, celery and garlic. Cook for 4 minutes, or until vegetables are softened. Add broth and potatoes; bring to a boil. Reduce heat to low. Simmer, uncovered, for about 45 minutes, stirring occasionally, or until soup is thick and only small chunks of potato remain. Add remaining ingredients except garnish; stir until cheese melts. Garnish as desired. Serves 8.

Kyle Fugate
Newburgh, IN

leftover love

Don't pass up delicious-sounding recipes that make enough to serve a farmhouse family when you only need to serve two. Leftovers are great for next-day meals. Soups, stews and casseroles make quick & easy lunches, or freeze leftovers for a heat-and-serve meal later when time is short.

Seafood Gumbo

This recipe serves a party-sized crowd. It freezes well, if you happen to have leftovers.

1 gal. water
2 lemons, sliced
3-oz. pkg. crab boil seasoning packet
3 t. salt, divided
2 lbs. unpeeled shrimp, uncooked
1 lb. bacon
1 c. all-purpose flour
2 onions, finely chopped
2 green peppers, finely chopped
4 cloves garlic, minced
1 lb. cooked ham, cubed
2 lbs. fresh crabmeat, drained and flaked
3 lbs. okra, sliced
28-oz. can whole tomatoes, undrained and
    chopped
½ c. Worcestershire sauce
1 t. pepper
hot cooked rice

Bring water, lemons, seasoning packet and one teaspoon salt to a boil in a large Dutch oven. Add shrimp and cook 3 to 5 minutes, until shrimp turn pink. Discard lemons and seasoning packet. Remove shrimp, reserving water. Peel shrimp. Chill.

Cook bacon in a large skillet until crisp; remove bacon, reserving drippings in skillet. Crumble bacon and set aside.

Add flour to drippings in skillet; cook over medium heat, stirring constantly, until caramel-colored, about 5 minutes. Stir in onion, green peppers and garlic; cook over low heat 10 minutes, or until vegetables are tender.

Add flour mixture and remaining salt to reserved water in Dutch oven. Stir in remaining ingredients except rice. Bring to a boil; reduce heat and simmer one hour and 50 minutes. Stir in chilled shrimp and cook 5 to 10 minutes. Serve gumbo over rice. Sprinkle with bacon. Makes 7½ quarts.

Seafood Gumbo

Big Bend Clam Chowder

This recipe was shared with me by my late Aunt Jo...it brings back so many wonderful memories! I loved to watch as she cut up the potatoes and onion. She always used home-canned tomatoes and fresh clams from Apalachicola, but it's good with canned clams, too.

4 c. potatoes, peeled and finely diced
1 c. onion, finely diced
2½ c. water
¾ c. salt pork, finely diced
¼ t. seasoned salt
3 c. tomatoes, finely diced
salt and pepper to taste
3 8-oz. cans minced clams, drained

Combine potatoes, onion and water in a large, heavy saucepan over medium heat. Meanwhile, cook salt pork in a skillet over medium-low heat until drippings have cooked out, being careful not to burn. Add salt pork, drippings and seasoned salt to potato mixture. Simmer until vegetables are tender. Stir in tomatoes; cook 3 to 5 minutes. Add salt and pepper. Add clams and simmer until heated through; do not boil. Serves 6 to 8.

Mary Smith
Jacksonville, FL

Simple Chicken Tetrazzini

One of my favorite recipes! It's delicious year-round and is equally good with leftover turkey.

8-oz. pkg. spaghetti, uncooked and divided
2 T. butter
2 T. all-purpose flour
salt and pepper to taste
½ c. chicken broth
1 c. milk
2 c. cooked chicken, diced
2-oz. jar chopped pimentos, drained
¼ c. shredded sharp Cheddar cheese

Divide pasta in half, reserving the remainder for a future use. Cook remaining pasta according to package directions; drain. Meanwhile, melt butter in a large saucepan over medium-low heat. Stir in flour, salt and pepper; blend until smooth. Gradually add broth and milk; blend well. Simmer until thickened, stirring constantly. Stir in chicken, pimentos and cooked spaghetti. Spoon into a lightly greased 2-quart casserole dish; sprinkle with cheese. Bake, uncovered, at 375 degrees for 15 to 25 minutes, until bubbly and cheese is melted. Serves 4 to 6.

Tonya Adams
Magnolia, KY

Garlicky Chicken & Redskin Potatoes

Roasted chicken with potatoes is a great hearty meal for cold winter days...what could be better?

8 chicken breasts
3 lbs. redskin potatoes, cut in half
20 cloves garlic, peeled
1 T. fresh thyme, chopped
salt and pepper to taste
¼ c. olive oil
Optional: fresh thyme sprigs

Place chicken in an ungreased roasting pan. Arrange potatoes and garlic around chicken. Sprinkle with seasonings and drizzle with oil. Bake, uncovered, at 425 degrees for 20 minutes. Reduce oven temperature to 375 degrees. Continue baking 45 minutes to one hour, until chicken is golden and juices run clear. Transfer chicken to a platter. Spoon potatoes and garlic around edges. Garnish with thyme sprigs, if desired. Serves 8.

Vickie
Gooseberry Patch

Garlicky Chicken &
Redskin Potatoes

Easy Chicken Divan

Busy-Day Chicken Paprikash

When my kids come home from college, this dish is what they always want me to make. It's a real comfort-food dinner!

4 to 5 chicken tenderloins
1 onion, sliced
1½ c. water, divided
2½ t. paprika
2 10¾-oz. cans cream of chicken soup
2 to 2½ T. French onion sour cream dip
hot cooked egg noodles

Sauté chicken and onion in one cup water in a large skillet over medium heat about 10 to 12 minutes. When chicken is almost done, remove and cut into bite-size pieces. Return chicken to skillet and continue cooking until done, about 3 to 5 minutes. Mix in paprika. Stir in soup; add enough of remaining water to make a semi-thick consistency. Simmer for 5 minutes. Stir in dip until smooth. Simmer just until heated through; do not boil. Serve over hot cooked noodles. Serves 6.

Bev Sajna
Rocky River, OH

Easy Chicken Divan

Quick, tasty and economical. Try it with asparagus and Swiss cheese...yum!

3 boneless, skinless chicken breasts, cooked
    and diced
10-oz. pkg. frozen chopped broccoli, cooked
    and drained
2 10¾-oz. cans cream of chicken soup
¾ c. mayonnaise
1 t. lemon juice
1 c. shredded Cheddar cheese
½ c. Italian-flavored dry bread crumbs
¼ c. butter, melted

Toss together cooked chicken and broccoli. Mix together soup, mayonnaise and lemon juice; add to chicken mixture. Pour into a greased 13"x9" baking pan; top with cheese. Toss bread crumbs in butter; sprinkle over cheese. Bake, uncovered, at 350 degrees for 25 to 30 minutes. Serves 6 to 8.

Bethi Hendrickson
Danville, PA

Nut-Crusted Baked Chicken

Everyone loves this supper...it's really good for any occasion! Just add rice pilaf and steamed, buttered broccoli for an elegant meal that's oh-so easy to prepare.

6-oz. pkg. cornbread stuffing mix
¼ c. almonds
¼ c. walnuts
¼ c. French fried onions
½ t. pepper
1 egg, beaten
3 T. warm water
10¾-oz. can cream of mushroom soup
4 boneless, skinless chicken breasts

Combine stuffing mix, almonds, walnuts, onions and pepper in a blender or food processor. Pulse until mixture is the texture of cornmeal; place in a shallow bowl. Whisk together egg and water in a separate shallow bowl. Add soup to egg mixture and beat until well blended. Dip chicken breasts into egg mixture and then into stuffing mixture until well coated. Place in a greased 13"x9" baking pan. Bake, uncovered, at 400 degrees until chicken juices run clear, about 45 minutes. Serves 4.

Micah Tannehill
Springfield, MO

Chilly-Day Chicken Pot Pie

*This is my family's favorite chicken pot pie recipe...
everyone who tries it asks me for the recipe.*

2 9-inch pie crusts
¼ c. butter or margarine
¼ c. all-purpose flour
¼ c. poultry seasoning
⅛ t. pepper
1 c. chicken broth
⅔ c. milk
2 c. cooked chicken, cubed
2 c. frozen mixed vegetables, thawed

Place one crust in an ungreased 9" pie plate; set
aside. Melt butter or margarine in a saucepan over
medium heat; stir in flour, seasoning and pepper.
Cook until mixture is smooth and bubbly. Gradually add broth and milk; bring to a boil. Reduce
heat and simmer, stirring constantly, until mixture
thickens. Stir in chicken and vegetables; cook until
heated through. Pour into pie plate. Place second
crust over filling; crimp edges and cut vents in top.
Bake at 400 degrees for 20 to 30 minutes, until
golden. Serves 4.

Jessica McAlister
Fort Worth, TX

cooking down memory lane
Use Mom's (or Grandma's) vintage
baking dishes from the 1950s to serve up
casseroles with sweet memories. If you
don't have any of hers, keep an eye out at
tag sales and thrift stores...you may find the
same kind of dishes she used.

Orange-Pecan Cornish Hens

*Great to make during the busy holiday season and
perfect served with wild rice.*

½ c. butter, melted and divided
4 1½-lb. Cornish game hens
1 t. salt
1 t. pepper
½ c. orange marmalade
¼ c. orange juice
1 t. cornstarch
½ c. chopped pecans
Garnish: orange slices

Spread one tablespoon butter equally over
hens; season with salt and pepper. Tie ends of legs
together, if desired, and place on a lightly greased
rack in a roasting pan. Bake at 400 degrees for one
hour, or until a meat thermometer inserted into
meaty part of thigh registers 180 degrees. Blend
together remaining butter, marmalade and orange
juice in a saucepan; bring to a boil. Blend together
a small amount of cornstarch and water in a bowl,
slowly adding remaining cornstarch until mixture
thickens. Slowly add cornstarch mixture to marmalade mixture, stirring constantly; add pecans.
Place hens in a greased 15"x10" jelly-roll pan. Pour
glaze over chicken and bake for 10 more minutes,
or until glaze begins to turn golden. Garnish with
orange slices. Serves 4.

Orange-Pecan
Cornish Hens

Grandma's Turkey à la King

This rich, creamy dish is so comforting!

½ c. sliced mushrooms
¼ c. butter
2 T. all-purpose flour
2 c. chicken broth
1 c. whipping cream
2 c. cooked turkey, cubed
⅔ c. frozen peas, thawed
salt and pepper to taste
6 to 8 frozen puff pastry shells, baked

Sauté mushrooms in butter in a skillet over medium-low heat until tender. Stir in flour until smooth. Whisk in broth; cook and stir until slightly thickened. Stir in remaining ingredients except puff pastry shells. Reduce heat to low; cook until thickened. Spoon into shells and serve. Serves 6 to 8.

Kelly Alderson
Erie, PA

My grandmother always served Turkey à la King with her homemade puff pastry shells. Now I use convenient bake & serve shells, but you can use split biscuits too.
—Kelly

Saucy Meatloaf

The tangy steak sauce is what gives this meatloaf its terrific flavor. (Pictured on page 8)

1½ lbs. ground beef
1 egg, beaten
1 c. soft bread crumbs
½ c. milk
3 T. red steak sauce
1¼ t. salt
⅛ t. pepper
Optional: additional red steak sauce

Combine all ingredients except additional steak sauce in a bowl; place in a lightly greased 9"x5" loaf pan. Bake at 350 degrees for one hour, brushing top with additional steak sauce, if desired. Let meatloaf stand 5 minutes before slicing. Serves 6 to 8.

Gloria Schantz
Breinigsville, PA

meatloaf sandwiches

Cut meatloaf into thick slices, wrap individually and freeze. Later, they can be thawed and rewarmed quickly for scrumptious meatloaf sandwiches at a few moments' notice.

Easy Gumbo Meatballs

*After baking, keep these warm in a slow cooker...
they're a potluck favorite!*

2 lbs. ground beef
4 slices bread, crumbled
¾ c. evaporated milk
10¾-oz. can chicken gumbo soup
10½-oz. can French onion soup
hot cooked rice
Optional: fresh parsley

Combine ground beef, crumbled bread and evaporated milk; form into one-inch balls. Arrange in an ungreased 13"x9" baking pan; pour soups on top. Bake, uncovered, at 350 degrees for 1½ hours. Serve over cooked rice. Garnish with parsley, if desired. Serves 6.

Brenda Flowers
Olney, IL

Easy Gumbo
Meatballs

Pot Roast & Dumplings

This is one of our favorite meals on a cold winter day. If you cook the roast in the slow-cooker overnight, you can make the dumplings the next morning. At the end of a busy day, dinner is practically ready!

2 c. baby carrots
5 potatoes, peeled and halved
4-lb. beef chuck roast
garlic salt and pepper to taste
2 c. water
1-oz. pkg. onion soup mix

Arrange carrots and potatoes in a 5 to 6-quart slow cooker. Place roast on top; sprinkle with garlic salt and pepper. Stir together water and soup mix in a small bowl, pour over roast. Cover and cook on low setting for 6 to 8 hours. Drain most of broth from slow cooker into a large soup pot; keep roast and vegetables warm in slow cooker. Bring broth to a boil over medium-high heat. Drop Dumplings batter into boiling broth by teaspoonfuls. Cover and cook for 15 minutes. Serve Dumplings with sliced roast and vegetables. Serves 8 to 10.

Dumplings:
2 c. all-purpose flour
½ t. salt
3 T. baking powder
1 c. light cream

Sift together dry ingredients. Add cream and stir quickly to make a medium-soft batter.

Wendy Sensing
Franklin, TN

Beef Stroganoff

With tender meat that's cooked with mushrooms and combined with a sour cream sauce, this main dish will top your family's menu list each week. Spoon over a heap of homestyle egg noodles to serve.

¼ c. all-purpose flour
1 t. paprika
½ t. salt
¼ t. pepper
1-lb. boneless sirloin steak, cubed
¼ c. butter
2 cloves garlic, minced
1 c. beef broth
½ c. water
2 c. sliced mushrooms
½ c. sour cream
hot cooked egg noodles

Combine flour, paprika, salt and pepper in a plastic zipping bag; add sirloin, shaking to coat. Melt butter in a 12" skillet over medium heat; brown sirloin with garlic. Add broth, water and mushrooms; mix well. Bring to a boil; reduce heat and simmer, covered, 30 minutes, or until meat is tender. Uncover and simmer 10 minutes, or until thickened. Stir in sour cream; heat thoroughly (do not boil). Serve over hot cooked over noodles. Serves 4.

Elizabeth Watters
Edwardsville, IL

antique flair
Recipe ads from vintage magazines make fun wall art for the kitchen. They're so easy to find at flea markets...look for ones featuring shimmery gelatin salads, golden macaroni & cheese or other favorites like the ones Mom used to make!

Beef Stroganoff

Flaky Beef Turnovers

Be sure to cut the potatoes in very small pieces so that they'll be done by the time the pastry shells are golden.

6-oz. boneless rib-eye steak, cut into large pieces
1 potato, peeled and diced
3 T. dry onion soup mix
2 T. catsup
1 t. Worcestershire sauce
1 T. fresh parsley, chopped
10-oz. pkg. puff pastry shells, thawed

Combine all ingredients except pastry shells in a large bowl. Roll out each pastry shell into a 7-inch circle on a lightly floured surface. Fill each pastry circle with approximately ¼ cup meat mixture. Lightly brush pastry edges with water. Fold circles in half and seal edges with tines of a fork. Cut several slits in the top of each turnover to vent; place on a lightly greased baking sheet. Bake at 400 degrees for 20 to 25 minutes, until golden. Serves 6.

Kay Marone
Des Moines, IA

My family loves it when I bake this dish... it's so tasty! —Kay

Roberta's Pepper Steak

A time-tested favorite...and so simple to prepare.

2 lbs. beef round steak, sliced into ½-inch strips
2 cloves garlic, pressed and divided
2 T. olive oil
2 green peppers, cut into thin strips
2 onions, coarsely chopped
8-oz. pkg. sliced mushrooms
2 t. salt
½ t. pepper
¾ c. red wine or beef broth
¼ t. to ½ t. curry powder
chicken broth, as needed

Brown steak strips and half the garlic in oil in a skillet over medium heat. Add green peppers and onions; cook until tender. Stir in mushrooms, salt, pepper and remaining garlic. Stir in wine or beef broth. Reduce heat to low and simmer for 30 minutes. Sprinkle with curry powder and continue simmering one hour. Add chicken broth as needed to prevent sticking and overbrowning. Serves 6 to 8.

Roberta Goll
Chesterfield, MI

growing garlic

While you're at the farmers' market, pick up a garlic bulb to plant in your own garden. (Don't use regular supermarket garlic, which was probably treated with a sprouting inhibitor.) Plant individual cloves two inches deep and one foot apart. When flower stalks begin to appear, cut them back. About midsummer, the leaves will begin to turn yellow...time to dig up your garlic and enjoy!

Spaghetti Casserole

This casserole feeds a crowd and can be made ahead and refrigerated before baking.

1 c. onion, chopped
1 c. green pepper, chopped
1 T. butter
28-oz. can tomatoes, undrained
4-oz. can mushrooms, drained
2 2¼-oz. cans sliced black olives, drained
2 t. dried oregano
½ t. salt
½ t. pepper
1 lb. ground beef, browned and drained
12 oz. spaghetti, cooked and drained
2 c. shredded Cheddar cheese
10¾-oz. can cream of mushroom soup
¼ c. water
¼ c. grated Parmesan cheese

Sauté onion and green pepper in butter in a large skillet until tender. Add tomatoes, mushrooms, olives, oregano, salt and pepper. Add ground beef and simmer, uncovered, for 10 minutes. Place half of the spaghetti in a greased 13"x9" baking dish. Top with half of the vegetable mixture. Sprinkle with one cup Cheddar cheese. Repeat layers. Combine soup and water; stir until smooth. Pour over casserole. Sprinkle with Parmesan cheese. Bake, uncovered, at 350 degrees for 35 minutes or until heated through. Serves 12.

Spaghetti Casserole

Special Grilled Cheese Sandwiches

These grown-up grilled cheese sandwiches are extra rich and delicious.

3-oz. pkg. cream cheese, softened
½ to ¾ c. mayonnaise
8-oz. pkg. shredded Colby Jack cheese
¾ t. garlic powder
¼ t. salt
8 slices French bread
2 T. butter, softened

Combine all ingredients except bread and butter; blend until smooth. Spread mixture on 4 slices of bread; top with remaining bread slices. Spread butter on outsides of sandwiches. Place sandwiches in a large skillet over medium heat. Cook until golden, about 4 minutes per side. Makes 4 sandwiches.

*Lynn Williams
Muncie, IN*

Heavenly Hot Ham & Cheese

This yummy recipe is from my grandmother.

1 lb. very thinly sliced deli ham
½ lb. American cheese, diced
⅓ c. mayonnaise
⅓ c. brown mustard
⅓ c. sweet pickle relish
1 onion, finely chopped
4 sandwich buns, split

Combine all ingredients except buns; spoon mixture onto buns. Wrap individually in aluminum foil; bake at 350 degrees for 20 minutes. Makes 4 sandwiches.

*Amy Jones
Buckhannon, WV*

Pepper Steak Sammies

Add your favorite steak sauce or seasoning salt... it's a great way to use leftover steak from last night's cookout, too!

1 to 1¼ lbs. beef sirloin or rib-eye steak
2 green peppers, thinly sliced
1 onion, sliced
4 cloves garlic, minced and divided
1 T. oil
salt and pepper to taste
⅓ c. butter, softened
4 French rolls, split and toasted

Grill or broil steak to desired doneness; set aside. Sauté green peppers, onion and half of garlic in oil in a skillet over medium heat until crisp-tender; drain. Slice steak thinly; add to skillet and heat through. Sprinkle with salt and pepper. Blend together butter and remaining garlic; spread over cut sides of rolls. Spoon steak mixture onto bottom halves of rolls; add tops. Makes 4 sandwiches.

*Vickie
Gooseberry Patch*

Pepper Steak Sammies

Creamy Chicken Sandwiches

Growing up in the country, we kids always looked forward to church and town socials where we could see our friends and eat some yummy homemade creamy chicken sandwiches. As we grew older, Mom would make these up and freeze portion sizes in muffin tins to send home with us as care packages!

27-oz. can chicken, drained
26-oz. can chicken broth
10¾-oz. can cream of chicken soup
1¼ c. saltine cracker crumbs
1 cube chicken bouillon
salt and pepper to taste
8 to 10 sandwich buns, split

Combine all ingredients except buns in a stockpot. Simmer over medium heat until thickened and heated through. If needed, add more cracker crumbs, or add water to thin. Serve on buns. Makes 8 to 10 sandwiches.

Karen Hazelett
Fort Wayne, IN

Mashed Root Vegetables

This side dish is so delicious, I often forget to eat whatever else is on my plate.

½ lb. sweet potatoes, peeled and cubed
½ lb. parsnips, peeled and cubed
½ lb. celery root, peeled and cubed
2 to 3 T. olive oil
salt and pepper to taste
1 lb. potatoes, peeled and cubed
3 T. butter, softened
½ c. milk

Toss together sweet potatoes, parsnips, celery root, oil, salt and pepper in a bowl. Place on an ungreased 15"x10" jelly-roll pan. Bake at 350 degrees for 20 to 25 minutes, until golden.

Meanwhile, place potatoes in a large saucepan and cover with salted water. Bring to a boil over medium-high heat; reduce heat to medium and cook until tender, about 12 to 15 minutes. Drain; return potatoes to the pot. Add roasted vegetables and butter; mash and stir until butter melts. Add milk; stir to mix. Season to taste with additional salt and pepper. Serves 6.

Mary Lou Thomas
Portland, ME

Carrot Pudding

My mother used to make this side dish for family holiday dinners in our metal gelatin mold pan. After inverting it onto a large platter, she put peas in the middle for a colorful look.

3 16-oz. pkgs. frozen sliced carrots
6 eggs, separated
1½ c. all-purpose flour
1 t. salt
1½ t. cream of tartar
1½ t. baking soda
¾ c. brown sugar, packed
¾ c. butter or margarine, softened

Prepare carrots according to package directions; drain and set aside. Beat egg whites in a bowl until stiff peaks form. In a separate bowl, sift together flour, salt, cream of tartar and baking soda. In another bowl, blend together brown sugar and butter or margarine. Beat egg yolks until light. Alternately add egg yolks and flour mixture to brown sugar mixture. Add carrots, mashing well. Fold in egg whites. Place in a greased 13"x9" baking pan. Bake, uncovered, at 350 degrees for 40 minutes. Serves 8.

Bonnie Zarch
Skokie, IL

Spicy Carrot French Fries

The sweet flavor that comes from roasting root vegetables mixed with the spicy seasonings is unusual and delicious.

2 lbs. carrots, peeled and cut into
   matchsticks
4 T. olive oil, divided
1 T. seasoned salt
2 t. ground cumin
1 t. chili powder
1 t. pepper
ranch salad dressing

Place carrots in a large plastic zipping bag. Sprinkle with 3 tablespoons oil and seasonings; toss to coat. Drizzle remaining oil over a baking sheet; place carrots in a single layer on sheet. Bake, uncovered, at 425 degrees for 25 to 35 minutes, until carrots are golden. Serve with salad dressing for dipping. Serves 4 to 6.

Kelly Gray
Weston, WV

My children didn't know until they were almost grown that this dish was healthy for you, or even that it was a vegetable! —Kelly

Spicy Carrot French Fries

Cheesy Cauliflower

Use spicy brown mustard for a bold flavor!

1¼ t. mayonnaise
1¼ t. mustard
1 head cauliflower, chopped and cooked
¼ c. butter, sliced
¾ c. grated Parmesan cheese

Combine mayonnaise and mustard in a small mixing bowl. Place cauliflower in an ungreased 2-quart casserole dish; spread with mustard mixture and dot with butter. Sprinkle with cheese. Bake, uncovered, at 375 degrees for 30 minutes. Serves 4 to 6.

John Alexander
New Britain, CT

Crispy French Fried Parsnips

My mom knew how important it was to get us to eat veggies and looked for new ways to serve them. We found we liked them this way…"fried" in the oven!

2 lbs. parsnips, peeled and cut into strips
3 T. olive oil
½ t. sea salt or garlic salt
chili powder to taste

Toss parsnip strips in oil. Place on ungreased baking sheets and sprinkle with seasonings. Bake at 350 degrees for 30 minutes, turning halfway through, or until tender. Serves 6 to 8.

Bev Fisher
Mesa, AZ

Roasted Brussels Sprouts

Orange zest and juice give these Brussels sprouts a pleasing hint of citrus.

1 T. orange juice
2 t. olive oil
1 t. grated orange zest
1 lb. Brussels sprouts, halved
½ t. salt
¼ t. pepper
Garnish: orange zest strips

Combine orange juice, olive oil and orange zest in a small bowl. Place Brussels sprouts on a 15"x10" jelly-roll pan coated with non-stick vegetable spray; drizzle orange juice mixture over sprouts and toss gently to coat. Sprinkle with salt and pepper. Bake at 450 degrees for 15 to 20 minutes, until edges of sprouts look lightly browned and crisp. Garnish with orange zest strips. Serves 4.

paint to perfection

Vintage glass milk bottles and vases can be dressed up with paint...many craft paints are made just for glass. Add festive polka dots and stripes in old-fashioned colors or create a whimsical checkerboard.

Roasted Brussels Sprouts

Golden Crumb Broccoli Casserole

If you like, use six cups steamed fresh broccoli instead of frozen broccoli.

10¾-oz. can cream of mushroom soup
¼ c. mayonnaise
1 c. shredded Cheddar cheese
1½ t. lemon juice
3 10-oz. pkgs. frozen broccoli, cooked and drained
1 c. cheese crackers, crushed

Combine soup, mayonnaise, cheese and lemon juice in a large bowl. Add broccoli and toss well. Transfer mixture to a greased, shallow 1½-quart casserole dish. Top with crackers. Bake, uncovered, at 350 degrees for 35 minutes, or until hot and bubbly. Serves 6 to 8.

Pam Glover
Castle Rock, CO

"I've been making this saucy broccoli dish for special occasions for about 20 years now, and it's still a favorite! Even people who are not crazy about broccoli, like my husband, enjoy it. —Pam"

Golden Crumb Broccoli Casserole

Good-for-You Southern Greens

On a wonderful trip down to North Carolina, our friends took us for authentic eastern North Carolina barbecue. We had some of the most delicious food we'd ever eaten. My husband loved the Southern collard greens but not all the fat they were cooked with. This recipe is my effort to make them a bit more healthy but still serve up that down-home country flavor.

½ c. cooked ham, finely chopped
½ c. onion, finely chopped
1 bunch kale, trimmed
½ c. chicken broth
⅛ t. salt
⅛ t. pepper
red wine vinegar to taste

Cook ham in a large skillet over medium heat until slightly browned. Add remaining ingredients except vinegar. Cover; simmer for 15 minutes, or until kale turns soft and dark. Drizzle with vinegar to taste. Serves 4 to 6.

Aubrey Dunne
Piscataway, NJ

Loaded Baked Potato Casserole

All your favorite baked potato toppings are mixed together to create one fabulous casserole that's bursting with flavor. Save time by microwaving your potatoes on high about 15 to 20 minutes…you can even leave the skins on. (Pictured on page 8)

3 lbs. potatoes, peeled, cubed and boiled
16-oz. container sour cream
½ c. butter, melted
8-oz. pkg. shredded sharp Cheddar cheese
5 slices bacon, crisply cooked and crumbled
Optional: additional shredded sharp Cheddar
   cheese

Mash together potatoes, sour cream and butter. Spoon mixture into a lightly greased 13"x9" baking dish; stir in cheese and bacon. Top with additional cheese, if desired. Bake, uncovered, at 350 degrees for 20 minutes, or until thoroughly heated and cheese is melted. Serves 6 to 8.

Shannon Franklin
Hartsville, SC

Mushroom-Rice Pilaf

My mother made this rice dish for as long as I can remember. We all loved its buttery onion-and-mushroom flavor. Now it's a favorite of mine for family meals, covered-dish dinners and picnics.

½ c. butter, sliced
1½ c. long-cooking rice, uncooked
10½-oz. can French onion soup
1¼ c. water
1 cube beef bouillon, crumbled
7-oz. can sliced mushrooms, drained

Place butter in an 11"x7" baking pan; place pan in a 350 degree oven until butter is melted. Stir in uncooked rice until evenly coated. Add remaining ingredients and stir slowly until well mixed. Bake, covered, at 350 degrees for 40 minutes, stirring occasionally. Serves 6.

Cathy Toogood
Clinton, PA

Spinach-Pecan Salad

Spinach-Pecan Salad

1 T. butter or margarine
1 T. brown sugar, packed
½ c. pecan halves
7-oz. pkg. baby spinach, washed
1 Granny Smith apple, cored and thinly sliced
½ c. crumbled blue cheese
3 T. olive oil
2 T. white vinegar
⅛ t. salt
⅛ t. pepper

Melt butter or margarine and sugar in a small skillet over low heat, stirring constantly. Add pecan halves; cook 2 to 3 minutes, turning to coat. Remove coated pecans from skillet and cool on wax paper.

Toss spinach, apple, cheese and pecans in a serving bowl. Whisk together oil, vinegar, salt and pepper; drizzle over salad, tossing gently to coat. Serves 4.

Vickie
Gooseberry Patch

Warm Bacon Salad

Toss together and enjoy.

1 head lettuce, torn
¼ to ½ c. vinegar
4 slices bacon, crisply cooked and crumbled
salt and pepper to taste

Place lettuce in a large serving bowl. Heat vinegar and bacon in a large saucepan until boiling; add to lettuce and toss to coat. Return to serving bowl. Sprinkle with salt and pepper. Serves 6 to 8.

Elaine Conway
Buffalo, NY

Spiced Oranges

This is an easy fruit side that can also be an unusual topping for a salad or even ice cream. In a hurry? Substitute drained canned mandarin oranges. (Pictured on page 8)

1 T. powdered sugar
1 T. lemon juice
¼ t. cinnamon
2½ c. oranges, peeled and thinly sliced
¼ c. slivered almonds
2½ T. chopped dates

Mix together powdered sugar, lemon juice and cinnamon in a medium bowl until well blended. Add oranges and toss to coat evenly. Cover and chill for 20 minutes. Just before serving, stir in almonds and dates. Serves 4.

Kim Hinshaw
Cedar Park, TX

Festive Broccoli Salad

This cold broccoli dish is super in the summer with burgers or steaks and gorgeous at Christmas served in a vintage crystal bowl from Grandma.

2 bunches broccoli, chopped into flowerets
1 red onion, chopped
½ to ¾ c. sweetened dried cranberries
3-oz. jar bacon bits
1 c. mayonnaise
2 T. red wine vinegar
½ c. sugar

Mix together broccoli, onion, cranberries and bacon bits in a large bowl. Whisk together remaining ingredients in a separate bowl and pour over broccoli mixture just before serving. Toss well. Serves 8.

Carol Shrum
Gastonia, NC

sew easy!

Aprons are a great project for a beginning seamstress...who wouldn't love a gift of a sweet or spunky new apron? There are lots of simple patterns and charming fabrics available. If you're making an apron for a child, use the scraps to make a tiny apron for her favorite doll too.

Christmas Cherry-Berry Pie

Christmas Cherry-Berry Pie

The cranberry sauce adds a special flavor to the all-time favorite cherry pie.

21-oz. can cherry pie filling
16-oz. can whole-berry cranberry sauce
¼ c. sugar
3 T. quick-cooking tapioca, uncooked
1 t. lemon juice
¼ t. cinnamon
2 T. butter
2 T. milk

Combine all ingredients except butter and milk; let stand 15 minutes. Divide Flaky Pastry in half; set one half aside. Roll one half of the dough out and place into a 9" pie plate; add filling mixture. Dot with butter. Roll remaining dough into a 12-inch circle; cut into ¾-inch-wide strips. Lay strips on pie at one-inch intervals; fold back alternate strips as you weave crosswise strips over and under. Trim crust even with outer rim of pie plate. Dampen edge of crust with water; fold crust edge over strips, seal and crimp. Brush lattice with milk. Bake at 400 degrees for 40 to 45 minutes, covering edge of crust with aluminum foil after 15 minutes to prevent browning. Serves 8.

Flaky Pastry:

3 c. all-purpose flour
1 c. plus 1 T. shortening
⅓ c. cold water
1 egg, beaten
1 T. vinegar
½ t. salt

Blend together flour and shortening. Add remaining ingredients; blend with an electric mixer on low speed.

Joyce LaMure
Reno, NV

Cinnamon Pear Crisp

I combined several recipes to come up with the perfect formula. My daughter loves helping me with this, because pears are softer and easier to peel and chop than apples.

3 c. Bartlett pears, peeled, cored and sliced
3 T. water
1 T. lemon juice
½ c. sugar, divided
½ c. plus 2 T. all-purpose flour, divided
1 t. cinnamon, divided
5 T. chilled butter
¼ c. brown sugar, packed

Combine pears, water, lemon juice, ¼ cup sugar, 2 tablespoons flour and ½ teaspoon cinnamon in a bowl. Toss to mix. Spread in a lightly greased 8"x8" baking pan. Cut butter into brown sugar and remaining sugar, flour and cinnamon in a separate bowl until crumbly. Sprinkle over pear mixture. Bake at 350 degrees for 45 minutes, or until pears are tender. Serves 6.

Elizabeth Shultz
Ankeny, IA

on-hand à la mode

Scoops of ice cream are perfect alongside warm apple dumplings, cobblers and pies. To make them ahead of time, simply scoop servings, arrange on a baking sheet and pop into the freezer. When frozen, store scoops in a freezer bag and then remove as many as needed at dessert time.

Cherry Brownie Cobbler

I found this recipe while looking for something new to make for a Sunday dessert. Your friends & family will love this cobbler…it's delicious! The chocolate and cherries really complement each other.

20-oz. pkg. brownie mix
½ c. water
½ c. oil
1 egg, beaten
21-oz. can cherry pie filling
¼ c. butter, softened
8½-oz. pkg. yellow cake mix
Garnish: vanilla ice cream

Prepare brownie mix according to package directions, using water, oil and egg. Spread batter in a lightly greased 13"x9" baking pan. Bake at 350 degrees for 15 minutes; remove from oven. Spread pie filling over brownie layer; set aside. Cut butter into dry cake mix until crumbly. Sprinkle mixture over pie filling. Return to oven and bake an additional 45 to 50 minutes, until filling is set. Cool completely; cut into squares. Serve topped with scoops of ice cream. Serves 10 to 12.

Amy Hunt
Traphill, NC

Pumpkin Gingerbread Trifle

Pumpkin Gingerbread Trifle

Something different from that same old pumpkin pie! This luscious dessert goes quickly at every covered-dish supper…try it and see!

14½-oz. pkg. gingerbread cake mix
3.4-oz. pkg. instant vanilla pudding mix
2 c. milk
15-oz. can pumpkin
½ t. cinnamon
16-oz. container frozen whipped topping,
    thawed and divided
3 1.4-oz. chocolate-covered toffee candy bars,
    crushed

Prepare and bake cake mix according to package directions. Cool; tear or cut cake into large chunks and set aside. Whisk together dry pudding mix and milk for 2 minutes, or until thickened; gently stir in pumpkin and cinnamon. Layer half each of cake chunks, pudding mixture and whipped topping in 12 tall glasses. Repeat layers, ending with topping. Garnish with crushed candy bars. Cover and refrigerate at least 3 hours before serving. Serves 12.

Cathy Forbes
Hutchinson, KS

Moist Chocolate Cake

I got this recipe from my mother, who got it from her mother, who we believe got it from her mother! Now I'm sharing it with my own soon-to-be-married daughter. It has been baked for many family birthdays and shared with co-workers, too...everyone who tries this cake requests the recipe!

2 c. sugar
½ c. shortening
2 eggs, beaten
2 c. all-purpose flour
1 t. salt
1 t. baking powder
1 T. baking soda
⅔ c. baking cocoa
2 c. boiling water
1 t. vanilla extract
Garnish: favorite frosting
Optional: shredded coconut

Blend together sugar, shortening and eggs in a large bowl. Add flour, salt, baking powder and baking soda; beat well. Add cocoa, water and vanilla; pour into a greased 13"x9" baking pan. Bake at 350 degrees for 25 to 30 minutes, until a toothpick inserted near center comes out clean. Cool; garnish as desired. Serves 8 to 10.

Suzanne Ruminski
Johnson City, NY

Coconutty Pecan Frosting

This scrumptious topping is perfect for German chocolate cake.

1 c. evaporated milk
1 c. agave syrup or sugar
3 egg yolks
½ c. butter
1 t. vanilla extract
2 c. sweetened flaked coconut
1½ c. chopped pecans

Combine all ingredients except coconut and pecans in a saucepan over medium-low heat. Cook for about 12 minutes, until thickened, stirring constantly. Remove from heat. Stir in coconut and pecans; beat until cool. Makes about 6 cups.

Sarah Mae Emack
Hildale, UT

gorgeous garnish
Decorate cakes and trifles with a sparkling bunch of sugared grapes...it's easier than it looks, and it's so pretty on a dessert buffet. Brush grapes with light corn syrup and then sprinkle generously with sanding sugar and let dry.

Peppermint Ice Cream

Christmas to me: sitting in front of the Christmas tree after decorating it, my mom sitting in my dad's lap, Christmas carols on the radio, us kids lined up on the couch, each with a bowl of peppermint ice cream, and no one saying a word, just admiring the glow of the pretty lights and the twinkle of tinsel...magical!

1 c. milk
⅔ c. sugar
2 c. whipping cream
½ t. vanilla extract
½ t. peppermint extract
⅔ c. peppermint candies, crushed
Optional: peppermint sticks

Whisk together milk and sugar until sugar is completely dissolved. Add cream and extracts. Pour into an ice cream maker. Churn about 20 to 25 minutes, according to manufacturer's instructions, until thick and creamy. Add crushed peppermint candies; churn an additional 5 minutes. Garnish, if desired. Makes 1½ quarts.

Tori Willis
Champaign, IL

Peppermint Ice Cream

Delectable Date-Nut Cookies

My great-grandmother always kept these sweet date-filled cookies in her freezer for when company would drop by. You couldn't leave her house without taking home a care package of these cookies!

1 c. butter or margarine, softened
2 c. brown sugar, packed
3 eggs, beaten
4 c. all-purpose flour
1 t. baking soda
⅛ t. salt

Blend together butter or margarine and brown sugar. Add remaining ingredients; mix well. Cover and chill dough for one hour; divide into 4 parts. Roll out each part ½-inch thick on a floured surface. Spread with Date Filling; roll up, jelly-roll fashion. Chill again. Cut roll into ¼-inch-thick slices; place on lightly greased baking sheets. Bake at 400 degrees for 12 minutes. Makes 2 dozen.

Date Filling:

1 lb. dates, chopped
½ c. water
½ c. sugar
½ c. black walnuts, chopped

Combine dates, water and sugar in a saucepan over medium-low heat. Cook 5 minutes, stirring frequently. Add walnuts; cool.

Shannon Bishop
Kingsport, TN

Chocolate-Cappuccino Brownies

Chewy and chocolatey together...delicious! (Pictured on page 8)

½ c. butter, melted
1 c. brown sugar, packed
2 T. instant coffee granules
3 eggs, lightly beaten
1 t. vanilla extract
½ c. brewed coffee, cooled
1 t. baking powder
½ t. salt
1¼ c. all-purpose flour, sifted
⅓ c. plus 1 T. baking cocoa
1 c. walnuts, chopped
1 c. semi-sweet chocolate chips
Garnish: powdered sugar

Combine butter, brown sugar and coffee granules in a bowl; blend well. Add eggs, vanilla and cooled coffee; stir. Combine baking powder, salt, flour and cocoa in a separate bowl; add to butter mixture. Stir in walnuts and chocolate chips. Pour batter into a greased 13"x9" baking pan. Bake at 350 degrees for 25 to 30 minutes. Let cool and cut into squares. Dust with powdered sugar before serving. Makes 1½ to 2 dozen.

Stuffed Strawberries (page 60)

Egg Salad Minis (page 86)

Spinach & Clementine Salad (page 95)

Mexican Tea Cookies (page 105)

IN THE GARDEN

Sensational spring favorites everyone will love

Lynda's Spinach-Feta Dip

This is a favorite dip enjoyed with bread cubes or crackers. Try garnishing with some farm-fresh chopped tomatoes.

8-oz. container Greek yogurt
¾ c. crumbled feta cheese
¼ c. cream cheese, softened
¼ c. sour cream
1 clove garlic, pressed
1½ c. baby spinach, finely chopped
1 T. fresh dill, minced, or 1 t. dill weed
⅛ t. pepper
Optional: additional fresh dill, minced
pita or bagel chips

Combine yogurt, cheeses, sour cream and garlic in a food processor. Process until smooth, scraping sides once. Spoon yogurt mixture into a bowl; stir in spinach, dill and pepper. Cover and refrigerate for several hours, until chilled. Let stand for 10 minutes at room temperature before serving. Garnish with additional dill, if desired. Serve with chips. Makes 2 cups.

Lynda McCormick
Burkburnett, TX

Stuffed Strawberries

Try using pecans in place of the walnuts for added variety. (Pictured on page 58)

20 strawberries, hulled and divided
8-oz. pkg. cream cheese, softened
¼ c. walnuts, finely chopped
1 T. powdered sugar
Optional: fresh mint leaves

Dice 2 strawberries; set aside. Cut a thin layer from the stem end of the remaining strawberries, forming a base. Starting at opposite end of strawberry, slice into 4 wedges, being careful not to slice through the base; set aside.

Beat remaining ingredients except mint together until fluffy; fold in diced strawberries. Spoon 1½ tablespoonfuls into the center of each strawberry. Refrigerate until ready to serve. Garnish with fresh mint leaves, if desired. Makes 18.

Barbara Parham Hyde
Manchester, TN

Marinated Shrimp Appetizer

If you're looking for a really special appetizer for your party, this is it! It's delicious but simple to prepare.

2 onions, thinly sliced
1½ c. oil
1½ c. white vinegar
½ c. sugar
¼ c. capers with juice
1½ t. celery seed
1½ t. salt
2 lbs. medium shrimp, cooked
    and peeled with tails intact

Combine all ingredients except shrimp in a large bowl; mix well. Add shrimp. Cover and refrigerate for at least 6 hours, stirring about every hour. Drain shrimp, discarding marinade. Arrange shrimp on a serving platter. Serves 8 to 10.

Gail Konschak
Millville, NJ

I'm asked for the recipe every time I serve it! —Gail

Marinated Shrimp
Appetizer

Three-Cheese Artichoke Bites

Mini appetizers filled with Cheddar, Parmesan and mozzarella cheese...scrumptious!

1 onion, chopped
1 clove garlic, minced
1 T. oil
2 6½-oz. jars marinated artichokes, drained
    and chopped
6 eggs, beaten
1 c. shredded Cheddar cheese
1 c. shredded mozzarella cheese
1 c. grated Parmesan cheese
½ t. Italian seasoning
¼ c. fresh parsley, chopped
¼ t. pepper
⅛ t. Worcestershire sauce
⅛ t. hot pepper sauce
¼ c. Italian-flavored dry bread crumbs
Optional: additional fresh parsley, chopped

Sauté onion and garlic in oil in a skillet over medium heat until tender; drain and set aside. Combine artichokes, eggs, cheeses, seasonings and sauces in a large bowl; mix well. Stir in onion mixture and bread crumbs. Fill greased mini muffin cups ⅔ full. Bake at 325 degrees for 15 to 20 minutes, until firm and golden. Serve warm. Sprinkle with additional parsley, if desired. Makes 3½ to 4 dozen.

Della Jones
Georgetown, KY

choosing 'chokes
To choose the best artichokes, look for ones that are dark green and heavy with tightly closed leaves. If they look dry or the leaves are open, the artichokes will be tough.

Incredible Mini Burger Bites

My family adores these...yours will, too! We make them for football parties and summer get-togethers.

2 lbs. lean ground beef
1½-oz. pkg. onion soup mix
2 eggs, beaten
½ c. dry bread crumbs
3 T. water
½ t. garlic salt
1 t. pepper
24 dinner rolls, split
6 slices American cheese, quartered
Garnish: catsup, mustard, lettuce leaves,
    thinly sliced onion, dill pickles

Mix together all ingredients except rolls, cheese and garnish in a bowl; refrigerate for one hour. Spread meat mixture over a greased large baking sheet. Cover with plastic wrap and roll out evenly with a rolling pin. Discard plastic wrap; bake at 400 degrees for 12 minutes. Slice into 24 squares with a pizza cutter. Top each roll with a burger square, a cheese slice and desired garnishes. Makes 24 mini sandwiches.

Megan Besch
Omaha, NE

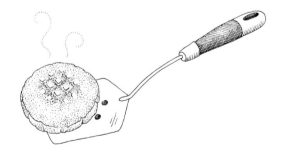

Incredible Mini Burger Bites

Grand Ma-Ma's Deviled Eggs

The best method for boiling eggs is to place them in a single layer in a saucepan and add enough water to cover one inch above the eggs. Bring water to a boil; immediately cover pan and remove from heat. Let eggs sit, covered, 15 minutes. Drain and immediately place eggs under cold running water. (Pictured on page 80)

4 eggs, hard-boiled, peeled and halved
1½ t. vinegar
½ t. dry mustard
¼ t. salt
⅛ t. pepper
½ t. sugar
1½ T. butter, melted
¼ t. Worcestershire sauce
Garnish: paprika

   Scoop egg yolks into a bowl. Arrange egg whites on a serving platter; set aside. Mash yolks well with a fork. Add remaining ingredients except paprika; mix well. Spoon into egg whites; sprinkle with paprika. Serves 8.

Maureen Gillet
Manalapan, NJ

"This recipe, which was handed down to me more than 30 years ago, is in memory of my very special mother-in-law, Charlotte." —Maureen

Minty Orange Iced Tea

Sometimes I find ginger mint or pineapple mint at the farmers' market and always pick up a bunch. It's fun to try a new herb in this tea recipe.

6 c. water
8 teabags
¼ c. fresh mint, chopped
3 T. sugar
2 c. orange juice
juice of 2 lemons
ice

   Bring water to a boil in a saucepan. Remove from heat and add teabags, mint and sugar; steep for 20 minutes. Discard teabags; strain out mint. Chill for at least 2 hours. Pour into a large pitcher; add juices. Serve in tall glasses over ice. Serves 6 to 8.

Barb Stout
Delaware, OH

Chrissy's Ravishing Rhubarb Slush

My good friend, Chrissy, gave me this recipe.

8 c. rhubarb, sliced
2 qts. water
6-oz. pkg. strawberry gelatin mix
½ c. lemon juice
3 c. sugar
2 2-ltr. bottles lemon-lime soda, chilled

   Combine rhubarb and water in a large pot; bring to a boil. Cook for 15 to 20 minutes. Strain, reserving juice. Add gelatin mix to juice; stir in lemon juice and sugar. Pour into a freezer-safe container. Freeze, stirring every couple of hours, until set. Spoon slush into glasses, filling ½ full; pour soda over top, filling glasses. Serves 25 to 30.

Jen Sell
Farmington, MN

Sweetheart Shakes

Surprise your sweetheart with a frosty treat!

3 c. milk, divided
1 c. vanilla ice cream, softened
3½-oz. pkg. instant vanilla pudding mix,
    divided
1 c. strawberry ice cream, softened
3 drops red food coloring

Pour 1½ cups milk into blender; add vanilla ice cream and ⅓ of the package of instant pudding mix. Cover; blend on high until smooth, about 15 seconds. Pour into four 8-ounce freezer-safe glasses; freeze for 30 minutes. Pour remaining ingredients into blender; cover and blend until smooth, about 15 seconds. Pour into glasses on top of vanilla portion and serve. Serves 4.

Jessica Parker
Mulvane, KS

Grandma McKindley's Waffles

Grandma McKindley's Waffles

You can't go wrong with an old-fashioned waffle breakfast...the topping choices are endless!

2 c. all-purpose flour
1 T. baking powder
¼ t. salt
2 eggs, separated
1½ c. milk
3 T. butter, melted

Sift together flour, baking powder and salt; set aside. Beat egg whites with an electric mixer at high speed until stiff; set aside. Stir together egg yolks, milk and melted butter; add to dry ingredients, stirring just until moistened. Fold in egg whites. Ladle batter by ½ cupfuls onto a lightly greased preheated waffle iron; cook according to manufacturer's instructions. Makes 8 to 10 waffles.

Nicole Millard
Mendon, MI

"My great-grandmother lived to be almost 100 years old. She was a genuinely kind person as well as a great cook. She made her home such a nice place to visit." —Nicole

Rise & Shine Sandwiches

Sure, you could get these from your local drive-through, but it's easy to make them at home...and you can adapt them to your own taste!

2¼ c. buttermilk biscuit baking mix
½ c. water
8 pork sausage breakfast patties
8 eggs, beaten
1 T. butter
salt and pepper to taste
8 slices American cheese

Combine biscuit mix with water in a bowl until just blended. Turn out onto a floured surface and knead for one minute. Roll out to ½-inch thickness. Cut out 8 biscuits with a 3-inch round biscuit cutter. Arrange on an ungreased baking sheet. Bake at 425 degrees for 8 to 10 minutes, until golden. Meanwhile, brown sausage patties in a skillet over medium heat; drain. Scramble eggs in butter in a separate skillet over low heat, to desired doneness; season with salt and pepper. Split biscuits; top each biscuit bottom with a sausage patty, a spoonful of eggs and a cheese slice. Add biscuit tops and serve immediately. Makes 8 sandwiches.

Dale Duncan
Waterloo, IA

less is best!
For the flakiest biscuits, stir the ingredients just to moisten and gently roll or pat the dough...don't overmix it.

Mile-High Buttermilk Biscuits

My secret? Use a sharp biscuit cutter and don't twist it when cutting out your biscuits…you'll be amazed how high they rise!

2 c. all-purpose flour
1 T. baking powder
1 t. salt
½ c. lard or shortening, chilled
⅔ to ¾ c. buttermilk
¼ c. butter, melted

Mix together flour, baking powder and salt. Cut in lard or shortening until mixture is crumbly. Stir in buttermilk until incorporated and dough leaves sides of bowl. Dough will be sticky. Knead dough 3 to 4 times on a lightly floured surface. Roll out to ½-inch thickness, about 2 to 4 passes with a rolling pin. Cut dough with a biscuit cutter, pressing straight down with cutter. Place biscuits on a parchment paper–lined baking sheet. Bake at 500 degrees for 8 to 10 minutes. Brush tops of warm biscuits with melted butter. Makes about one dozen.

Staci Meyers
Montezuma, GA

Sawmill Sausage Gravy

1 lb. ground pork sausage
2 T. all-purpose flour
1½ c. milk
salt and pepper to taste

Brown sausage in a skillet over medium heat. Drain on paper towels, reserving drippings in skillet. Add flour to reserved drippings and stir until browned. Slowly whisk in milk; cook and stir until smooth and thickened. Thin with hot water, if needed. Stir sausage into gravy; season with salt and pepper. Makes 3 cups.

Gretchen Phillips
Redkey, IN

Garden-Fresh Frittata

Pick vegetables fresh from your garden for this delicious meal!

3 egg whites
1 egg
2 T. chives, chopped
⅛ t. salt
⅛ t. pepper
½ c. red skin potatoes, cubed
½ c. broccoli flowerets
¼ c. yellow pepper, chopped
⅓ c. water
½ t. canola oil
Garnish: chives, diced tomatoes, grated
    Cheddar cheese

Beat together egg whites, egg, chives, salt and pepper until thoroughly combined; set aside. Add potatoes to a lightly greased oven-proof skillet; sauté 5 to 6 minutes, until browned. Add broccoli, yellow pepper and water; cover skillet with lid. Cook 3 minutes, or until potatoes are tender; remove cover and allow liquid to evaporate. Add oil to skillet, thoroughly coating all vegetables. Pour egg mixture over vegetables; allow to set slightly and then stir. Cover skillet and cook frittata 3 minutes, until eggs are set but not dry. Remove lid from skillet and place skillet under broiler, allowing the top to brown. Garnish as desired. Serves 4.

Garden-Fresh Frittata

Buttery Scones

Creamy Scrambled Eggs & Chives

Spoon onto buttered toast for a scrumptious light meal that's ready in a jiffy!

8 eggs
2 T. fresh chives, chopped
½ t. salt
¼ t. pepper
¼ c. water
2 t. butter
½ c. cream cheese, diced

Whisk eggs together with chives, salt, pepper and water; set aside. Melt butter in a skillet over medium-high heat; add egg mixture. As eggs begin to set, push them gently toward center with a spatula so that uncooked egg can flow toward sides of skillet. When eggs are partially set, add cream cheese. Continue cooking for one more minute, or until eggs are set but still moist, stirring occasionally. Serves 4.

Regina Vining
Warwick, RI

Buttery Scones

Serve warm with butter, honey, jam and, of course, your favorite tea!

1 c. buttermilk
1 egg
2 to 3 T. sugar
3½ c. all-purpose white flour, divided
2 t. baking powder
1 t. baking soda
½ t. salt
½ c. butter, melted
½ c. raisins

Beat buttermilk, egg and sugar with an electric mixer at medium speed. Sift 3 cups of flour with baking powder, baking soda and salt. Add two-thirds of the flour mixture to the buttermilk mixture and stir well. Gradually add melted butter, stirring well; add remaining flour mixture. Add raisins and a bit more flour if needed. Knead dough on a floured surface 2 to 3 times. Cut dough into 3 parts. Form each into a 1½-inch-thick circle and cut into 4 equal parts. Place on a greased baking sheet. Bake at 400 degrees for 15 minutes, or until tops are golden. Makes one dozen.

Quick Poppy Seed Muffins

Such an easy recipe! These are terrific at breakfast, with tea or for after-school snacks.

18¼-oz. pkg. lemon cake mix with pudding
½ c. poppy seed
Garnish: sugar

Prepare cake batter according to package directions. Add poppy seed; mix well. Fill greased muffin cups ⅔ full. Top each muffin with a sprinkle of sugar. Bake at 350 degrees for about 8 to 10 minutes, until a toothpick inserted near center comes out clean. Makes 2 dozen muffins.

Brenda Trnka
Manitoba, Canada

Orange Blossom Honey Butter

This is so yummy spread on hot muffins...what a treat!

½ c. butter, softened
2 T. honey
1 T. orange zest

Beat butter in a small bowl until light and fluffy. Beat in honey and orange zest until well blended. Cover and refrigerate. Makes ½ cup.

Sharon Demers
Dolores, CO

Orange Biscuits

My grandmother kept a journal and always included lots of recipes alongside her memories. I remember her always serving these with ham...oh, the aroma from the kitchen was wonderful!

½ c. orange juice
¾ c. sugar, divided
½ c. butter, divided
2 t. orange zest
2 c. all-purpose flour
1 t. baking powder
½ t. salt
⅓ c. shortening
¾ c. milk
½ t. cinnamon

Combine orange juice, ½ cup sugar, ¼ cup butter and orange zest in a medium saucepan. Cook and stir over medium heat for 2 minutes. Fill 12 ungreased muffin cups each with 1¼ tablespoons of mixture; set aside. Sift together flour, baking powder and salt; cut in shortening until mixture resembles coarse crumbs. Stir in milk, and mix with a fork until mixture forms a ball. On a heavily floured surface, knead dough for one minute. Roll into a 9-inch square, about ½-inch thick; spread with remaining ¼ cup softened butter. Combine cinnamon and remaining ¼ cup sugar; sprinkle over dough. Roll up dough and cut into 12 slices, about ¾-inch thick. Place slices, cut sides down, in muffin cups. Bake at 450 degrees for 14 to 17 minutes. Cool for 2 to 3 minutes; remove from pan. Makes one dozen.

Peg Baker
La Rue, OH

Orange Biscuits

Sweet Strawberry Bread

I taught for 41 years, and every Friday one of our faculty members served breakfast. When it was my turn, I loved to bake breads…this was one recipe everyone enjoyed.

3 c. all-purpose flour
1 t. baking soda
1 t. salt
1½ t. cinnamon
2 c. sugar
4 eggs
1½ c. oil
2 c. strawberries, hulled and sliced
1¼ c. chopped walnuts

Combine flour, baking soda, salt, cinnamon and sugar in a large bowl. Add eggs, one at a time, beating well after each addition. Stir in oil; add remaining ingredients. Divide batter between 2 greased and floured 9"x5" loaf pans. Bake at 350 degrees for one hour. Makes 2 loaves.

Caroline Schiller
Bayport, NY

Whole-Wheat-Chocolate Chip-Banana Bread

Even with the whole-wheat flour and oats, this bread is surprisingly moist. It's an irresistible way to add these healthy ingredients to your family's diet.

3 bananas, mashed
2 eggs, beaten
¼ c. oil
½ c. brown sugar, packed
1 c. whole-wheat flour
1 c. quick-cooking oats, uncooked
1 t. baking soda
1 c. semi-sweet chocolate chips

Combine bananas, eggs, oil and brown sugar in a large bowl. Blend well with an electric mixer at medium speed. Add flour, oats and baking soda; beat just until dry ingredients are mixed in. Stir in chocolate chips. Pour batter into a greased 9"x5" loaf pan. Bake at 350 degrees for 55 to 60 minutes. Remove bread from pan; cool completely on a wire rack. Makes one loaf.

Barbie Hall
Salisbury, MD

berry mix & match
Blueberries, raspberries, mulberries and strawberries are all scrumptious. For a flavorful change, mix & match berries in muffin, coffee cake and quick bread recipes.

"This recipe is a staple at our house!" —Barbie

Cream of Broccoli-Cheese Soup

Whenever I'm running short on time for supper, this is one of the first recipes I think of.

1 c. onion, chopped
½ t. garlic powder
1 T. butter or margarine
5 c. chicken broth
8-oz. pkg. medium egg noodles, uncooked
10-oz. pkg. frozen chopped broccoli
6 c. milk
12-oz. pkg. shredded Cheddar cheese

Sauté onion and garlic in butter or margarine in a large stockpot over medium heat until onion is tender. Add broth and bring to a boil. Reduce heat and add noodles; cook for 5 minutes. Stir in broccoli. Cover and cook for 5 more minutes. Stir in milk and cheese. Heat slowly, stirring, until cheese melts; do not boil. Serves 6 to 8.

Geneva Rogers
Gillette, WY

Blue-Ribbon Crab & Asparagus Chowder

If you like asparagus, you will love this chowder! The recipe has become a tradition at my friend's annual Barn Bash every fall. Recently, I won the blue ribbon at the state fair in the Chili vs. Chowder Cook-off. Yee-haw!

½ c. butter
1 sweet onion, chopped
2 carrots, peeled and chopped
3 stalks celery, chopped
1 t. salt
½ t. pepper
¼ c. all-purpose flour
4 c. water
½ t. nutmeg
1 t. seafood seasoning
1 T. chicken bouillon granules
3 to 4 redskin potatoes, peeled and cubed
4 c. half-and-half
2 t. fresh parsley, chopped
2½ to 3 c. asparagus, trimmed and chopped
1 lb. crabmeat, flaked
Optional: additional half-and-half

Melt butter in a large stockpot over medium heat; add onion, carrots, celery, salt and pepper. Continue to cook until vegetables are softened, about 10 minutes. Stir in flour to coat vegetables. Slowly whisk in water; stir in nutmeg, seafood seasoning, bouillon and potatoes. Bring to a boil; reduce heat and simmer, covered, 10 minutes or until potatoes are tender. Add half-and-half, parsley and asparagus. Simmer 10 more minutes. Gently fold in crabmeat. Heat through. If chowder is too thick, thin with additional half-and-half, if desired. Serves 8 to 10.

Patti Bogetti
Magnolia, DE

Blue-Ribbon Crab & Asparagus Chowder

Caroline's Leek Soup

After many trips to the farmers' market, I began to chat with Caroline. She always has the same corner spot that's bursting with herbs and fresh produce. One Saturday she shared this recipe with me, and our family's been enjoying it ever since.

1 leek, halved lengthwise and sliced
1 t. butter
1 T. water
1 head cauliflower, cut into 1-inch pieces
¾ t. coriander
14½-oz. can chicken broth
1¼ c. milk
1¼ t. salt
¼ t. pepper
Garnish: 1 T. sliced almonds

Rinse leek well in cold water; pat dry. Combine butter and water in a saucepan over medium-high heat. Add leek and cauliflower; cook for 5 minutes. Stir in remaining ingredients except garnish; bring to a boil. Reduce heat to low and simmer, covered, for 20 minutes. Transfer soup in batches to a blender; purée until smooth. Garnish servings with almonds. Serves 4.

Laura Fuller
Fort Wayne, IN

Cheesy Chicken Chalupas

Everybody loves this hearty Mexican dish! Toss hot cooked rice with salsa and cheese for a quick & easy side dish.

2 10¾-oz. cans cream of chicken soup
16-oz. container sour cream
4½-oz. can diced green chiles
2¼-oz. can chopped black olives, drained
3 green onions, chopped
1 onion, chopped
3 c. shredded Cheddar cheese
4 to 5 chicken breasts, cooked and diced
10 to 12 10-inch flour tortillas
2 c. shredded Monterey Jack cheese
Garnish: shredded lettuce, chopped tomato, chopped fresh cilantro

Mix together soup, sour cream, vegetables and Cheddar cheese in a large bowl. Set aside 1½ cups of soup mixture for topping; add chicken to remaining mixture. Spoon chicken mixture into tortillas; roll up and place in a lightly greased 13"x9" baking pan. Spoon reserved soup mixture over tortillas; sprinkle with Monterey Jack cheese. Bake, covered, at 350 degrees for one hour. Garnish with shredded lettuce, chopped tomato and chopped fresh cilantro. Serves 10 to 12.

Carrie Kiiskila
Racine, WI

feeding a crowd?

Consider serving festive Mexican-, Italian- or Chinese-style dishes that everybody loves. They usually feature rice or pasta, so they're filling yet budget-friendly. A theme also makes it a snap to put together the menu and table decorations.

Cheesy Chicken Chalupas

Crispy Herbed Chicken

Crispy Herbed Chicken

Easy to make and ready to pack up for your picnic at a moment's notice!

½ c. cornmeal
½ c. all-purpose flour
1½ t. salt
1 t. dried oregano
¼ t. pepper
3 lb. fryer chicken, cut up
½ c. milk
⅓ c. butter, melted

Combine cornmeal, flour, salt, oregano and pepper on a large plate. Dip chicken pieces in milk; dredge in cornmeal mixture. Place chicken pieces in a greased 13"x9" baking dish; drizzle butter over top. Bake for one hour at 350 degrees, or until juices run clear when chicken pieces are pricked. Serves 4.

Stuffed Artichoke Chicken

This is one of my husband's favorite meals. The filling was originally served as an appetizer...one day I decide to try stuffing chicken cutlets with it, and it was a big hit!

1 c. mayonnaise
1 onion, chopped
1 c. grated Parmesan cheese
14-oz. can artichoke hearts, drained and chopped
1 T. lemon juice
½ t. pepper
2 lbs. boneless chicken cutlets
salt and pepper to taste
3 T. olive oil
¾ c. seasoned dry bread crumbs

Combine mayonnaise, onion, cheese, artichokes, lemon juice and pepper in a bowl; set aside. Flatten chicken cutlets between 2 pieces of wax paper until thin; sprinkle with salt and pepper. Spread artichoke mixture onto each chicken cutlet. Roll up; secure with a wooden toothpick. Drizzle roll-ups with oil; coat with bread crumbs. Place in an ungreased 13"x9" baking pan. Bake, uncovered, at 350 degrees for 30 minutes. Serves 8.

Michelle Marckesano
East Meadow, NY

Pan-Fried Pork Chops

My son always requests these pork chops for his birthday dinner.

½ c. all-purpose flour
1 t. seasoned salt
⅛ t. pepper
4 center-cut pork chops
1 egg, beaten
2 T. milk
½ c. dry bread crumbs
2 T. shortening
¼ c. chicken broth

Mix together flour, salt and pepper; coat pork chops in mixture, and set aside. Whisk together egg and milk; dip chops into egg mixture and then into bread crumbs. Heat shortening in a skillet over medium heat. Add chops and cook for 3 minutes on each side, or until golden. Add broth; reduce heat, cover and simmer about 45 minutes, or until tender. Uncover for last 5 minutes of cooking time. Serves 2.

Annette Ingram
Grand Rapids, MI

Country Glazed Ham

Serve this ham on a large platter surrounded by pomegranate seeds or cranberries and orange-peel twists.

10 to 12-lb. fully cooked smoked ham,
    skin removed and fat trimmed
1 c. water

Place ham in a shallow roasting pan and add water. Bake at 325 degrees for approximately 16 minutes per pound. If ham browns too quickly, tent with aluminum foil. Do not seal. When done, remove from oven and allow to cool. Spread Glaze over ham. Serves 15.

Glaze:
thinly sliced peels of 6 oranges
2 c. water
⅓ c. currant jelly
¾ c. orange marmalade
¼ c. red wine

Bring orange peels and water to a boil in a saucepan; boil 10 minutes. Drain; return orange peels to saucepan. Add jelly and marmalade to orange peels in saucepan; simmer 10 minutes. Remove from heat and stir in wine.

Juanita Williams
Jacksonville, OR

Country Glazed Ham
Grand Ma-Ma's Deviled Eggs (page 64)
Country-Style Baked Potato Salad (page 97)

Steak Diane

Add some tiny new potatoes and fresh steamed asparagus...delicious!

1 clove garlic, sliced
2 T. butter
2 beef rib-eye steaks
¼ t. salt
⅛ t. pepper
1 T. fresh parsley, minced
1 T. fresh chives, minced
1½ t. Worcestershire sauce

Sauté garlic in butter in a skillet over medium-low heat until tender. Remove garlic with a slotted spoon; discard. Add steaks and lightly brown to desired doneness, about 3 to 4 minutes per side. Remove steaks to 2 dinner plates; sprinkle with salt and pepper. Add parsley, chives and Worcestershire sauce to pan juices; stir and heat through. Drizzle pan juices over steaks. Serves 2.

Vickie
Gooseberry Patch

keep it fresh!

Until they're ready for your best recipe, tuck sprigs of fresh herbs into water-filled Mason jars or votive holders for a few days. Not only will they stay fresh longer, but they'll also look lovely.

Beef & Snow Pea Stir-Fry

My husband and I went to a Chinese restaurant on our first date. This is my version of the dish he ordered. We have it for our anniversary every year, and it's simply divine!

3 T. soy sauce
2 T. rice wine or rice vinegar
1 T. brown sugar, packed
½ t. cornstarch
1 T. oil
1 T. fresh ginger, minced
1 T. garlic, minced
1 lb. beef round steak, cut into thin strips
1 to 1½ c. snow peas
hot cooked rice

Combine soy sauce, rice wine or vinegar, brown sugar and cornstarch in a small bowl; set aside. Heat oil in a wok or skillet over medium-high heat. Add ginger and garlic; sauté for 30 seconds. Add steak and stir-fry for 2 minutes, or until evenly browned. Add snow peas and stir-fry for an additional 3 minutes. Add the soy sauce mixture; bring to a boil, stirring constantly. Reduce heat and simmer until sauce is thick and smooth. Serve over hot cooked rice. Serves 4.

Rhonda Reeder
Ellicott City, MD

Family-Favorite Chili Mac

Family-Favorite Chili Mac

Kids love this quick & easy dinner. Serve with a tossed salad and cornbread sticks.

2 7¼-oz. pkgs. macaroni & cheese, uncooked
10-oz. can diced tomatoes with green chiles
1 to 2 lbs. ground beef
1¼-oz. pkg. taco seasoning mix
chili powder to taste
salt and pepper to taste

Prepare macaroni & cheese according to package directions. Stir in tomatoes with green chiles; set aside. Brown beef in a skillet; drain and mix in taco seasoning. Stir beef mixture into macaroni mixture. Add seasonings as desired; heat through. Serves 8.

Stephanie McNealy
Talala, OK

Right after my husband and I were married, we were living on a tight budget. One weekend our cupboard was so bare that I just started tossing food into pots and hoping for something tasty to happen. My husband, his kids and our new little girl sure love this very inexpensive dish... thank goodness! —Stephanie

Pasta Bake Florentine

This dish is a huge hit at our church dinner events and is always the first to go. It's not only delicious but is also so colorful and appealing.

2 T. olive oil
1 onion, finely chopped
¼ c. red pepper, chopped
½ c. mushrooms, coarsely chopped
1 lb. ground beef
½ t. salt
¼ t. garlic salt
¼ t. pepper
2 26-oz. jars pasta sauce
1 c. marinated artichokes, drained and
    chopped
10-oz. pkg. frozen chopped spinach, thawed
    and drained
16-oz. pkg. rotini pasta, cooked
8-oz. pkg. shredded mozzarella cheese

Heat olive oil in a Dutch oven over medium heat. Sauté onion, red pepper and mushrooms until tender, about 5 minutes. Stir in ground beef, salt, garlic salt and pepper. Cook until beef is browned, about 5 to 7 minutes; drain. Stir in pasta sauce, artichokes and spinach until well combined. Stir in cooked pasta. Transfer to a lightly greased 13"x9" baking pan; sprinkle with cheese. Bake, uncovered, at 350 degrees for 15 to 20 minutes, until heated through and cheese is melted. Serves 8.

Jenny Flake
Gilbert, AZ

freezing extra pasta
So often there's cooked macaroni or pasta left over. It's fine to freeze it for later. Drain well, toss with a little oil and freeze in a plastic zipping bag. To reuse, place the frozen pasta in a colander, rinse it with hot water to separate and stir into a skillet or casserole dish. Heat until warmed through.

Scallops & Shrimp with Linguine

Scallops & Shrimp with Linguine

Everyone will love this!

3 T. butter or margarine, divided
3 T. olive oil, divided
1 lb. uncooked large shrimp, peeled and cleaned
3 cloves garlic, minced and divided
1 lb. uncooked sea scallops
8-oz. pkg. sliced mushrooms
2 c. snow peas, trimmed
2 tomatoes, chopped
½ c. green onion, chopped
1 t. salt
½ t. red pepper flakes
¼ c. fresh parsley, chopped
2 T. fresh basil, chopped
10 oz. linguine, cooked and kept warm
Parmesan cheese

Heat one tablespoon each of butter or margarine and olive oil in a large skillet over medium-high heat. Add shrimp and half of garlic; cook 2 to 3 minutes, until shrimp turn pink. Remove shrimp from skillet; keep warm. Repeat with scallops, oil, butter or margarine and remaining garlic. Heat remaining one tablespoon each of butter or margarine and oil in same skillet over medium heat. Add mushrooms, snow peas, tomatoes, green onion, and seasonings; cook 4 to 5 minutes. Combine linguine, mushroom mixture, shrimp and scallops in a large bowl; toss well. Sprinkle with Parmesan cheese. Serves 8.

Red Snapper with Fennel

Set out your fennel a few days before grilling to allow it time to dry out.

4 to 6 dried fennel branches
½ c. butter
juice of 1 lime
1½ lbs. red snapper, cleaned

Prepare grill by placing coals in grill and topping with fennel branches. Bring grill to medium heat while preparing the marinade. Melt butter in a saucepan; remove from heat and add lime juice, mixing well. Place fish on a lightly greased grill rack. Baste with lime marinade and grill 10 minutes, or until cooked through. Remaining marinade can be used as a dipping sauce. Serves 4 to 6.

Pepper-Crusted Salmon

You'll want to use freshly ground pepper for a crispy crust.

¼ c. soy sauce
2 cloves garlic, pressed
4 t. lemon juice
2 t. sugar
4 6-oz. salmon fillets
1 T. pepper
¼ c. olive oil

Combine soy sauce, garlic, lemon juice and sugar in a plastic zipping bag; add salmon. Refrigerate 10 minutes. Remove salmon from marinade; discard marinade. Pat salmon dry. Press pepper into both sides of salmon.
Heat oil in a large, heavy skillet over medium heat; sauté salmon 2 to 3 minutes per side, until it flakes easily with a fork. Drain on paper towels. Serves 4.

Stacie Avner
Delaware, OH

Pepper-Crusted Salmon
Savory Orzo Dish (page 90)
Garlic-Roasted Asparagus (page 93)

Egg Salad Minis

Farm-fresh eggs are a farmers' market treat...don't pass them up! (Pictured on page 58)

4 eggs, hard-boiled, peeled and chopped
¼ c. onion, finely chopped
mayonnaise to taste
salt and pepper to taste
butter to taste, softened
14 slices soft sandwich bread, crusts trimmed

Mash eggs with a fork. Stir in onion. Add mayonnaise, salt and pepper. Spread butter on half the bread slices and spread mayonnaise on remaining bread slices. Spoon egg mixture evenly onto buttered bread slices. Top with remaining bread slices and cut diagonally into quarters. Makes 28 mini sandwiches.

Jennifer Niemi
Nova Scotia, Canada

Watercress & Cream Cheese Sandwiches

Dainty and light...perfect for an afternoon tea!

⅓ c. fresh watercress
¼ c. fresh parsley
8-oz. pkg. cream cheese, softened
¼ c. butter, softened
2 T. fresh chives, chopped
salt and pepper to taste
8 slices white bread

Chop watercress and parsley in a food processor. Add cream cheese, butter, chives, salt and pepper. Continue processing until mixture is thoroughly blended. Remove from food processor and spread on 4 bread slices; top with remaining slices. Cut sandwiches into thirds or quarters using a sharp knife or a decorative cookie cutter. Place on a tray, cover and refrigerate until ready to serve. Makes 12 to 16 mini sandwiches.

Turkey & Berry Sandwiches

I served these sandwiches to several friends while we were vacationing at the beach. Everyone raved and requested the recipe!

2 lettuce leaves
2 slices Swiss cheese
¼ lb. thinly sliced deli turkey
4 strawberries, hulled and sliced
4 slices whole-wheat bread
2 T. whipped cream cheese spread
2 t. pecans, finely chopped

Layer lettuce, cheese, turkey and strawberries on 2 slices of bread. Combine cream cheese and pecans and spread on remaining bread slices; place on bottom halves of sandwiches. Makes 2 sandwiches.

Kim Hinshaw
Austin, TX

Rosemary-Dijon Chicken Croissants

Pair with fruit salad cups and sweet tea for a delightful brunch.

3 c. cooked chicken breast, chopped
⅓ c. green onion, chopped
¼ c. smoked almonds, chopped
¼ c. plain yogurt
¼ c. mayonnaise
1 t. fresh rosemary, chopped
1 t. Dijon mustard
⅛ t. salt
⅛ t. pepper
10 mini croissants, split
Optional: leaf lettuce

Combine all ingredients except croissants and lettuce; mix well. Arrange lettuce leaves inside croissants, if desired; spread with chicken mixture. Makes 10 mini sandwiches.

Jo Ann
Gooseberry Patch

chicken salad in a snap
For a quick & easy chicken salad recipe, combine shredded deli chicken with snipped fresh cilantro, lime juice, halved grapes, chopped red onion and mayonnaise to taste.

Rosemary-Dijon Chicken Croissants

Church Ladies' Ham Salad Sandwiches

The women of Saint James have been making this recipe ever since I can remember. Bring along a variety of breads so everyone can choose their favorite for spreading with ham salad and sandwich spreads. Sliced bagels, Hawaiian sweet bread, party rye, pita pockets, wraps and hearty country white bread all make delicious sandwiches.

6 lbs. bologna, chopped
1 stalk celery, finely chopped
1 doz. eggs, hard-boiled, peeled and diced
pickle relish to taste
32-oz. jar sweet pickles, drained and chopped
3 onions, minced
32-oz. jar mayonnaise-type salad dressing
9 to 10 loaves sliced white, wheat or
    sourdough bread

Place bologna in a food processor; process until well ground. Combine ground bologna with remaining ingredients except bread; mix well. Spread mixture on half the bread slices; top with remaining bread slices. Makes 7 to 8 dozen sandwiches.

Ruby Shepley
Shamokin, PA

Triple-Cheese Mac

This is a great dish no matter the season…my family loves it!

6 T. butter or margarine
2 cloves garlic, pressed
¼ c. all-purpose flour
3½ c. milk
1 T. spicy mustard
salt and pepper to taste
1 c. shredded sharp Cheddar cheese
½ c. shredded American cheese
¼ c. grated Parmesan cheese
16-oz. pkg. elbow macaroni, cooked
¼ c. bread crumbs

Whisk together butter or margarine, garlic and flour in a saucepan over medium heat. Stir in milk, mustard, salt and pepper to taste. Cook and stir until thickened and smooth. Add cheeses, blending well. Stir in macaroni. Transfer to a greased 13"x9" baking pan. Top with bread crumbs and bake, uncovered, at 350 degrees about 35 minutes, until golden. Serves 6.

Linda Duffy
Mashpee, MA

Savory Mashed Potatoes

This recipe can be prepared a day in advance, if you wish.

5 potatoes, peeled and diced
¼ c. milk
½ t. seasoned salt
3 T. butter, divided
1 c. sour cream
3-oz. package cream cheese, softened
2 t. dried chives
½ c. round buttery crackers, crushed
⅔ c. shredded Cheddar cheese

Cook potatoes in salted water until tender; drain. Beat potatoes, milk, seasoned salt and 2 tablespoons butter in a mixing bowl until fluffy. Mix in sour cream, cream cheese and chives. Pour into a greased 13"x9" baking pan. Combine remaining one tablespoon of butter with crushed cracker crumbs; sprinkle over potato mixture. Bake, uncovered, at 350 degrees for 30 minutes. Top with shredded cheese during last 10 minutes of baking. Serves 5.

Savory Mashed Potatoes

Savory Orzo Dish

Orzo is actually tiny, rice-shaped pasta. Flavored with garlic and herb soup mix, it's a good pick to complement your favorite main dish. (Pictured on page 85)

2 T. butter
2 cloves garlic, minced
¼ t. salt
1½ c. orzo pasta, uncooked
1½-oz. pkg. savory herb soup mix
4 c. water
8-oz. pkg. sliced mushrooms
2 T. fresh parsley, chopped

Melt butter in a skillet over medium heat; add garlic, salt and pasta; heat until garlic is golden, stirring constantly. Stir in soup mix and water; simmer 10 minutes. Add mushrooms; simmer 10 more minutes, or until liquid is absorbed. Stir in parsley. Serves 2 to 4.

Bev Eckert
Jonesboro, AR

Marinated Sugar Snap Peas

Prepare this dish ahead of time if you need to.

1½ lbs. sugar snap peas
½ red onion, thinly sliced
1 clove garlic, crushed
⅓ c. olive oil

Add enough water to cover peas in a large stockpot. Bring to a boil and cook until crisp-tender, approximately one minute. Drain and rinse with cool water. Place in a large mixing bowl with remaining ingredients; gently toss. Cover and refrigerate 30 minutes. When ready to serve, remove from refrigerator and allow to come to room temperature. Serves 8.

Orange-Maple Glazed Carrots

This dish always impresses guests...they don't have to know you made it in the microwave.

⅔ c. orange juice
16-oz. pkg. baby carrots
2 T. orange zest
⅓ c. maple syrup
1 t. fresh nutmeg, grated
⅓ c. butter

Microwave orange juice in a 2-quart microwave-safe casserole dish on high for 1½ minutes. Add carrots and orange zest; stir to coat. Cover dish and microwave on high for 7 minutes. Stir in the remaining ingredients and microwave, uncovered, for 2 to 4 minutes, until carrots are crisp-tender. Serves 3 to 4.

Lemony Broccoli

A tang of lemon with fresh broccoli...a winning combination.

1½ lbs. broccoli, cut into spears
½ clove garlic, minced
2 T. olive oil
2 T. lemon juice

Add broccoli to a saucepan with a small amount of water. Cook broccoli over medium-high heat for 6 to 8 minutes, until crisp-tender. Drain. Sauté garlic in oil over medium heat until tender. Add lemon juice; mix well. Pour over broccoli, tossing gently to blend. Serves 6.

Irene Robinson
Cincinnati, OH

Orange-Maple Glazed Carrots

Spring Spinach Sauté

Spring Spinach Sauté

This delicious vegetarian dish is also great with pork chops.

1 to 2 cloves garlic, minced
2 T. olive oil
6-oz. pkg. baby spinach
½ c. feta cheese, crumbled
¼ c. slivered almonds

Sauté garlic in hot oil until golden; add spinach, stirring until crisp-tender. Add feta cheese and almonds; heat through. Serves 4.

Beth Childers
Urbana, OH

Garlic-Roasted Asparagus

Roasting really brings out the flavor of fresh asparagus. (Pictured on page 85)

1 lb. asparagus, trimmed
1 T. olive oil
3 cloves garlic, pressed
¼ t. salt
¼ t. pepper

Toss together all ingredients; arrange in a single layer on a lightly greased baking sheet. Bake at 450 degrees for 8 minutes, or until tender. Serves 4.

Jeanne Calkins
Midland, MI

Michele's Fruit Sticks

So simple and yet so good, these are a refreshing snack everyone loves.

1 c. orange segments
1 c. seedless green grapes
1 c. seedless red grapes
1 c. watermelon, cubed
1 c. cantaloupe, cubed
1 c. honeydew, cubed
½ c. maraschino cherries, drained
6 to 8 extra-long bamboo skewers
crushed ice

Thread fruit onto skewers, leaving bottom 2 to 3 inches of each skewer unfilled. Fill a large serving bowl with crushed ice and insert the bottom of each stick into crushed ice. Serves 6 to 8.

Michele Pappagallo
London, AR

Years ago, I needed a quick recipe for a family picnic. After running out of ideas, I tossed these together, and they were a hit! —Michele

jump-start your garden

Start cool-weather veggies such as lettuce and spinach indoors in old wooden drawers. Just line drawers with plastic, add gravel for drainage and plant away! The plants can go directly outside when the days warm up.

Berry Fruit Toss

Berry Fruit Toss

For a pretty presentation, serve in a carved watermelon basket or trifle bowl.

2 qts. strawberries, sliced
2 whole pineapples, peeled, cored and chopped
½ c. orange marmalade
¼ c. orange juice
2 T. lemon juice
½ c. blueberries
Optional: fresh mint sprigs

Combine strawberries and pineapple in a large mixing bowl; set aside. Combine orange marmalade, orange juice and lemon juice, mixing well. Add to strawberry mixture, mixing well. Add blueberries before serving. Garnish with mint sprigs, if desired. Serves 10 to 12.

Honeyed Mango Salad

We love this simple fruit-filled salad...it's yummy, quick & easy.

2 mangoes, peeled, pitted and sliced
2 oranges, sectioned
1 banana, sliced
2 T. lemon juice
juice of 1 lime
2 T. honey
¼ c. oil
⅛ t. salt
Garnish: 6 lettuce leaves, 6 maraschino cherries

Combine fruit and lemon juice in a large bowl; toss to coat. Cover and chill until serving time. Blend lime juice and honey in a small bowl; stir in oil and salt. Drizzle honey mixture over fruit mixture; stir gently. To serve, place lettuce leaves in individual salad bowls; fill with fruit mixture. Top with cherries and any fruit juice remaining in bowl. Serves 6.

Phyl Broich Wessling
Garner, IA

Spinach & Clementine Salad

This fresh, crunchy salad is the perfect way to use a Christmas gift box of clementines. (Pictured on page 58)

2 lbs. clementines, peeled and sectioned
2 lbs. baby spinach
4 stalks celery, thinly sliced
1 c. red onion, thinly sliced
½ c. pine nuts or walnuts, toasted
¼ c. dried cherries
¼ c. olive oil
2 T. red wine vinegar
1 clove garlic, minced
1 t. Dijon mustard
⅛ t. sugar
salt and pepper to taste

Place clementines in a large salad bowl with spinach, celery, onion, nuts and cherries. Toss well. Whisk together remaining ingredients in a small bowl; drizzle over salad. Serve immediately. Serves 8.

Sharon Jones
Oklahoma City, OK

beat the heat

If it looks like it's going to be hot weather, whip up a basket full of hand fans for everyone to pick and choose from. Wallpaper scraps, fabric snippets and copies of handwritten recipes are perfect for arranging on poster board. Use spray adhesive to secure them and then glue on a paint-stirring stick for the handle.

Artichoke-Tortellini Salad

A make-ahead salad that's perfect for toting to a picnic in the park, a girlfriends' lunch or a backyard cookout.

9-oz. pkg. refrigerated cheese tortellini
1 c. broccoli flowerets
½ c. fresh parsley, finely chopped
1 T. pimento, chopped
6-oz. jar marinated artichoke hearts
2 green onions, chopped
2½ t. fresh basil, chopped, or ¼ t. dried basil
½ t. garlic powder
½ c. Italian salad dressing
5 to 6 cherry tomatoes, cut in half
Garnish: sliced black olives, shaved Parmesan
    cheese

Cook tortellini according to package directions. Drain and rinse with cool water. Combine tortellini and remaining ingredients except tomatoes and garnish, in a large bowl. Cover and refrigerate 4 to 6 hours to blend flavors. When ready to serve, add tomatoes and toss lightly. Garnish with olives and cheese. Serves 6.

Kay Barg
Sandy, UT

Artichoke-Tortellini Salad

Chinese Coleslaw

Crunchy, colorful and full of flavor…but it's the dressing that really makes this a standout!

9 c. napa cabbage, shredded
4 c. green cabbage, shredded
1 c. red or green pepper, sliced
1 c. snow pea pods
1 c. bean sprouts
5 green onions, sliced
Garnish: 2 T. toasted sesame seed

Combine vegetables in a large bowl. Drizzle with Sesame-Ginger Dressing; toss and sprinkle with sesame seed. Toss once more before serving. Serves 12.

Sesame-Ginger Dressing:

1 clove garlic, minced
⅛-inch-thick slice fresh ginger, peeled and minced
¼ c. sesame oil or peanut oil
3 T. soy sauce
3 T. rice wine vinegar
1 t. sugar
Optional: 4 drops chili oil

Combine all ingredients in a jar with a tight-fitting lid. Secure lid and shake well to blend.

Carolyn Ayers
Kent, WA

cookie cutter creations

Cookie cutter topiaries make sweet centerpieces for spring flings. Just secure a dowel in a terra cotta pot using sand or floral foam, glue a flower-shaped cookie cutter on top and tie on a ribbon for the "leaves."

Country-Style Baked Potato Salad

A truly tasty salad…a spin on a loaded baked potato. Use any or all of your favorite toppings! (Pictured on page 80)

4 lbs. potatoes, peeled, cubed and cooked
1 lb. bacon, sliced into ½-inch pieces and crisply cooked
8-oz. pkg. shredded Cheddar cheese
½ c. butter, softened
½ c. green onions, chopped
1½ c. sour cream
1 t. salt
1 t. pepper

Combine all ingredients in a large bowl, tossing gently. Chill for 2 hours before serving. Serves 10 to 12.

Deanna Lyons
Roswell, GA

Icebox Carrot Salad

So refreshing…don't let anyone know how easy it is!

3 16-oz. cans shoestring carrots, drained
½ c. green pepper, thinly sliced
2 to 3 green onions, thinly sliced
¾ c. sugar
⅔ c. cider vinegar
½ c. oil
1 t. salt

Combine all ingredients in a large serving bowl; let marinate overnight in refrigerator. Serves 4 to 6.

Sheree Haskins
La Mirada, CA

Oma's Lemon Cheesecake

This is a treasured recipe, handed down from my Oma (German for Gramma) all the way to my daughter. This wonderful treat has been present at every Christmas in my life...not a crumb is ever left on the plate! The cake crust makes this so elegant, and the cheesy, light lemony goodness shines through. It is so worth the extra steps!

½ c. butter, softened
2¼ c. sugar, divided
4 eggs, divided
2 t. vanilla extract, divided
1½ c. all-purpose flour
1 t. baking powder
½ t. salt
2 8-oz. pkgs. cream cheese, softened
16-oz. container sour cream, divided
zest of 1 lemon, divided

Beat butter and ⅔ sugar together until creamy. Add one egg and one teaspoon vanilla. Combine flour, baking powder and salt; add to butter mixture. Mix well. Press evenly into the bottom and partially up the sides of a lightly greased 9" round springform pan. For filling, blend cream cheese with 1⅓ cups sugar until smooth. Beat in remaining 3 eggs, one at a time; stir in one cup sour cream, remaining vanilla and two-thirds of lemon zest. Pour filling into crust; bake at 325 degrees for one hour. Turn off oven; leave pan in oven for 15 minutes. Remove cake from oven and return oven to 325 degrees. For topping, mix together remaining sour cream, ¼ c. sugar and zest until smooth. Spread topping over filling. Bake at 325 degrees for an additional 15 minutes. Cool before serving. Serves 12.

Cora Wilfinger
Manitowoc, WI

Easiest-Ever Cheesecake

You can also drizzle melted chocolate on top for a rich and flavorful twist.

12-oz. pkg. vanilla wafers, crushed
1 c. plus 2 T. sugar, divided
½ c. butter, melted
2 8-oz. pkgs. cream cheese, softened
12-oz. container frozen whipped topping, thawed
Optional: fresh raspberries

Combine vanilla wafers, 2 tablespoons sugar and butter; press into the bottom of a 13"x9" baking pan. Blend together remaining sugar and cream cheese in a separate bowl; fold in whipped topping. Spread over wafer crust; chill until firm. Garnish with fresh raspberries, if desired. Serves 12 to 15.

Linda Lewanski
Cosby, TN

Friends will think you spent hours on this simple cheesecake. —Linda

---

edible petals
Accent a dessert with edible flowers...rose petals, nasturtiums, violets and pansies are some colorful choices. Make sure your flowers are pesticide-free and rinse them well before using.

Easiest-Ever Cheesecake

Grandmother's Pound Cake

Try this old-fashioned favorite with fresh sliced strawberries on top.

1 c. butter, softened
1⅔ c. sugar
5 eggs
½ t. vanilla extract
2 c. all-purpose flour

Beat butter until creamy. Blend in sugar, eggs and vanilla. Gradually mix in flour; pour into a greased and floured 9"x5" loaf pan. Bake at 300 degrees for one to 1½ hours, until a toothpick inserted near the center comes out clean. Serves 8 to 10.

Teri Naquin
Melville, LA

Grandmother's Pound Cake

Triple-Chocolate-Sour Cream Cake

A chocolate lover's dream!

1 c. all-purpose flour
1 t. baking powder
½ t. baking soda
½ t. salt
2 1-oz. sqs. unsweetened chocolate, broken
1 T. baking cocoa
1¼ c. sugar
⅓ c. water
2 eggs
¾ c. butter, softened
½ c. sour cream
1 t. vanilla extract

Combine flour, baking powder, baking soda and salt in a mixing bowl. Set aside. Mix unsweetened chocolate, baking cocoa and sugar in a food processor or blender; process until crumbly. Bring water to a boil and add to chocolate mixture. Blend until chocolate melts. Break eggs into processor and mix well. Add butter, sour cream and vanilla; process again. Add flour mixture to food processor, pulsing until ingredients are well blended. Lightly grease and flour an 8" springform pan; add cake batter. Bake at 350 degrees for one hour or until cake begins to pull away from pan. When cake has cooled, remove sides of pan. Spread Frosting over cake. Refrigerate to allow icing to completely set before serving. Serves 8 to 10.

Frosting:
½ c. whipping cream
6 1-oz. sqs. semi-sweet chocolate, broken

Scald cream in a saucepan, add chocolate and stir for one minute. Remove pan from heat and continue to stir until chocolate is completely melted. Allow to cool slightly before spreading on cake.

Bee Sting Cake

This is a shorter version of an all-time favorite.

2 eggs, beaten
1 c. sugar
1 t. vanilla extract
1 c. all-purpose flour
1 t. baking powder
½ c. milk
2 T. butter

Beat together eggs, sugar, vanilla, flour and baking powder in a large bowl; set aside. Bring milk and butter to a boil in a saucepan over medium heat; mix well. Add to egg mixture; pour into a greased and floured 8"x8" baking pan. Bake at 350 degrees for 30 minutes, or until a toothpick inserted near center comes out clean. Spread Topping over warm cake. Broil until topping is bubbly and warm. Serves 10.

Topping:
½ c. plus 2 T. brown sugar, packed
¼ c. butter, melted
¼ c. whipping cream
1 c. sweetened flaked coconut
1 t. vanilla extract

Combine all ingredients; mix well.

Jo Ann
Gooseberry Patch

> ### cake keeper
> To keep cakes fresh for up to one week, they should be wrapped or covered and stored in the refrigerator. If stored on the counter under a cake dome or cake keeper, they'll stay fresh for about three days.

Black-Bottom Cupcakes

Black-Bottom Cupcakes

Chocolate and cream cheese...what a scrumptious combination!

2 8-oz. pkgs. cream cheese, softened
2 eggs, beaten
2⅔ c. sugar, divided
1¼ t. salt, divided
1½ c. semi-sweet chocolate chips
3 c. all-purpose flour
½ c. baking cocoa
2 t. baking soda
2 c. water
⅔ c. oil
2 T. vinegar
2 t. vanilla extract

Combine cream cheese, eggs, ⅔ cup sugar, ¼ teaspoon salt and chocolate chips; mix well and set aside.

Combine remaining 2 cups sugar, remaining one teaspoon salt and remaining ingredients in a large bowl; fill paper-lined muffin cups ¾ full with chocolate batter. Top each with ¼ cup cream cheese mixture. Bake at 350 degrees for 25 to 30 minutes. Makes 2 dozen.

Gretchen Brown
Forest Grove, OR

Grandma's Banana Cupcakes

My grandma used to make these often...they were so yummy!

½ c. butter, softened
1¾ c. sugar
2 eggs, beaten
2 c. all-purpose flour
1 t. baking soda
1 t. baking powder
1 c. buttermilk
2 bananas, mashed
1 t. vanilla extract
Optional: ½ c. chopped pecans

Blend butter with an electric mixer at medium speed for 5 minutes. Slowly add sugar; beat in eggs. Combine flour, baking soda and baking powder. Add flour mixture to butter mixture alternately with buttermilk. Stir in bananas, vanilla and pecans, if desired. Fill paper-lined muffin cups ½ full. Bake at 350 for 18 to 25 minutes, until a toothpick inserted near the center comes out clean. Allow to cool; frost with Cream Cheese Frosting. Keep refrigerated. Makes 1½ to 2 dozen.

Cream Cheese Frosting:
8-oz. pkg. cream cheese, softened
½ c. butter, softened
2 t. vanilla extract
16-oz. pkg. powdered sugar

Blend all ingredients with an electric mixer at medium speed, until spreadable.

Kelly Marcum
Rock Falls, IL

I like to drizzle a little caramel sauce over the tops to make them extra special. —Kelly

Nichole's Cake Mix Cookies

These are a moist, but not-too-sweet, cookie.

¼ c. butter, softened
8-oz. pkg. cream cheese, softened
1 egg yolk, beaten
½ t. vanilla extract
18¼-oz. pkg. butter pecan cake mix

Beat butter and cream cheese with an electric mixer at medium speed. Add egg yolk and vanilla; blend thoroughly. Gradually beat in dry cake mix. Dough will be slightly stiff. Cover and refrigerate for 20 minutes. Drop dough by rounded teaspoonfuls onto greased or parchment paper–lined baking sheets. Bake at 350 degrees for 14 minutes, or until lightly golden. Makes about 3 dozen.

Nichole Martelli
Santa Fe, TX

I wanted to make a new cookie to add to the usual ones I share with family and friends. After the first taste, my husband said, 'Now that's a recipe that you have to send to Gooseberry Patch!' —Nichole

the best batch

For best results when baking cookies, set out butter and eggs on the kitchen counter an hour ahead of time so that they can come to room temperature.

Mexican Tea Cookies

Dusted in powdered sugar, these cookies are heavenly. (Pictured on page 58)

1 c. butter, softened
¼ c. powdered sugar
2 t. vanilla extract
1 T. water
2 c. all-purpose flour
1 c. chopped pecans
Garnish: additional powdered sugar

Beat butter and powdered sugar with an electric mixer at medium speed; add vanilla, water and flour. Stir in pecans. Shape dough into one-inch balls. Arrange on an ungreased baking sheet. Bake at 300 degrees for 20 minutes. Remove from oven. When cool, roll in powdered sugar. Makes about 40 cookies.

Kimberly Pfleiderer
Galion, OH

Strawberry-Rhubarb Pie

Last year my family moved from Germany to North Carolina, where strawberries are plentiful. I decided to make a pie using the best of what is grown locally, and this is the result. The combination of a sweet crust with a tart filling is the perfect taste of summer.

5 c. strawberries, hulled and chopped
2 stalks rhubarb, peeled and diced
¾ c. brown sugar, packed
½ c. sugar
¼ c. all-purpose flour
2 T. cornstarch
⅛ t. salt
½ t. cinnamon
9-inch pie crust
1½ T. butter, diced

Combine strawberries and rhubarb; set aside. Sift together sugars, flour, cornstarch, salt and cinnamon. Stir into strawberry mixture. Place crust in a 9" pie plate; chill for 10 minutes. Spoon strawberry mixture into crust; dot with butter. Sprinkle Crumb Topping over filling. Bake at 400 degrees for 50 to 60 minutes, until topping is golden. Set pie on a wire rack to cool for 2 hours. Serves 8.

Crumb Topping:
3 T. all-purpose flour
1 T. sugar
⅛ t. salt
1 T. butter, softened

Mix together flour, sugar and salt; cut in butter until crumbly.

Shar Toliver
Böblingen, Germany

Aunt Elaine's Pink Lemonade Pie

The recipe for this delicious pie was handed down to us from my husband's great-aunt Elaine…we think of her every time we make it. It's so easy and so refreshing. Our daughter even won an award at a dessert competition with this wonderful concoction.

6-oz. can frozen pink lemonade concentrate, thawed
14-oz. can sweetened condensed milk
8-oz. container frozen whipped topping, thawed
¼ t. red food coloring
Optional: ¼ to 1 t. lemon extract
9-inch graham cracker crust
Garnish: red decorating sugar

Mix together lemonade concentrate, condensed milk, whipped topping and food coloring until well blended. Stir in lemon extract to taste, if desired, for a more tart flavor. Pour into graham cracker crust; sprinkle with decorating sugar. Cover and freeze for 4 hours to overnight. Thaw slightly before serving to make slicing easier. Serves 8 to 12.

Kathy Sharp
Westerville, OH

Chocolate Chip Cookie Dough Pie

Sometimes there is nothing better than chocolate chip cookie dough!

16½-oz. tube refrigerated chocolate chip cookie
    dough
2 8-oz. pkgs. cream cheese, softened
2 eggs
½ c. sugar
5 1.4-oz. chocolate-covered toffee candy bars,
    crumbled and divided

Press cookie dough into an ungreased 9" pie plate to make crust. Combine cream cheese, eggs, sugar and 3 crumbled candy bars in a large bowl; pour into crust. Bake, uncovered, at 325 degrees for 30 to 35 minutes. Cool completely. Sprinkle top with remaining 2 crumbled candy bars. Chill until ready to serve. Serves 8.

Chocolate Chip
Cookie Dough Pie

Coconut Cream Pie

I have such fond memories of when my dad's family would all get together to eat at a local restaurant. Their coconut cream pie was my favorite! This is my own version of it.

2 c. milk
⅔ c. sugar
¼ c. cornstarch
¼ t. salt
3 egg yolks, beaten
2 T. butter or margarine
½ t. vanilla extract
1½ c. sweetened flaked coconut,
   divided
9-inch pie crust, baked

Combine milk, sugar, cornstarch and salt in a saucepan; cook over medium heat until thickened. Cook for 2 additional minutes, stirring constantly. Remove from heat. Stir a small amount of hot mixture into egg yolks in a small bowl. Pour yolks back into saucepan; simmer gently for 2 minutes. Add butter or margarine, vanilla and one cup coconut; pour into crust. Spread Meringue over pie; seal to edges. Sprinkle with remaining coconut. Bake at 350 degrees for 12 minutes. Serves 8.

Meringue:
4 egg whites
7-oz. jar marshmallow creme

Beat egg whites with an electric mixer at high speed until very stiff peaks form. Add marshmallow creme; beat for 4 minutes.

Lauren Williams
Kewanee, MO

French Bread Pudding

A soul-satisfying treat the whole family will love!

2½ c. milk
½ c. whipping cream
4 eggs
½ c. sugar
1½ t. vanilla extract
½ t. cinnamon, or to taste
½ t. nutmeg
Optional: 1 t. orange zest, finely grated
⅛ t. salt
7 c. cinnamon, French or rich egg bread,
   cubed and with crusts trimmed
3 T. butter, melted
Garnish: powdered sugar

Whisk together all ingredients except bread, butter and garnish in a medium mixing bowl until well blended. Toss milk mixture with bread in a bowl to coat. Spoon into greased 2-quart casserole dish; drizzle with melted butter. Bake at 325 degrees for one hour, or until knife inserted near center comes out clean. Sprinkle with powdered sugar before serving. Serve warm or chilled. Serves 6.

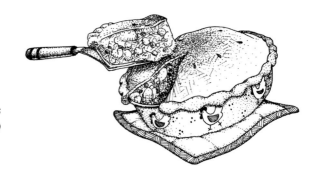

French Bread Pudding

Open-Face Peach Pie (page 155)

Louisiana Shrimp (page 132)

Mother's Fried Chicken (page 129)

Skyscraper Banana Splits (page 157)

PICNICS & MORE

Garden-fresh summertime recipes to share with family & friends

Mom's Summer Salsa

This colorful salsa has a burst of fresh flavor in every bite. I love making it for my family each summer, and whenever I do, I'm reminded of all the good times and happy meals we've shared. It brings a good tear to my eye.

4 c. seedless watermelon, diced
1 c. green pepper, diced
½ c. red pepper, diced
½ c. orange pepper, diced
½ c. sweet onion, diced
½ c. red onion, diced
½ c. carrots, peeled and diced
½ c. celery, diced
2 jalapeño peppers, seeded and sliced
2 T. rice vinegar
1 T. oil
1 c. fresh cilantro, chopped
2 T. fresh mint, chopped
2 T. fresh basil, chopped
Garnish: ¼ c. unsalted cashews, chopped

Combine all ingredients except cashews in a large bowl. Cover and refrigerate until ready to serve. Sprinkle with cashews just before serving. Makes 8½ cups.

Paula Marchesi
Lenhartsville, PA

Roasted Red Pepper Salsa

Fry up some quartered corn tortillas for your own fresh chips.

2 c. corn
2 tomatoes, diced
7-oz. jar roasted red peppers, drained and chopped
2 green onions, finely chopped
1 jalapeño pepper, seeded and minced
3 T. fresh cilantro, minced
2 T. lime juice
1 T. white vinegar
½ t. salt
¼ t. pepper
¼ t. ground cumin
2 avocados, pitted, peeled and chopped
multicolored tortilla chips

Gently stir together all ingredients except chips; cover and refrigerate at least 2 hours before serving. Serve with chips. Makes 2½ cups.

easy swap
If you're substituting frozen corn for fresh kernels, a 10-ounce package of frozen equals 1¾ cups fresh.

Roasted Red Pepper Salsa

Heather's BLT Bites

I discovered this recipe when my husband was in the military. He loved it, and I always made it for him when he came home from long tours. Now he travels a lot for work, but he still comes home to these little bites after he's been away. It's a true family favorite.

1 lb. bacon, crisply cooked and crumbled
1 c. mayonnaise-type salad dressing
1½ c. green onions, chopped
½ c. grated Parmesan cheese
10 to 12 roma tomatoes

Stir together bacon, salad dressing, onions and Parmesan until well blended; set aside. Cut a small slice from the top of each tomato; scoop out and discard pulp of tomatoes. Fill each tomato with bacon mixture; refrigerate for one hour. Makes 10 to 12.

Heather Werner
Paxton, IL

Mango Chutney Chicken Bites

This is a fantastic summertime appetizer...a tasty, lighter version of chicken salads that contain mayonnaise. So quick & easy, and once your family & friends get a taste, they'll want more!

12½ oz. can chicken, drained
2 to 3 T. mango chutney
⅛ t. ground ginger
⅛ t. pepper
2 T. green onions, chopped
crackers or thinly sliced French bread
Garnish: chopped green onions

Mix together all ingredients except crackers or bread and garnish; cover and refrigerate overnight. Serve on crackers or bread; sprinkle with green onions. Makes 3 to 4 dozen.

Lisanne Miller
Canton, MS

Honey-Glazed Snack Mix

Pack in plastic zipping bags for school-day snacks or pour in a bowl for a movie-night treat.

5 c. corn & rice cereal
3 c. mini pretzel twists
2 c. pecan halves
½ c. honey
½ c. butter, melted

Combine cereal, pretzels and pecans in a large bowl; set aside. Blend together honey and butter. Pour over cereal mixture; toss to coat. Spread on ungreased baking sheets. Bake at 300 degrees for 10 minutes. Stir and bake an additional 10 to 15 minutes. Pour onto wax paper and cool completely. Store in airtight containers. Makes about 10 cups.

Cindy Elliott
Modesto, IL

"This recipe is from my friend Mary Beth Mitchell. I like the taste of this best when I use fresh honey from the farmers' market or orchard." —Cindy

Honey-Glazed Snack Mix

Homemade Root Beer

Always wear gloves when handling the dry ice. Be careful not to seal the container tightly after adding the dry ice, as it makes the pressure build up inside.

4 lbs. sugar
4 gal. water
2-oz. bottle root beer concentrate
4 lbs. dry ice

Combine sugar, water and root beer concentrate in a large clear plastic container. Add dry ice; cover loosely. Let stand for 45 minutes to one hour. Serve immediately or store in an airtight container. Makes 4 gallons.

Lynn Williams
Muncie, IN

Strawberry-Watermelon Slush

A luscious combination of fresh summer fruit. Slip a plump strawberry onto a drinking straw for a fun garnish.

1 pt. strawberries, hulled and halved
2 c. watermelon, seeded and cubed
⅓ c. sugar
⅓ c. lemon juice
2 c. ice cubes

Combine strawberries, watermelon, sugar and lemon juice in a blender. Blend until smooth. Gradually add ice and continue to blend. Serve immediately. Serves 5 to 6.

Sandy Benham
Sanborn, NY

buzz off!

It's easy to keep pesky bugs away from pitchers of root beer or lemonade...simply stitch buttons or charms to the edges of tea towels and drape over the pitchers.

Raspberry Sun Tea

Let the sun do the work!

6 raspberry-herb teabags
3 qts. cold water
¼ c. sugar or to taste
ice
Garnish: fresh mint sprigs

Place teabags into a one-gallon glass container; add cold water. Set the container on your sunny porch, patio or windowsill for several hours. Discard teabags, add sugar to taste, stir well and chill. Pour into tall chilled glasses filled with ice; garnish with mint sprigs. Makes 12 cups.

Strawberry-Watermelon Slush

Crab, Corn & Pepper Frittata

You may also use fresh crabmeat if you'd like.

6 eggs, beaten
¼ c. milk
⅓ c. mayonnaise
1 c. imitation crabmeat, flaked
2 T. green onion, chopped
2 T. red pepper, chopped
⅓ c. corn
salt and pepper to taste
1 c. shredded Monterey Jack cheese

Whisk together all ingredients except cheese. Pour into a greased 10" pie plate. Bake at 350 degrees for 15 to 20 minutes. Sprinkle with cheese and bake for an additional 5 minutes, or until cheese is melted. Serves 4 to 6.

Stacie Avner
Delaware, OH

This is an adaptation of one of my mom's recipes. In the summertime, I like to use fresh corn. —Stacie

Farmers' Market Omelet

I love visiting the farmers' market bright & early on Saturday mornings…a terrific way to begin the day!

1 t. olive oil
2 T. bacon, diced
2 T. onion, chopped
2 T. zucchini, diced
5 cherry tomatoes, quartered
¼ t. fresh thyme, minced
3 eggs, beaten
¼ c. fontina cheese, shredded

Heat oil in a skillet over medium-high heat. Add bacon and onion; cook and stir until bacon is crisp and onion is tender. Add zucchini, tomatoes and thyme. Cook until zucchini is soft and juice from tomatoes has slightly evaporated. Reduce heat to medium and add eggs. Cook, lifting edges to allow uncooked egg to flow underneath. When eggs are almost fully cooked, sprinkle cheese over top and fold over. Serves one to 2.

Vickie
Gooseberry Patch

garden party centerpiece

For a garden party, arrange flowers or even vegetables in produce baskets or miniature watering cans. Insert seed packets attached to bamboo skewers into arrangements, or use skewers to identify the dishes you're serving.

Country Breakfast
Casserole

Country Breakfast Casserole

*A small bag of frozen hashbrowns can be used
instead of the potatoes, onion and diced peppers.*

1 T. oil
4 potatoes, diced
1½ t. salt, divided
1 red pepper, diced
1 green pepper, diced
1 onion, minced
8-oz. pkg. breakfast sausage links, chopped,
    browned and drained
1½ c. egg substitute
1 c. milk
2 T. all-purpose flour
½ t. pepper
1 c. shredded Cheddar cheese

Heat oil in medium skillet. Fry potatoes with
one teaspoon salt in oil until golden. Add red and
green peppers and onion; cook 5 minutes. Spoon
into a greased 3-quart casserole dish; top with
sausage. Mix together egg substitute, milk, flour,
½ teaspoon salt and pepper in a mixing bowl.
Pour egg mixture over potato mixture; sprinkle
with cheese. Bake, uncovered, at 350 degrees for
30 minutes. Serves 8.

Blueberry Buckle
Coffee Cake

Blueberry Buckle Coffee Cake

Fresh blueberries are a summertime treat to be savored.

2 c. all-purpose flour
¾ c. sugar
2½ t. baking powder
¾ t. salt
¼ c. shortening
¾ c. milk
2 c. blueberries
½ c. powdered sugar
¼ t. vanilla extract
½ to 2 t. hot water

Mix together flour, sugar, baking powder, salt, shortening and milk. Beat for 30 seconds; carefully fold in berries. Spread batter into a greased 9"x9" baking pan; sprinkle with Crumb Topping. Bake at 375 degrees for 45 to 50 minutes. Combine remaining ingredients in a small bowl; drizzle over warm cake. Serves 9.

Crumb Topping:
½ c. sugar
⅓ c. all-purpose flour
¼ c. butter, softened
½ t. cinnamon

Mix all ingredients together until crumbly.

Kathy Grashoff
Fort Wayne, IN

Rise & Shine Bacon Waffles

*Bacon adds a terrific flavor to morning waffles…
you'll love 'em served alongside scrambled eggs.*

1¾ c. all-purpose flour
1 T. sugar
2 t. baking powder
½ t. salt
3 eggs, separated
1½ c. milk
¼ c. butter, melted
1 lb. bacon, crisply cooked and crumbled

Combine flour, sugar, baking powder and salt in a large bowl; set aside. Beat together egg yolks, milk and butter; stir into dry ingredients until smooth. Beat egg whites in a mixing bowl until stiff peaks form; fold into batter. Stir in bacon. Pour ½ to ¾ cup batter onto a lightly greased waffle iron; cook according to manufacturer's instructions until golden. Makes 8 waffles.

Tonya Sheppard
Galveston, TX

make mine crispy!
To prepare crispy bacon easily, try baking it in the oven. Place bacon slices on a broiler pan, place the pan in the oven and turn the temperature to 400 degrees. Bake for 12 to 15 minutes, turn bacon over and bake for another 8 to 10 minutes.

Peachy Oat Bread

*So yummy made with fresh peaches just off the tree!
I've also used canned peaches, drained very well.*

2 c. whole-wheat flour
1 c. quick-cooking oats, uncooked
¾ c. sugar
3 T. baking powder
½ t. baking soda
½ t. salt
½ t. cinnamon
2 c. peaches, pitted and chopped
2 eggs, beaten
1 c. milk
¼ c. oil

Stir together flour, oats, sugar, baking powder, baking soda, salt and cinnamon in a large bowl. Add peaches and stir gently to coat; set aside. Whisk together eggs, milk and oil in a separate bowl. Add to peach mixture; stir just until moistened. Pour batter into a greased 9"x5" loaf pan. Bake at 350 degrees for one hour. Cool in pan 10 minutes. Remove from pan and cool completely on a wire rack. Makes one loaf.

*Sharon Velenosi
Stanton, CA*

get to the core
An easy way to core apples and peaches... slice fruit in half and then use a melon baller to scoop out the core.

Connie's Pretzel Buns

There is so much you can do with this recipe! You can coat them with butter after baking and sprinkle the tops with coarse salt or cinnamon-sugar. You can make mini sandwiches out of them, too...cut when completely cool. Or, they're delicious just the way they are!

1 T. instant yeast
2 T. sugar
1½ t. salt
2¾ c. bread flour
3 T. butter, softened
1 c. warm water
6 c. cold water
5 t. baking soda
melted butter
coarse salt

Place yeast, sugar, salt, flour and butter in a food processor. Pulse until butter is cut into dry ingredients. Add warm water, 110 to 115 degrees. Process until a soft dough forms, adding a little more water if needed. Dough should feel soft and elastic to the touch. Turn out into a greased bowl; cover and let rise until double in bulk. Punch down dough; form into golf ball–size buns. Press a finger almost, but not quite, through the center of each bun. Place buns on parchment paper–lined baking sheets; cover and let rise again until almost double in bulk. Place cold water in a non-aluminum saucepan over high heat. Add baking soda; bring to a boil. Drop buns, 2 to 3 at a time, into boiling water. Boil for about 40 seconds on each side. Remove buns from water with a slotted spoon and return to parchment paper–lined baking sheets. Brush buns with butter and sprinkle with coarse salt. Bake at 475 degrees for 8 to 12 minutes, until golden, watching closely to avoid overbrowning. Cool buns on a wire rack. Makes 2 to 3 dozen.

*Connie Mrazik
Saint Charles, MO*

Connie's Pretzel Buns

Grilled Herb Bread

Try different herb combinations such as marjoram, chives or basil.

2 c. warm water (110 to 115 degrees)
2 envs. active dry yeast
⅓ c. plus 1 t. sugar, divided
⅓ c. oil
2 t. salt
6 c. all-purpose flour
¼ c. chopped herbs

Combine water, yeast and one teaspoon sugar in a mixing bowl; let stand 10 minutes. Gently stir in remaining sugar, oil and salt. Add 3 cups flour and stir. Gradually add remaining flour, one cup at a time, working well. Place dough on a lightly floured surface and knead, adding more flour if sticky. Lightly oil a large bowl and place dough inside. Turn dough once to coat with oil. Allow to rise until double in bulk. Before rolling dough out, oil rolling pin and work surface. Cut dough in half; roll each half out to a ¼-inch thickness. Coat one side of each dough portion with oil and place on grill, oiled sides down. Oil top sides and sprinkle with herbs to taste. Grill 2 minutes, flip and grill another 2 minutes or until golden. Makes 2 loaves.

Strawberry-Peach Soup

This is great on hot summer days or for a ladies' luncheon. Not only does it taste great, it looks great!

2 c. strawberries, hulled and chopped
8-oz. container strawberry yogurt
½ c. sugar, divided
1 t. lemon juice, divided
2 peaches, peeled, pitted and chopped
8-oz. container peach yogurt
Garnish: whipped cream, strawberries

Combine strawberries, strawberry yogurt, ¼ cup sugar and ½ teaspoon lemon juice in a blender. Process until smooth. Transfer to a bowl and set aside. Repeat with peaches, peach yogurt, remaining sugar and remaining lemon juice. To serve, pour each mixture at the same time into individual shallow soup bowls. Garnish servings with whipped cream and a strawberry. Serves 6.

Kathy Majeske
Denver, PA

Garden-Fresh Gazpacho

I learned to make this when I was managing a restaurant. It can be very addictive in the summer months!

6 to 8 tomatoes, chopped
1 onion, finely chopped
1 cucumber, peeled and chopped
1 green pepper, chopped
2 T. fresh parsley or cilantro, chopped
1 clove garlic, finely chopped
1 to 2 stalks celery, chopped
2 T. lemon juice
salt and pepper to taste
4 c. tomato juice
4 drops hot pepper sauce
Garnish: cucumber slices, fresh parsley sprigs

Combine all ingredients except garnish in a large lidded container or gallon-size Mason jar. Refrigerate until well chilled. Top servings with cucumber slices and fresh parsley sprigs. Serves 12 to 15.

Patsy Johnson
Salem, MO

simple switch
Swap out the tomatoes for avocados in your favorite gazpacho recipe, or try stirring in a little unflavored yogurt for a yummy white gazpacho.

Garden-Fresh Gazpacho

Too-Simple Tortilla Soup

Tomato & Basil Bisque

Garnish servings with a swirl of cream and a sprig of basil leaves.

2 onions, chopped
2 carrots, peeled and shredded
1 T. butter
8 tomatoes, peeled and chopped
½ t. sugar
½ t. salt
¼ t. pepper
½ c. fresh basil, chopped
2 c. chicken broth

Sauté onions and carrots in butter in a large saucepan over medium heat until tender. Stir in tomatoes, sugar, salt and pepper; bring to a boil. Reduce heat; cover and simmer for 10 minutes. Cool soup slightly; transfer to a blender. Add basil; cover and process until smooth. Pour soup back into saucepan. Stir in broth; heat through. Serves 4.

Zoe Bennett
Columbia, SC

Too-Simple Tortilla Soup

Top this soup with fresh cilantro and a diced avocado and serve with tortilla chips.

2 10-oz. cans chicken, drained
2 14½-oz. cans chicken broth
2 15-oz. cans white hominy, drained
16-oz. jar salsa
1 T. cumin

Combine all ingredients in a stockpot; bring to a boil. Reduce heat, and warm through. Serves 6 to 8.

Paulette Cunningham
Lompoc, CA

Hawaiian Grilled Chicken

If fresh herbs aren't available, simply substitute ½ to ¾ teaspoon dried. This dish is also terrific grilled outside!

½ c. olive oil
⅓ c. lemon juice or white wine vinegar
½ c. soy sauce
3 to 4 cloves garlic, minced
1 to 2 t. fresh oregano, chopped
1 to 2 t. fresh rosemary, chopped
4-lb. roasting chicken, halved
Optional: 1 to 2 t. fresh basil, chopped
1 t. salt
¼ t. black or lemon pepper
non-stick olive oil spray
Garnish: rosemary sprigs, lemon wedges

Combine olive oil, lemon juice, soy sauce, garlic, oregano and rosemary in a large plastic zipping bag. Close and shake to blend. Add chicken to bag. Refrigerate up to 6 hours; turn occasionally to coat chicken with marinade. Remove chicken from bag; reserve marinade. Brush chicken with marinade and sprinkle with basil, if desired, salt and pepper. Discard marinade. Place chicken, skin-side down, on a broiler rack about 7 inches from heat. Broil chicken 20 minutes, or until golden. Lightly coat all sides of chicken with non-stick olive oil spray. Turn chicken and continue to broil 10 minutes, or until juices run clear. Garnish as desired. Serves 4.

Kristine Coburn
Dansville, NY

Mother's Fried Chicken

Mother's Fried Chicken

This recipe was given to me by my mother 30 years ago. It is always asked for when I cook for church get-togethers and Sunday dinners. The first time I made this for my pastor and his wife, it brought back memories for them of their own mothers' fried chicken.

4 c. self-rising flour
2 T. salt
2 T. pepper
8 lbs. chicken
4 to 5 c. shortening, divided

Combine flour, salt and pepper in a shallow pan. Dredge chicken in flour mixture. Heat 3 cups shortening to 350 degrees in a large cast-iron skillet over medium-high heat. Working in batches, fry chicken, covered, about 10 minutes. Reduce heat to medium-low; fry 30 minutes per side. Add shortening as needed. Uncover during last 5 minutes of cooking time. Drain on paper towels. Serves 8.

Evelyn Russell
Dallas, TX

Tangy BBQ Chicken

The barbecue sauce in this recipe is our family favorite...I could almost drink it! The recipe makes about 1½ cups sauce, and it's tasty on chicken, beef and pork.

1 c. brewed coffee
1 c. catsup
½ c. sugar
½ c. Worcestershire sauce
¼ c. cider vinegar
⅛ t. pepper
8 chicken legs with thighs

Combine all ingredients except chicken in a saucepan. Bring to a boil over medium heat; reduce heat to low. Simmer, uncovered, for 30 to 35 minutes, until thickened, stirring occasionally. Grill chicken as desired, brushing with sauce as it cooks. Serves 8.

Jewel Sharpe
Raleigh, NC

portable place setting

A wheelbarrow or wagon is just right for holding paper plates, cups, flatware and napkins. It's easy to take right to the picnic spot and keeps picnic tables free for holding all the scrumptious food!

Ribs with Espresso Barbecue Sauce

The ribs and barbecue sauce can be prepared one day ahead. Just cool slightly, cover separately and refrigerate.

2 T. hot Mexican-style chili powder
1 T. paprika
1 T. ground cumin
1½ t. salt
¾ t. pepper
4 lbs. baby back pork ribs, cut into
    serving-size pieces
12-oz. bottle dark beer
18-oz. bottle favorite barbecue sauce
½ c. water
2 T. brown sugar, packed
1 T. instant coffee granules

Whisk together seasonings in a small bowl to blend; rub mixture over ribs. Place ribs in a large heavy roasting pan. Bring beer to a boil over medium heat in a large saucepan; cook until reduced to one cup, about 5 minutes. Pour beer around ribs; cover tightly with aluminum foil. Bake at 400 degrees until fork-tender, about 1½ hours. Combine remaining ingredients in a saucepan over medium heat. Simmer until slightly thickened, stirring occasionally, about 10 minutes. Brush ribs with barbecue sauce; grill over medium-hot coals for 3 minutes. Turn ribs; brush again with sauce and grill for an additional 3 to 4 minutes, until heated through. Bring remaining sauce to a boil; serve with ribs. Serves 4 to 6.

Jo Ann
Gooseberry Patch

Easy Southern-Style Pork Barbecue

This Southern slow-cooker favorite is known as pulled-pork barbecue.

3- to 4-lb. pork roast
¼ c. water
2 T. smoke-flavored cooking sauce
pepper to taste
6 to 8 sandwich buns, split
Optional: favorite barbecue sauce, coleslaw

Place pork roast in a 4 to 5-quart slow cooker. Add water; sprinkle evenly with cooking sauce and pepper to taste. Cover and cook on high one hour and then on low 6 to 8 hours. Remove roast from slow cooker; shred meat with a fork. Place meat on buns; top with barbecue sauce and a scoop of coleslaw, if desired. Serves 6 to 8.

Marilyn Morel
Keene, NH

To really experience the true Southern-style pork barbecue sandwich, add a generous dab of coleslaw before you add the top bun. Yum! —Marilyn

Easy Southern-Style Pork Barbecue

Family-Favorite Pork Tacos

My kids liked to order tacos just like these at our neighborhood Mexican restaurant, so I recreated the recipe to make at home. It's a great way to save money and is such a hit...everyone in my family actually prefers them!

2 t. oil
1 lb. pork tenderloin, cubed
1 t. ground cumin
2 garlic cloves, minced
1 c. green or red salsa
Optional: ½ c. fresh cilantro, chopped
8 10-inch corn tortillas, warmed
Garnish: shredded lettuce, diced tomatoes,
    sliced avocado, sliced black olives, sour cream,
    shredded Cheddar cheese

Heat oil in a non-stick skillet over medium-high heat. Add pork cubes and cumin; cook until pork is done, about 5 minutes. Add garlic and cook for one minute; drain. Stir in salsa and heat through; stir in cilantro, if desired. Using 2 forks, shred pork. Fill warmed tortillas with pork mixture; garnish as desired. Serves 4.

Carol Lytle
Columbus, OH

Louisiana Shrimp

Serve lots of French bread with these shrimp to soak up the saucy seasonings. (Pictured on page 110)

2 T. butter
½ c. Worcestershire sauce
5 cloves garlic, chopped
6 bay leaves, broken in half
2 t. seafood seasoning
hot pepper sauce to taste
pepper to taste
2 T. lemon juice
1 lb. uncooked shrimp, peeled and cleaned

Combine all ingredients except shrimp in a saucepan; mix well. Bring to a boil; reduce heat and simmer 5 minutes. Place shrimp in an ungreased 3-quart casserole dish; pour mixture over shrimp. Bake at 400 degrees for 10 minutes. Remove and discard bay leaves. Serves 2.

Deborah DeVaughn
Martin, TN

Herbed Shrimp Tacos

These tacos are great to make in the summer...simply grill the shrimp on metal skewers after marinating. They're so good!

juice of 1 lime
½ c. plus 1 T. fresh cilantro, chopped and divided
½ t. salt
½ t. pepper
⅛ t. dried thyme
⅛ t. dried oregano
1 lb. uncooked medium shrimp, peeled and cleaned
½ c. radishes, shredded
½ c. green cabbage, shredded
½ c. red onion, chopped
Optional: 2 T. oil
10 6-inch flour tortillas, warmed
Optional: guacamole, fresh salsa

Combine lime juice, one tablespoon cilantro, salt, pepper and herbs in a large plastic zipping bag; mix well. Add shrimp; close bag and refrigerate at least one hour. Mix together radishes, cabbage, onion and remaining cilantro; set aside. Thread shrimp onto skewers and grill over medium-high heat until pink and cooked through, or heat oil in a skillet over medium heat and sauté shrimp until done. Spoon into warm tortillas; serve with guacamole, fresh salsa, if desired, and cabbage mixture. Serves 10.

Lori Vincent
Alpine, UT

Herbed Shrimp Tacos

Honey-Garlic Steak

The honey-garlic sauce is the secret...what a blend of flavors!

1 lb. boneless beef steak
6 T. honey-garlic barbecue sauce, divided
2 T. olive oil
1 clove garlic, pressed
1 c. mushrooms, chopped
1 c. green pepper, sliced
1 c. onion, sliced
2 T. soy sauce
hot cooked rice

Brush each side of steak with one tablespoon barbecue sauce; set aside. Heat oil in a skillet over medium-high heat; stir in garlic, mushrooms, green pepper and onion. Sauté 10 minutes, or until vegetables are crisp-tender. Meanwhile, grill steak over medium-low coals for 15 minutes, turning once halfway through cooking time. Add soy sauce and remaining barbecue sauce to vegetables; reduce heat to medium-low. Simmer 15 minutes. Transfer steak to a serving platter, cover with aluminum foil and set aside 5 minutes. To serve, uncover and slice steak and spoon vegetables over top. Serve with rice. Serves 4.

Athena Colegrove
Big Spring, TX

Bacon-Stuffed Burgers

These go so fast I have to double the recipe!

4 slices bacon, crisply cooked and crumbled,
    drippings reserved
¼ c. onion, chopped
4-oz. can mushroom pieces, drained and diced
1 lb. ground beef
1 lb. ground pork sausage
¼ c. grated Parmesan cheese
½ t. pepper
½ t. garlic powder
2 T. steak sauce
8 sandwich buns, split
Optional: lettuce, tomato, provolone cheese

Heat 2 tablespoons reserved drippings in a skillet over medium heat. Add onion and sauté until tender. Add bacon and mushrooms; heat through and set aside. Combine beef, sausage, Parmesan cheese, pepper, garlic powder and steak sauce in a large bowl. Shape into 16 patties. Spoon bacon mixture over 8 patties. Place remaining patties on top and press edges tightly to seal. Grill over medium coals to desired doneness. Serve on buns with lettuce, tomato and cheese, if desired. Makes 8.

Molly Cool
Gooseberry Patch

summertime scrapbook
Put everyone's favorite summertime photos together in a scrapbook to be enjoyed year-round! Add postcards from family trips, ticket stubs from the county fair and other mementos.

Bacon-Stuffed Burgers

Angie's Pasta & Sauce

Boycott-Your-Grill Beef Kabobs

Skewers that bake in the oven...perfect for a rained-out cookout!

1 c. oil
⅔ c. soy sauce
½ c. lemon juice
¼ c. Worcestershire sauce
¼ c. mustard
2 cloves garlic, minced
1 T. pepper
⅛ t. hot pepper sauce
3 lbs. beef sirloin steak, cut into 2-inch cubes
2 green peppers, cut into 1-inch squares
2 8-oz. pkgs. mushrooms
20-oz. can pineapple chunks, drained

Combine all ingredients except steak, vegetables and pineapple. Pour over steak; cover and refrigerate for 24 hours. Thread steak, vegetables and pineapple onto skewers. Arrange on greased baking sheets. Bake at 400 degrees for 8 to 10 minutes. Turn and continue baking until steak is done. Serves 4.

Kathy Solka
Ishpeming, MI

Angie's Pasta & Sauce

Homemade sauce is so simple to prepare. You'll love the taste of both the sauce and the freshly grated Parmesan on top.

6 to 8 roma tomatoes, halved, seeded
    and diced
1 to 2 cloves garlic, minced
½ c. butter, melted
1 T. dried basil
8-oz. pkg. angel hair pasta, cooked
Garnish: freshly grated Parmesan cheese

Combine tomatoes and garlic in a saucepan. Simmer over medium heat 15 minutes; set aside. Blend together butter and basil; add to pasta. Toss to coat. Stir in tomato mixture and garnish. Serves 4 to 6.

Angie Whitmore
Farmington, UT

Carol's Veggie Panini

A stop at a roadside market yielded a basket brimming with fresh veggies. This is the super-simple recipe I created to use them up.

2 T. balsamic vinegar
1 T. olive oil
½ t. salt
⅛ t. pepper
1 eggplant, cut into ¼-inch slices
1 zucchini, cut into 8 slices
1 red pepper, quartered
8 slices ciabatta bread
1 c. shredded mozzarella cheese
8 fresh basil leaves

Whisk together vinegar, oil, salt and pepper in a bowl; set aside. Brush both sides of eggplant, zucchini and red pepper with vinegar mixture. Arrange in a single layer on a lightly greased baking sheet. Coat all vegetables with vegetable spray. Broil about 4 inches from heat for 7 to 8 minutes, turning once and coating vegetables with spray as needed. Lightly brush one side of each bread slice with remaining vinegar mixture; turn and coat second side with spray. Place bread, sprayed-side down, on an ungreased baking sheet. Top 4 bread slices with vegetables, cheese and basil. Top with remaining bread slices, sprayed-side up. Place sandwiches, one at a time, in a skillet; set a bacon press or other weight on top. Cook sandwiches over medium-high heat for about 4 minutes, turning once, until lightly golden on both sides. Makes 4 sandwiches.

Carol Lytle
Columbus, OH

Grilled Salmon BLTs

Lemony dill mayonnaise is the secret ingredient in this recipe!

⅓ c. mayonnaise
2 t. fresh dill, chopped
1 t. lemon zest
4 1-inch-thick salmon fillets
¼ t. salt
⅛ t. pepper
8 ½-inch slices country-style bread
4 romaine lettuce leaves
2 tomatoes, sliced
6 slices bacon, crisply cooked and halved

Stir together mayonnaise, dill and zest; set aside. Sprinkle salmon with salt and pepper; place on a lightly greased hot grill, skin-side down. Cover and cook about 10 to 12 minutes, without turning, until cooked through. Slide a thin metal spatula between salmon and skin; lift salmon and transfer to plate. Discard skin. Arrange bread slices on grill; cook until lightly toasted on both sides. Spread mayonnaise mixture on one side of 4 toasted bread slices. Top each with one lettuce leaf, 2 tomato slices, one salmon fillet, 3 half-slices bacon and remaining bread slice. Makes 4 sandwiches.

Edie DeSpain
Logan, UT

Grilled Salmon BLTs

Caesar Focaccia Sandwich

Now that I'm retired after 28 years of federal service, I enjoy being able to try new recipes on my family. This one was a big winner!

2 c. mixed salad greens
¼ c. Caesar salad dressing
8-inch round focaccia bread, halved
    horizontally
4 slices Cheddar cheese
¼ lb. deli ham, thinly shaved
¼ lb. deli turkey, thinly shaved
1 tomato, sliced
1 slice red onion, separated into rings
Garnish: pickles, potato chips

  Toss salad greens with salad dressing; set aside. Layer the bottom half of focaccia with greens mixture and remaining ingredients except garnish. Cover with top half of focaccia; cut into halves or quarters. Serve with pickles and chips on the side. Serves 2 to 4.

Wendy Ball
Battle Creek, MI

Chili Crescent Cheese Dogs
Buffalo Potato Wedges (page 147)

Chili Crescent Cheese Dogs

So easy to make, the kids will love to help out! Serve with Buffalo Potato Wedges. (Recipe on page 147)

8-oz. tube refrigerated crescent rolls
8 hot dogs
1 c. shredded Cheddar cheese
1 c. chili

  Separate crescent rolls into triangles. Place one hot dog in the center of each dough triangle; sprinkle each with cheese. Spoon chili over cheese. Fold dough corners inward to partially cover each hot dog, pressing ends. Arrange on an ungreased baking sheet. Bake at 425 degrees for 10 to 12 minutes, until crescents are golden and hot dogs are heated through. Serves 8.

Jen Martineau
Delaware, OH

plan a picnic

An old-fashioned picnic lunch is a terrific way to relax on a sunny afternoon. Pack sandwiches along with fresh fruits & veggies in vintage tins for easy toting.

Grandma Dumeney's
Baked Beans

Grandma Dumeney's Baked Beans

My Grandma Dumeney brought her sweet baked beans to every family reunion. Everyone really looked forward to them! Grandma was 84 when she shared this simple recipe with me, and I'm so glad she did!

3 28-oz. cans pork & beans
1 lb. bacon, crisply cooked and crumbled
1 c. brown sugar, packed
1 c. catsup
1 onion, diced
Garnish: additional crisply cooked and
    crumbled bacon

Combine all ingredients except garnish in a large bowl and mix well. Transfer to a lightly greased 4-quart casserole dish with a lid. Bake, covered, at 400 degrees for one hour. Reduce temperature to 350 degrees; uncover dish and bake for an additional hour. Garnish with bacon. Serves 8.

Susan Fountain
Stanton, MI

campfire fun
A fun idea for a family get-together...serve up baked beans Western style. Enjoy them with a dinner 'round a campfire. Roast hot dogs, grill corn on the cob, roast potatoes in the coals and finish off the meal with warm biscuits and honey.

Fried Dill Pickle Coins

We tried these crunchy pickles at a restaurant and later found the recipe. They're a family favorite!

2 c. all-purpose flour
½ t. salt
¼ t. pepper
2 eggs, beaten
1 c. milk
3 c. dill pickles, thinly sliced
oil for deep frying
ranch salad dressing for dipping

Combine flour, salt and pepper in a bowl. Whisk together eggs and milk in a separate bowl. Drain pickles well on paper towels. Coat pickles with flour mixture and then dip in egg mixture. Heat oil to 375 degrees in a large deep fryer. Add pickles, about 10 at a time, and cook for 3 minutes, or until golden, turning once. Drain on paper towels. Serve warm with ranch dressing. Serves 6.

Maria Hostettler
Fredonia, PA

Sweet & Tangy Cucumbers

I used to work at a deli that served these fantastic "pickled" cucumbers. This is the secret recipe!

2 c. sugar
1 c. white vinegar
10 to 12 cucumbers, peeled and
    thinly sliced
1 to 2 onions, thinly sliced

Whisk together sugar and vinegar until sugar is dissolved. Toss with remaining ingredients. Refrigerate until ready to serve. Serves 12 to 15.

Kathie Poritz
Burlington, WI

Country-Fried Green Tomatoes

These are a must-have side dish in the summer when green tomatoes are plentiful in the garden.

1 c. buttermilk
1 egg, beaten
1 c. cornmeal
½ c. all-purpose flour
2 T. sugar
⅛ t. salt
¼ t. pepper
2 to 3 green tomatoes, sliced ½-inch thick
vegetable oil for frying

Whisk together buttermilk and egg in a shallow bowl. Combine cornmeal, flour, sugar, salt and pepper in another shallow bowl. Dip tomato slices in buttermilk mixture; coat in cornmeal mixture. Heat oil, about one-inch deep, in a large skillet over medium-high heat. Cook tomatoes 4 minutes on each side, or until golden. Serves 4.

Angie Stone
Argillite, KY

Country-Fried Green
Tomatoes

Tomato Pie

This tastes like homemade pizza.

3 to 4 tomatoes, diced
salt and pepper to taste
½ c. mayonnaise
1 c. shredded sharp Cheddar cheese
1 c. shredded Colby Jack cheese
1 T. dried chives
1 T. dried basil
9-inch pie crust, baked

Place tomatoes between paper towels to absorb some of the moisture. Sprinkle tomatoes with salt and pepper in a bowl. Combine mayonnaise, cheeses, chives and basil in a separate bowl; carefully add tomatoes. Pour mixture into pie crust. Bake, uncovered, at 400 degrees for 20 to 30 minutes. Serves 8.

Lynette Edmondson
Dickson, TN

first come, first served

For the best selection, plan to be at the farmers' market first thing in the morning. Bring along a roomy shoulder bag or basket so that it's easy to tote all your goodies.

Grilled Market Veggies

I just love to take my roomy basket to the farmers' market. It's great fun to bring home a bushel of veggies, herbs and new recipes to try!

2 to 3 zucchini, sliced ¾-inch thick
2 to 3 yellow squash, sliced ¾-inch thick
1 to 2 baby eggplant, sliced ¾-inch thick
1 sweet onion, sliced ¾-inch thick
2 tomatoes, sliced 1-inch thick
½ c. balsamic vinegar
1½ c. oil
2 cloves garlic, minced
1 T. fresh rosemary, minced
1 T. fresh oregano, chopped
1 T. fresh basil, chopped
1 T. fresh parsley, minced
1 T. sugar
salt and pepper to taste

Combine vegetables in a large bowl. Whisk together remaining ingredients and pour over vegetables. Toss to coat. Marinate for 30 minutes to one hour. Remove vegetables from marinade with a slotted spoon. Arrange on a grill over medium-high heat. Grill 2 to 5 minutes on each side, basting often with marinade, until tender. Serves 4 to 6.

Regina Wickline
Pebble Beach, CA

Old-Fashioned Creamed Corn

This recipe was given to me by my grandmother when I first got married, 37 years ago. She has been making her creamed corn this way for 60 years. It always goes first at our church and family suppers, and we always run out, no matter how much I make! This is the best creamed corn you will ever eat!

6 ears corn, husked
¼ c. bacon drippings
¼ c. water
2 T. all-purpose flour
½ c. milk
sugar to taste
salt and pepper to taste

Remove kernels from corn, reserving as much liquid as possible. Set aside. Heat drippings in a cast-iron skillet over medium heat. Add corn and reserved liquid. Stir in water, and cook for 15 minutes. Whisk flour into milk; slowly add to corn. Reduce heat to low and cook, stirring frequently, until mixture thickens. Sprinkle with sugar, salt and pepper; stir to blend. Serves 6.

Beverly Tanner
Crouse, NC

Smoky Grilled Corn

You'll find smoked paprika in the spice aisle at your grocery.

8 ears corn, husked
4 T. olive oil, divided
I T. kosher salt, divided
I T. pepper, divided
I T. smoked paprika, divided

Divide corn between 2 large plastic zipping bags. Add 2 tablespoons oil, 1½ teaspoons salt, 1½ teaspoons pepper and 1½ teaspoons paprika to each bag. Close bags and gently toss to coat corn. Remove corn from bags; arrange on a campfire grate or grill over medium-high heat. Grill corn, turning often, until lightly golden, about 25 minutes. Serves 8.

Mary Ann Dell
Phoenixville, PA

Smoky Grilled Corn

Green Beans Supreme

Buffalo Potato Wedges

These potatoes are irresistible as either a side dish or an appetizer. (Pictured on page 139)

6 to 8 potatoes, sliced into wedges
1 to 2 T. olive oil
salt, pepper and garlic powder to taste
¼ c. butter
½ c. hot pepper sauce
Optional: blue cheese salad dressing

Arrange potato wedges on a lightly greased baking sheet. Drizzle with oil; sprinkle with salt, pepper and garlic powder. Bake at 375 degrees for about 30 minutes, or until tender, tossing occasionally. Remove pan from oven. Combine butter and hot sauce in a microwave-safe bowl. Microwave on high until butter is melted, about one minute; mix well. Drizzle butter mixture over potato wedges; bake 15 more minutes. Serve with salad dressing for dipping, if desired. Serves 8 to 10.

Victoria Francis
McHenry, IL

Green Beans Supreme

This isn't your usual green bean casserole. Loaded with cheese and sour cream, it will be your new favorite!

1 onion, sliced
1 T. fresh parsley, snipped
3 T. butter, divided
2 T. all-purpose flour
½ t. lemon zest
½ t. salt
⅛ t. pepper
½ c. milk
8-oz. container sour cream
16-oz. pkg. frozen French-style green beans, cooked
½ c. shredded Cheddar cheese
¼ c. soft bread crumbs

Cook onion slices and parsley in 2 tablespoons butter until onion is tender. Blend in flour, lemon zest, salt and pepper. Stir in milk; heat until thick and bubbly. Add sour cream and beans; heat through. Spoon into an ungreased 2-quart baking dish; sprinkle with cheese. Melt remaining butter and toss with bread crumbs; sprinkle over beans. Broil 3 to 4 inches from heat for 3 minutes, or until golden. Serves 4 to 6.

Joan's Ratatoûille

I created this recipe from the abundant supply of fresh vegetables my father grows every year. He so enjoys sharing his garden bounty with family & friends! This is a delicious side dish, but I enjoy serving it in rimmed soup plates as soup.

2 c. onion, chopped
4 cloves garlic, minced
½ c. olive oil
8 c. tomatoes, peeled and coarsely chopped
4 to 6 c. zucchini, cut into ½-inch-thick slices
2 green peppers, cut into thin strips
2 red peppers, cut into thin strips
1 T. chili powder, or to taste
salt to taste

Sauté onion and garlic in oil in a large saucepan over medium heat, for about 3 to 4 minutes. Add tomatoes, zucchini and peppers. Reduce heat; cover and simmer, stirring occasionally, until vegetables are tender, about 20 minutes. Stir in seasonings. Simmer, uncovered, an additional 15 minutes, stirring occasionally. Serves 6.

Joan Shaffer
Chambersburg, PA

Zucchini Pancakes

You'll love these tender pancakes...they're super for a brunch buffet!

½ c. biscuit baking mix
¼ c. grated Parmesan cheese
salt and pepper to taste
2 eggs, beaten
2 c. zucchini, shredded
oil for frying
Garnish: butter, maple syrup, sour cream

Combine all ingredients except oil and garnish; stir until mixed. Heat oil in a skillet over medium-high heat. Drop batter by 2 tablespoonfuls into skillet. Cook and flip until golden on both sides. Serve warm; garnish as desired. Serves 4.

Nancy Dearborn
Erie, PA

Skillet-Toasted Corn Salad

The corn for this salad is cooked until toasty brown and tossed with peppers and Parmesan cheese...yummy!

⅓ c. plus 1 T. olive oil, divided
⅓ c. lemon juice
1 T. Worcestershire sauce
3 cloves garlic, minced
3 to 4 dashes hot pepper sauce
¼ t. salt
½ t. pepper
6 ears sweet corn, husks and kernels removed
4 red, yellow and green peppers, coarsely chopped
½ c. grated Parmesan cheese
1 head romaine lettuce, cut crosswise into
    1-inch pieces

Combine ⅓ cup oil, lemon juice, Worcestershire sauce, garlic, hot pepper sauce, salt and pepper in a jar with a tight-fitting lid. Cover and shake well; set aside. Heat remaining oil in a large skillet over medium-high heat. Add corn kernels; sauté 5 minutes, or until corn is tender and golden, stirring often. Remove from heat. Combine corn, peppers and cheese in a large bowl. Pour dressing over corn mixture; toss lightly to coat. Serve over lettuce. Serves 6 to 8.

Sherri Cooper
Armada, MI

Whenever my father comes to visit, this salad is one that he requests. He usually stops by the local farmers' vegetable stand on his way to our house and picks up fresh ears of corn...just for this salad! —Sherri

Skillet-Toasted Corn Salad

Granny's Macaroni Salad

My family loves this cheesy macaroni salad made from my grandmother's own recipe. She was a very good granny to me!

48-oz. pkg. seashell pasta, uncooked
8-oz. pkg. pasteurized process cheese spread, cubed
1 green pepper, chopped
1 cucumber, shredded
4 to 5 carrots, peeled and shredded
2 tomatoes, chopped

Cook pasta according to package directions. Drain and rinse with cold water. Mix cheese and vegetables together in a large serving bowl; add pasta. Toss together. Add Dressing and mix well. Chill 8 hours to overnight to allow flavors to combine. Serves 15 to 20.

Dressing:

2 c. mayonnaise-style salad dressing
2 T. sugar
2 T. vinegar
1 T. mustard

Mix all ingredients together in a small bowl.

Suzanne Morrow
Moorhead, MN

Louise's Potato Salad

This recipe was handed down in my husband's family. His Portuguese grandma would make this often...it's one of the things they remember best about her cooking.

5 lbs. potatoes, peeled, cubed and cooked in salted water
4 eggs, hard-boiled, peeled and divided
¼ c. mayonnaise
½ red onion, chopped
2 stalks celery, chopped
1 T. sweet pickle relish
½ t. celery salt
½ t. dried parsley
Garnish: paprika, fresh parsley

Keep potatoes warm while preparing other ingredients. Slice one egg and set aside for garnish. Dice remaining eggs; place in a large bowl and add remaining ingredients except garnish. Add potatoes to bowl while still warm; toss gently to coat. Refrigerate until serving time. Garnish with sliced egg, paprika and parsley. Serves 10.

Denise Neal
Castle Rock, CO

don't toss it!
Next time you finish a jar of pickles, save the leftover juice! It makes a tasty addition to potato salad and deviled eggs.

Chunky Tomato-Avocado Salad

Chunky Tomato-Avocado Salad

Chill this flavorful salad for at least two hours if you don't have time to refrigerate it overnight.

1 avocado, pitted, peeled and cubed
3 plum tomatoes, chopped
¼ c. sweet onion, chopped
1 T. fresh cilantro, chopped
2 to 3 T. lemon juice

Gently stir together all ingredients; cover and refrigerate overnight. Serves 4.

Alma Evans
Patrick Air Force Base, FL

Crunchy Veggie Salad

Mmm...with crunchy veggies, crisp bacon and creamy dressing, this salad will have people asking for the recipe wherever you take it!

6 slices bacon, crisply cooked and crumbled
I head cauliflower, cut into flowerets
I bunch broccoli, cut into flowerets
I c. radishes, sliced
¾ c. green onion, diced
I c. sour cream
I c. favorite creamy salad dressing
0.65-oz. pkg. cheese-garlic salad dressing mix

Combine bacon and vegetables in a large bowl; set aside. Mix together remaining ingredients in a separate bowl. Pour salad dressing mixture over vegetables; toss to mix well. Chill 30 minutes before serving. Serves 6 to 8.

Janie Branstetter
Duncan, OK

Blueberry-Chicken Salad

Fresh blueberries and lemony yogurt add a fresh spin to the usual chicken salad.

2 c. chicken breast, cooked and cubed
¾ c. celery, chopped
½ c. red pepper, diced
½ c. green onions, thinly sliced
2 c. blueberries
6-oz. container lemon yogurt
3 T. mayonnaise
½ t. salt
Optional: Bibb lettuce

Combine chicken and vegetables in a large bowl. Gently stir in blueberries. Combine yogurt, mayonnaise and salt. Drizzle over chicken mixture and gently toss to coat. Cover and refrigerate 30 minutes. Spoon onto lettuce-lined plates, if desired. Serves 4.

Debi DeVore
Dover, OH

Lemon-Dill Pea Salad

Creamy and delicious!

8-oz. container sour cream
I T. lemon juice
I green onion, chopped
2 t. sugar
I t. dill weed
2 c. fresh peas, shelled

In a bowl, combine sour cream, lemon juice, green onion, sugar and dill weed; blend well. Using a steamer, steam peas 3 to 4 minutes, until tender; rinse and cool. Fold into sour cream mixture. Refrigerate until serving time. Serves 4.

the berry best
Fresh-picked berries are a special country pleasure. Store them in a colander in the refrigerator to let cold air circulate around them. Wash when you're ready to use.

Blueberry-Chicken Salad

Tangy Watermelon Salad

Tangy Watermelon Salad

I won first prize at a Ladies' Day salad contest during our county fair with this recipe. Everyone is surprised to see watermelon and onions together, but when they taste the salad, they really like it and always ask for the recipe.

14 c. watermelon, cubed
1 red onion, halved and thinly sliced
1 c. green onions, chopped
¾ c. orange juice
5 T. red wine vinegar
2 T. plus 1½ t. honey
1 T. green pepper, finely chopped
½ t. salt
¼ t. pepper
¼ t. garlic powder
¼ t. onion powder
¼ t. dry mustard
¾ c. oil

Combine watermelon and onions in a large bowl; set aside. Combine orange juice, vinegar, honey, green pepper and seasonings in a small bowl; slowly whisk in oil. Pour over watermelon mixture; toss gently. Cover and refrigerate for at least 2 hours. Serve with a slotted spoon. Serves about 10.

Belva Conner
Hillsdale, IN

Key Lime Pie

Cool and tangy...perfect after a grilled dinner.

4 extra-large eggs, separated
14-oz. can sweetened condensed milk
¼ c. Key lime juice
9-inch pie crust, baked
¼ t. cream of tartar
¼ c. sugar

Beat egg yolks with an electric mixer at medium speed until foamy; add condensed milk, blending

thoroughly. Add lime juice and continue to beat until mixture is thick. Pour into crust and bake at 350 degrees for about 6 minutes, until filling is set. Meanwhile, beat egg whites in a small bowl until foamy; blend in cream of tartar. Slowly add sugar, and continue to beat until egg whites are stiff; spread over hot filling, spreading meringue to edges to seal. Bake at 450 degrees for 4 minutes, or until meringue is golden. Serves 6 to 8.

Open-Face Peach Pie

Bring this to the next summer backyard party, and you'll be popular! (Pictured on page 110)

1 c. sugar
2 T. cornstarch
9-inch pie crust
6 peaches, peeled, pitted and halved
1 c. whipping cream

Mix together sugar and cornstarch; spread three-fourths of mixture into pie crust. Arrange peaches on top; sprinkle with remaining sugar mixture. Pour cream evenly over peaches; bake at 400 degrees for 10 minutes. Reduce heat to 350 degrees; bake an additional 40 minutes. Serves 8.

Christy Hughes
Provo, UT

This favorite pie recipe was handed down to me from my grandmother. —Christy

Berry Crumble

Quick-cooking oats are the secret to the scrumptious topping, making it extra-crunchy.

4 c. blackberries or blueberries
1 to 2 T. sugar
3 T. butter, softened
3 1½-oz. pkgs. quick-cooking oats with maple
  and brown sugar

Toss berries and sugar together in an ungreased 9" pie plate; set aside. Cut butter into quick-cooking oats until mixture resembles coarse crumbs; sprinkle over berries. Bake at 375 degrees for about 30 to 35 minutes, until topping is golden. Serves 6.

Sandy Bernards
Valencia, CA

Berry Crumble

Yummy Plum Dumplings

This dessert is also a delicious and unusual side dish for roast pork...the recipe makes its own sauce! The amount of water sounds like a lot, but it is correct.

4 c. plums, pitted and halved
4 c. all-purpose flour
1 T. baking powder
1 t. salt
2 c. milk
3 to 4 c. water
½ c. butter, diced
2 c. sugar

Arrange plum halves in the bottom of a lightly greased 13"x9" baking pan; set aside. Combine flour, baking powder, salt and milk; stir until dough forms. Pat dough evenly over plums. Pour enough water down the side of dough to just reach the top of dough. Dot with butter; sprinkle with sugar. Bake, uncovered, at 350 degrees for 1½ hours. Serve warm. Serves 8 to 10.

Andrea Ford
Montfort, WI

I scream, you scream!
An ice cream social is made for kids big or little! It's easy to plan and is a get-together that kids of all ages can set up and enjoy with family & friends.

Rocky Road Frozen Sandwiches

A snap to prepare...you can have a frosty treat anytime!

1 c. chocolate frosting
½ c. mini marshmallows
32 graham cracker squares, divided
½ c. marshmallow creme
½ gal. chocolate ice cream, softened

Mix together frosting and marshmallows; spread over each of 16 graham crackers. Spread marshmallow creme over each of remaining graham crackers. Spread ½ cup ice cream onto each of the graham crackers coated with frosting mixture. Top with remaining graham crackers. Wrap individually in plastic wrap, and freeze until firm. Makes 16.

Stacie Avner
Delaware, OH

Skyscraper Banana Splits

Everyone will line up for these piled-high sundaes! (Pictured on page 110)

¼ c. chocolate syrup, divided
4 scoops vanilla ice cream, divided
4 bananas, halved lengthwise and crosswise
4 scoops chocolate ice cream, divided
½ c. strawberry syrup, divided
Garnish: whipped cream, cherries

Pour one tablespoon chocolate syrup into each of 4 parfait glasses; add one scoop vanilla ice cream to each. Arrange 4 banana pieces, cut-side out, in each glass; top each with one scoop chocolate ice cream. Drizzle each evenly with strawberry syrup; top each with whipped cream and a cherry. Serves 4.

Beth Kramer
Port Saint Lucie, FL

Homemade Banana Pudding

My grandma was the cook at a small country school. She would make this dessert for the students and for family gatherings. It was a favorite for all. I think you'll love it, too!

2 eggs, beaten
2 c. milk
1½ c. brown sugar, packed
2 T. all-purpose flour
2 T. creamy or crunchy peanut butter
1 t. vanilla extract
1 to 2 bananas, sliced and divided
Optional: chopped peanuts

Whisk together eggs and milk in a bowl; set aside. Mix together brown sugar and flour in a saucepan. Add egg mixture to brown sugar mixture. Cook over medium-low heat, stirring constantly, until thickened. Add peanut butter and vanilla; whisk until creamy. Cool; transfer to a serving bowl. Fold banana slices into pudding, reserving a few slices for top of pudding. Garnish with reserved banana slices and sprinkle with peanuts, if desired. Serves 6.

Traci Rodgers
Gas City, IN

brown sugar fix
If a plastic bag of brown sugar has hardened, try this: Add a dampened paper towel to the bag, close it and microwave for 20 seconds. Press out the lumps with your fingers. If that doesn't do the trick, microwave for another 10 seconds.

Best-Ever Strawberry Shortcake

My mom always made this shortcake when our strawberries ripened in early June. She received this recipe from her mother, and it has always been a family favorite. In fact, this dessert is so good, it has even been featured at my brother-in-law's fine-dining restaurant!

½ c. butter, softened
1 c. sugar
2 eggs, beaten
1 t. vanilla extract
½ c. milk
2 c. all-purpose flour
1 T. baking powder
¼ t. salt
Garnish: sliced strawberries, whipped cream

Beat butter and sugar with an electric mixer at medium speed until smooth; beat in eggs, vanilla and milk. Mix flour, baking powder and salt in a separate bowl. Gradually add flour mixture to butter mixture; mix well. Spoon batter into a greased 9"x9" baking pan. Bake at 350 degrees for 40 to 50 minutes, until a toothpick inserted near the center comes out clean. Cut shortcake into squares; top with strawberries and whipped cream. Serves 9.

Emma Johnson
Lithopolis, OH

Farmgirl Chocolate Chippers

A great recipe when you need a lot of cookies!

2 c. butter, softened
2 c. sugar
2 c. brown sugar, packed
4 eggs, beaten
2 t. vanilla extract
5 c. long-cooking oats, uncooked
4 c. all-purpose flour
2 t. baking powder
2 t. baking soda
1 t. salt
2 12-oz. pkgs. semi-sweet chocolate chips
7-oz. pkg. chocolate candy bar, grated
3 c. chopped pecans

Blend together butter, sugar and brown sugar in a large bowl; mix well. Add eggs and vanilla; set aside. Working in batches, process oats in a blender or food processor until powdery. Combine oats, flour, baking powder, baking soda and salt in a large bowl; mix into butter mixture. Stir in chocolate chips, grated chocolate and pecans. Shape into 2-inch balls; arrange 2 inches apart on ungreased baking sheets. Bake at 375 degrees for 6 minutes. Makes 10 dozen.

Mary Murray
Mount Vernon, OH

Farmgirl Chocolate Chippers

Creamy Coffee Granita

Purée honeydew cubes in a food processor or blender. Place in a large mixing bowl with remaining ingredients. Stir well until sugar is thoroughly dissolved. Spoon into an ice-cream maker and freeze according to manufacturer's instructions. Serves 6.

Hot Fudge Brownie Sundaes

Homemade brownies, ice cream and hot fudge sauce…can it get any better? Try cutting the brownies with a round cookie cutter just for fun!

¼ c. butter
2 1-oz. sqs. semi-sweet baking chocolate, chopped
1 egg
½ c. brown sugar, packed
1 t. vanilla extract
¼ t. salt
¼ c. all-purpose flour
4 scoops vanilla ice cream, softened
Garnish: chocolate sauce, warmed

Combine butter and chocolate in a microwave-safe container; microwave on high until melted, stirring every minute. Stir; cool 10 minutes. Mix together egg, brown sugar, vanilla and salt in a small bowl. Stir into chocolate mixture. Add flour; mix well. Spread batter in an 8"x8" baking pan lined with lightly greased aluminum foil. Bake at 350 degrees for 15 minutes, or until a toothpick inserted near center comes out clean. Cool completely on a wire rack. Cover; chill until firm. Cut brownies into 8 squares. Spread 4 brownies with ice cream; top with remaining brownies. Wrap in plastic wrap; freeze overnight. To serve, drizzle with warm chocolate sauce. Serves 4.

Robin Hill
Rochester, NY

Creamy Coffee Granita

Start this about three hours before you'd like to serve it.

6 c. hot, strong brewed coffee
½ c. sugar
Garnish: whipped cream

Pour coffee and sugar into a 13"x9" baking pan, stirring to dissolve sugar. Cover with plastic wrap; place in freezer. Freeze 3 hours, scraping occasionally, until frozen. Serve topped with whipped cream. Serves 8 to 10.

Fresh Melon Sorbet

Light and delicious.

1 medium honeydew, seeded, peeled and cubed
¼ c. sugar
¼ c. lime juice

Hot Fudge Brownie Sundaes

Pumpkin Pie Ice Cream Fantasy (page 207)

Zesty Roasted Chicken & Potatoes (page 183)
Green Beans with Bacon & Garlic (page 202)

Slow-Cooker Country Chicken & Dumplings (page 179)

Old-Fashioned Ginger Beer (page 170)

BOUNTIFUL HARVEST

Comforting classics to welcome the autumn season

Robert's Corn Dip

Robert's Corn Dip

This dip is so delicious! The flavor is even better if it's made two days ahead of time.

3 11-oz. cans sweet corn & diced peppers, drained
2 4½-oz. cans chopped green chiles
6-oz. can chopped jalapeños, drained and
    liquid added to taste
½ c. green onion, chopped
1 c. mayonnaise
1 c. sour cream
1 t. pepper
½ t. garlic powder
16-oz. pkg. shredded sharp Cheddar cheese
Garnish: sliced jalapeño
corn chips

Mix together all ingredients except corn chips and jalapeño; refrigerate. Garnish, with sliced jalapeño. Serve with corn chips for scooping. Makes about 6 cups.

Carole Snodgrass
Rolla, MO

Claudia's Famous Wing Dip

8-oz. pkg. cream cheese, softened
16-oz. container sour cream
1 c. blue cheese salad dressing
½ c. hot wing sauce
2½ c. cooked chicken, shredded
1 c. shredded provolone cheese
tortilla chips
celery sticks

Beat cream cheese, sour cream, salad dressing and wing sauce in a large bowl until well blended. Stir in chicken and cheese. Transfer to a greased 2-quart casserole dish. Cover and bake at 350 degrees for 25 to 30 minutes, until hot and bubbly. Serve warm with tortilla chips and celery sticks. Makes 6½ cups.

Jason Keller
Carrollton, GA

Bacon Quesadillas

Bacon Quesadillas

These savory snacks have zing...what flavor!

1 c. shredded Colby Jack cheese
¼ c. bacon bits
¼ c. green onion, thinly sliced
Optional: 4½-oz. can green chiles
Optional: ¼ c. red or green pepper, chopped
4 6-inch flour tortillas
Garnish: sour cream, salsa

Combine cheese, bacon bits and onion in a small bowl; add chiles and peppers, if desired. Sprinkle mixture equally over one half of each tortilla. Fold tortillas in half; press lightly to seal edges. Arrange on a lightly greased baking sheet. Bake at 400 degrees for 8 to 10 minutes, until edges are lightly golden. Top with a dollop of sour cream and salsa. Serves 4.

Edward Kielar
Perrysburg, OH

Patricia's Super Nachos

These nachos are served at our home whenever we watch football bowl games on television. Make a double batch to feed a whole tailgating crowd!

1 lb. ground beef
1 onion, chopped
1 t. salt
½ t. pepper
2 16-oz. cans refried beans
4-oz. can diced green chiles
hot pepper sauce to taste
3 c. shredded Cheddar cheese
¾ c. taco sauce
1 c. guacamole
8-oz. container sour cream
¼ c. green onions, chopped
2¼-oz. can chopped black olives, drained
tortilla chips

Brown beef and onion in a skillet over medium heat. Drain; add salt and pepper and set aside. Spread beans in the bottom of an ungreased 15"x10" jelly-roll pan. Top with ground beef mixture, chiles, hot pepper sauce and cheese; drizzle taco sauce over the top. Bake, uncovered, at 400 degrees for 25 minutes, or until heated through and cheese is melted. Remove from oven; top with remaining ingredients except tortilla chips. Serve warm with tortilla chips. Serves 12.

Patricia Addison
Cave Junction, OR

Cheese-Olive Hot Snacks

My sister and I make these snacks as part of our Christmas Eve dinner celebration. Their cheesy goodness and surprise green olive center make them a popular appetizer any time.

5-oz. jar sharp pasteurized process
    cheese spread
¼ c. butter, softened
⅛ t. hot pepper sauce
⅛ t. Worcestershire sauce
⅔ to ¾ c. all-purpose flour
5¾-oz. jar green olives with pimentos,
    drained

Blend cheese and butter in a bowl until fluffy; add hot pepper and Worcestershire sauces, mixing well. Stir in enough flour to reach a dough consistency. Wrap each olive with a small piece of dough; roll so the olive is completely covered. Place on ungreased baking sheets. Bake at 400 degrees for 10 to 12 minutes, until lightly golden. Serves 15 to 20.

Bonnie Studler
Los Angeles, CA

fall fun
Jumping in leaf piles is a not-to-be-missed part of childhood fun! No fallen leaves in your yard? Ask some neighbors with a big maple tree or two for permission to rake up their leaves...you'll have a ball!

Pecan-Stuffed Dates with Bacon

Super quick and easy to make!

15 pecan halves
15 seedless dates
15 slices precooked packaged bacon

Heat pecan halves in a small non-stick skillet over medium-low heat, stirring often, 2 to 3 minutes, until toasted. Cut a lengthwise slit down the center of each date. Stuff one pecan half into each date and wrap each with one slice of bacon. Bake at 425 degrees for 8 minutes, or until bacon is crisp. Makes 15.

Pecan-Stuffed Dates with Bacon

Tropical Smoothies

Tropical Smoothies

A chilled, fruity smoothie really hits the spot on a hot day.

1 c. mango, peeled, pitted and cubed
¾ c. banana, sliced
⅔ c. milk
1 t. honey
¼ t. vanilla extract
Optional: 2 t. honey

Arrange mango in a single layer on a baking sheet; freeze for one hour. Place frozen mango and remaining ingredients in a blender. Process until smooth. Pour into glasses to serve. Serves 2.

Melissa Bordenkircher
Columbus, OH

spoonfuls of honey
Removing honey from measuring cups or spoons has never been easier...just coat your spoon or cup with vegetable oil before measuring the honey.

Mocha Coffee Smoothie

These delicious smoothies will give those expensive coffeehouse treats a run for their money.

1 c. milk
7 to 8 ice cubes
2 T. sugar
1 T. instant coffee granules
2 T. chocolate syrup
Garnish: whipped cream, grated chocolate

Combine all ingredients except garnish in a blender. Blend until smooth and creamy; pour into 2 tall glasses. Top with whipped cream and grated chocolate. Serves 2.

Kathleen Sturm
Corona, CA

Cinnamon Tea

Serve this tea in a crystal punch bowl with floating lemon and orange slices; add a rosemary wreath around the base of the bowl.

14 c. water
12 cinnamon-herb teabags
2 c. sugar
6-oz. can frozen pineapple juice concentrate
6-oz. can frozen lemonade concentrate
6-oz. can frozen orange juice concentrate
6 3-inch cinnamon sticks

Bring 12 cups water to a boil, add teabags and steep for 5 minutes. Discard teabags and add remaining water, sugar, juice concentrates and cinnamon sticks. Heat through, stirring well. Discard cinnamon sticks. Serves 30.

Old-Fashioned Ginger Beer

Our family always makes homemade root beer for family gatherings, but one year we tried this recipe. From then on, it's been a must-have right alongside our root beer.

4 lemons
¾ c. fresh ginger, peeled and coarsely chopped
¾ c. honey
¾ c. sugar
2 c. boiling water
1¼ c. orange juice
4 c. sparkling mineral water, chilled
crushed ice

Set one lemon aside and squeeze ⅓ cup lemon juice from remaining 3 lemons. Set juice aside. Grate 2 tablespoons of zest. Pulse ginger, honey and sugar in a food processor until just combined; place in a bowl or pitcher. Add lemon zest, boiling water, lemon juice, and orange juice; stir until sugar dissolves. Cool to room temperature. Cover and refrigerate for at least 24 hours and up to 5 days. To serve, strain ginger beer base into a pitcher. Thinly slice remaining lemon; add to pitcher. Stir in sparkling water. Serve over ice. Serves 8 to 10.

Amy Butcher
Columbus, GA

Old-Fashioned
Ginger Beer

Multi-Grain Waffles

Get off to a healthy start with these toasty, nutty-tasting waffles. Pair with Honey-Baked Bananas.

½ c. long-cooking oats, uncooked
2 c. buttermilk
⅔ c. whole-wheat flour
⅔ c. all-purpose flour
¼ c. toasted wheat germ
1½ t. baking powder
½ t. baking soda
¼ t. salt
1 t. cinnamon
2 eggs, beaten
¼ c. brown sugar, packed
1 T. oil
2 t. vanilla extract
Optional: butter, maple syrup

Mix oats and buttermilk in a large bowl; let stand for 15 minutes. Whisk together flours, wheat germ, baking powder, baking soda, salt and cinnamon in a separate bowl. Add eggs, brown sugar, oil and vanilla to oat mixture; mix well. Add oat mixture to flour mixture; stir just until moistened. Add batter by ½ cupfuls to a preheated, greased waffle iron. Bake according to manufacturer's instructions until crisp and golden, about 4 to 5 minutes. Serve with butter and maple syrup, if desired. Makes 12.

Kay Marone
Des Moines, IA

Honey-Baked Bananas

My mom shared this recipe for luscious honeyed bananas.

6 bananas, diagonally sliced
2 T. butter, melted
¼ c. honey
2 T. lemon juice

Arrange bananas in an ungreased 13"x9" baking pan. Blend remaining ingredients; brush over bananas. Bake, uncovered, at 350 degrees for about 15 minutes, turning occasionally. Serves 6.

Amy Greenlee
Carterville, IL

Overnight Apple
French Toast

Sausage & Potato Bake

One snowy weekend I wanted to fix something special for my family, so I tried this recipe and it is a real keeper! Just add sourdough toast and a fresh fruit salad for a hearty breakfast.

1 lb. mild ground pork sausage
1 lb. hot ground pork sausage
10¾-oz. can cream of chicken soup
8-oz. container French onion dip
8-oz. container sour cream
2 c. shredded sharp Cheddar cheese
30-oz. pkg. frozen shredded hashbrowns
   with onions and peppers, thawed

Brown sausage in a skillet over medium heat; drain and set aside. Combine remaining ingredients except hashbrowns in a large bowl; stir until well blended. Fold in hashbrowns and sausage; transfer to a greased 13"x9" baking pan. Bake, uncovered, at 350 degrees for 45 to 55 minutes, until bubbly and golden. Serves 10 to 12.

Lori Comer
Kernersville, NC

Overnight Apple French Toast

1 c. brown sugar, packed
½ c. butter
2 T. light corn syrup
4 Granny Smith apples, peeled, cored and sliced
   ¼-inch thick
3 eggs
1 c. milk
1 t. vanilla extract
9 slices day-old French bread

Combine brown sugar, butter and corn syrup in a small saucepan; cook over low heat until thick. Pour into an ungreased 13"x9" baking pan. Arrange apple slices on top of syrup. Beat eggs, milk and vanilla in a mixing bowl. Dip French bread in egg mixture and arrange over apple slices. Cover and refrigerate overnight. Remove from refrigerator

30 minutes before baking and uncover. Bake at 350 degrees for 35 to 40 minutes, until the top of the bread is browned. Serve French toast with apple slices on top and spoon warm Sauce over the apples. Serves 6 to 8.

Sauce:
1 c. applesauce
10-oz. jar apple jelly
½ t. cinnamon
⅛ t. ground cloves

Combine all ingredients in a saucepan and cook over medium heat until jelly is melted.

Baked Brown Sugar Oatmeal

We enjoyed this oatmeal at the first bed & breakfast we ever stayed in. Now it has become a staple for family breakfasts at Christmas and Easter. It tastes like a warm oatmeal cookie!

½ c. oil
2 eggs, beaten
½ c. brown sugar, packed
½ c. sugar
3 c. quick-cooking oats, uncooked
2 t. baking powder
1 t. salt
1 c. milk
Optional: raisins, brown sugar, milk

Whisk together oil, eggs and sugars; set aside. Combine oats, baking powder and salt in a separate bowl; add to oil mixture. Add milk and stir well. Pour into a greased 1½-quart casserole dish. Bake, uncovered, at 350 degrees for 45 minutes, or until top is golden. Serve warm, either plain or with raisins, brown sugar and milk, if desired. Serves 6.

Kim Travetti
Norristown, PA

Cornmeal-Cheddar
Biscuits

Morning Glory Muffins

You'll love these yummy muffins like I do...they're packed with good-for-you ingredients!

2 c. all-purpose flour
1¼ c. sugar
2 t. baking soda
½ t. salt
2 t. cinnamon
2 c. carrots, peeled and grated
1 c. apple, cored, peeled and chopped
½ c. raisins
½ c. unsalted sunflower kernels
½ c. sweetened flaked coconut
3 eggs, beaten
1 c. oil
2 t. vanilla extract

Combine flour, sugar, baking soda, salt and cinnamon in a large bowl. Stir in carrots, apple, raisins, sunflower kernels and coconut. Whisk together eggs, oil and vanilla in a separate bowl; stir into flour mixture until batter is just combined. Let batter rest for 4 minutes. Spoon into well-greased muffin cups, filling ⅔ full. Bake at 350 degrees for 20 to 25 minutes. Let muffins cool in pan for 10 minutes. Turn out onto a wire rack to finish cooling. Makes 16.

Michelle Campen
Peoria, IL

Cornmeal-Cheddar Biscuits

If you really like the flavor of Cheddar, try making these biscuits with extra-sharp Cheddar cheese.

1½ c. all-purpose flour
½ c. yellow cornmeal
2 t. sugar
1 T. baking powder
¼ to ½ t. salt
½ c. butter
½ c. shredded Cheddar cheese
1 c. milk

Combine flour, cornmeal, sugar, baking powder and salt; cut in butter until mixture resembles coarse crumbs. Stir in cheese and milk just until moistened. Drop dough by ¼ cupfuls onto an ungreased baking sheet. Bake at 450 degrees for 12 to 15 minutes, until lightly golden. Makes one dozen.

Mary Gage
Lakewood, CA

Farmhouse Pumpkin Bread

My Great-Grandmother Mayne used to make this at her home in the country. It is still a family favorite, especially around the holidays.

3½ c. all-purpose flour
3 c. sugar
2 t. baking soda
1½ t. salt
1 t. cinnamon
1 t. nutmeg
1 t. ground ginger
¾ c. oil
⅔ c. water
4 eggs, beaten
2 c. canned pumpkin
Optional: 1 c. chopped pecans or walnuts

Combine all ingredients except nuts in a large bowl; mix well. Fold in nuts, if desired. Divide batter between 2 lightly greased 9"x5" loaf pans. Bake at 350 degrees for about 30 minutes. Makes 2 loaves.

Brandi Divine
Forney, TX

Whole Acorn Squash Cream Soup

Whole Acorn Squash Cream Soup

This unique recipe celebrates the beauty of squash by using it as a serving bowl. Choose squash that stand upright for ease in baking and serving.

4 acorn squash
¼ c. cream cheese
1 c. heavy whipping cream
1 c. chicken broth
½ t. salt
1 t. ground cinnamon

Cut off about one inch of stem ends of squash to reveal seeds. Scoop out and discard seeds and pulp. Arrange squash in a 13"x9" baking pan.

Place one tablespoon cream cheese in each squash. Pour ¼ cup each heavy cream and chicken broth over cream cheese in each squash; sprinkle each with ⅛ teaspoon salt and ¼ teaspoon cinnamon. Add ½ inch of water to baking pan.

Bake, uncovered, at 350 degrees for one hour and 45 minutes, or until squash are very tender. To serve, carefully set each squash in a shallow soup bowl. Serves 4.

Slow-Cooker Autumn Stew

Served with buttermilk biscuits and honey, it's a yummy meal that will warm you to your toes.

2 butternut squash, peeled and diced
4 potatoes, peeled and quartered
2 sweet potatoes, peeled and quartered
2 c. buttermilk
14½-oz. can beef broth
⅛ t. ground cloves
½ t. cinnamon
28-oz. can turkey, drained
½ t. dried sage
1 t. dried parsley
¼ c. cornstarch

Arrange squash and potatoes in a 5-quart slow cooker; pour in buttermilk and beef broth. Sprinkle vegetables with cloves and cinnamon. Add turkey; sprinkle with sage and parsley. Cover and cook on high setting 5 hours, or until potatoes are tender. Whisk in cornstarch and cook until sauce thickens. Serves 8 to 10.

Rachel Boyd
Defiance, OH

save with slow cookers

Slow cookers use very little electricity...no more than a lightbulb, costing about 2 cents an hour. They're actually more economical than your oven.

One evening I made a campfire bundle out of chicken, potatoes, butternut squash and peppers. It was so good, I thought I would try it in the slow cooker with turkey, sweet potatoes, potatoes and squash...it turned out even better! —Rachel

Butternut Squash Soup

Butternut Squash Soup

2½ lbs. butternut squash, halved, seeded, peeled
    and cubed
2 c. leeks, chopped
2 Granny Smith apples, peeled, cored and diced
2 14½-oz. cans chicken broth
1 c. water
seasoned salt and white pepper to taste
Garnish: freshly ground nutmeg and sour cream

Combine squash, leeks, apples, broth and
water in a 4-quart slow cooker. Cover and cook
on high setting for 4 hours, or until squash and
leeks are tender. Carefully purée the hot soup, in
3 or 4 batches, in a food processor or blender until
smooth. Season with seasoned salt and white pepper. Garnish with nutmeg and sour cream. Serves 8.

Creamy Wild Rice Soup

*My kids love this soup…they're happy to eat it any
time of the year! It's also a delicious way to use up
the leftover rice from last night's dinner.*

6-oz. pkg. long-grain and wild rice, uncooked
1 lb. ground beef
14½-oz. can chicken broth
10¾-oz. can cream of mushroom soup
2 c. milk
1 c. shredded Cheddar cheese
⅓ c. carrot, peeled and shredded
1-oz. pkg. ranch salad dressing mix
Garnish: chopped green onions

Prepare rice mix according to package directions.
Measure out 1½ cups cooked rice and set aside, reserving the remainder for another use. Meanwhile,
brown beef in a Dutch oven over medium heat.
Drain; stir in cooked rice and remaining ingredients except garnish. Reduce heat to low and simmer for 15 to 20 minutes, stirring often. Sprinkle
servings with green onions. Serves 6 to 8.

Brooke Sottosanti
Brunswick, OH

Slow-Cooker Country Chicken & Dumplings

*Using refrigerated biscuits for the dumplings and
a slow cooker makes this recipe a lifesaver on busy
weeknights. (Pictured on page 162)*

4 boneless, skinless chicken breasts
2 10¾-oz. cans cream of chicken soup
2 T. butter, sliced
1 onion, finely diced
2 7½-oz. tubes refrigerated biscuits, torn

Place chicken, soup, butter and onion in a 4-quart
slow cooker; add enough water to cover chicken.
Cover and cook on high setting for 4 hours. Add
biscuits to slow cooker; gently push biscuits into
cooking liquid. Cover and continue cooking for
about 1½ hours, or until biscuits are done in the
center. Serves 6.

Joanne Curran
Arlington, MA

"This is absolutely delicious down-home
goodness with very little effort! —Joanne

Italian Sausage Soup

Truly a stick-to-your-ribs soup...hearty, filling and delicious.

1 onion, chopped
3 carrots, peeled and chopped
4 stalks celery, chopped
1 T. garlic, chopped
4 10½-oz. cans beef broth
1 T. Italian seasoning
1 lb. Italian pork link sausage, cooked,
    drained and sliced
6-oz. can tomato paste
10-oz. pkg. frozen chopped spinach,
    thawed and drained
8-oz. pkg. frozen cheese tortellini

Combine onion, carrots, celery, garlic, beef broth and Italian seasoning in a large stockpot; bring to a boil over medium heat. Reduce heat; simmer for 10 minutes. Add sausage, tomato paste and spinach; heat through, about 5 minutes. Stir in tortellini; cook, 15 to 20 minutes, until tender. Serves 6 to 8.

Alicia VanDuyne
Braidwood, IL

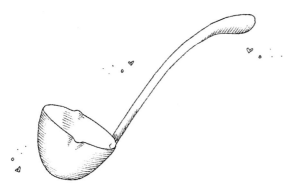

30-Minute Chili

A homemade seasoning mix gives this quick chili great taste.

2 lbs. lean ground beef
16-oz. can black beans, undrained
15½-oz. can small red beans, undrained
2 14.5-oz. cans diced tomatoes with green
    pepper, celery and onion
2 8-oz. cans tomato sauce
Optional: corn chips, shredded Cheddar cheese

Cook beef in a Dutch oven over medium-high heat, stirring often, 4 to 5 minutes, until beef crumbles and is no longer pink; drain well. Return beef to Dutch oven; sprinkle with ⅓ cup Chili Seasoning Mix. Cook one minute over medium-high heat.

Stir in beans and remaining ingredients except corn chips and cheese; bring to a boil over medium-high heat, stirring occasionally. Cover, reduce heat to low and simmer, stirring occasionally, 15 minutes. Top with corn chips and shredded Cheddar cheese, if desired. Serves 8.

Chili Seasoning Mix:

¾ c. chili powder
2 T. ground cumin
2 T. dried oregano
2 T. dried, minced onion
2 T. seasoned salt
2 T. sugar
2 T. dried, minced garlic

Combine all ingredients. Store in an airtight container up to 4 months at room temperature. Shake or stir well before using. Makes about 1⅓ cups.

Jo Ann
Gooseberry Patch

This versatile mix pairs perfectly with beef, pork, poultry or seafood! —Jo Ann

30-Minute Chili

Speedy Chicken Cordon Bleu

Speedy Chicken Cordon Bleu

Gourmet in a flash!

4 boneless, skinless chicken breasts
1 T. butter
¼ lb. cooked ham slices
1 c. shredded Swiss cheese, divided
½ c. white wine or chicken broth
10¾-oz. can cream of chicken soup
¾ c. water
8-oz. pkg. noodles, uncooked
Garnish: fresh parsley

Cook chicken in butter in a skillet over medium heat for 6 to 8 minutes per side, until no longer pink in the middle. Set pan aside. Wrap each chicken breast with one ham slice folded in half lengthwise. Transfer chicken to a lightly greased 13"x9" baking pan. Sprinkle with ½ cup cheese. Broil 3 to 5 minutes, until cheese is melted and lightly golden.

Add wine or broth to skillet; cook over medium heat, using a spoon to scrape up drippings. Add cream of chicken soup, water and ½ cup cheese. Whisk until smooth.

Prepare noodles according to package directions. Serve sauce over chicken and noodles. Garnish with parsley. Serves 4.

Balsamic Chicken & Pears

The flavors in this dish blend together so well...very, very tasty!

2 t. oil, divided
4 boneless, skinless chicken breasts
2 Bosc pears, cored and cut into 8 wedges
1 c. chicken broth
3 T. balsamic vinegar
2 t. cornstarch
1½ t. sugar
¼ c. dried cherries or raisins

Heat one teaspoon oil in a large non-stick skillet over medium-high heat; add chicken. Cook until golden and cooked through, about 4 to 5 minutes per side. Transfer to a plate; keep warm. Heat remaining oil in same skillet; add pears and cook until tender and golden. Combine remaining ingredients except cherries or raisins in a small bowl. Stir broth mixture into skillet with pears; add cherries or raisins. Bring to a boil over medium heat. Cook for one minute, stirring constantly. Return chicken to pan; heat through. Serve pear sauce over chicken. Serves 4.

Shirl Parsons
Cape Carteret, NC

Zesty Roasted Chicken & Potatoes

Just add a salad to round out this quick & easy one-dish meal. (Pictured on page 162)

6 boneless, skinless chicken breasts
1 lb. redskin potatoes, quartered
⅓ c. mayonnaise
3 T. Dijon mustard
½ t. pepper
2 cloves garlic, pressed
Optional: fresh chives, chopped, to taste

Arrange chicken and potatoes in a lightly greased 15"x10" jelly-roll pan. Blend mayonnaise and Dijon mustard, pepper and garlic in a small bowl; brush over chicken and potatoes.

Bake, uncovered, at 400 degrees for 25 to 30 minutes, until potatoes are tender and juices run clear when chicken is pierced with a fork. Sprinkle with chives, if desired. Serves 6.

Denise Mainville
Mesa, AZ

Spanish Paella

Make it extra special…add ½ pound frozen shrimp along with the chicken and cook until the shrimp turn pink.

3½-oz. pkg. sliced pepperoni
1 T. oil
1 lb. boneless, skinless chicken breasts, cubed
1 red pepper, diced
1 clove garlic, pressed
1½ t. dried thyme
8-oz. pkg. Spanish-style yellow rice mix, uncooked
2 c. water
10-oz. pkg. frozen peas

Cook pepperoni for 2 to 3 minutes in a skillet or wok over medium-high heat, stirring occasionally. Remove pepperoni to a plate; set aside. Add oil and chicken to skillet. Cook 3 to 4 minutes, until juices run clear when chicken is pierced with a fork. Drain; remove chicken to a plate. Add red pepper, garlic and thyme to skillet; cook and stir for one minute. Stir in rice mix, water and pepperoni; heat mixture to boiling. Reduce heat to medium-low; cover and simmer for 10 minutes, or until rice is nearly tender. Stir in frozen peas; cover and cook for 5 minutes. Return chicken to skillet; heat through. Serves 4.

Rhonda Reeder
Ellicott City, MD

fantastic frozen veggies

Don't hesitate to stock up on frozen vegetables when they go on sale. Flash-frozen soon after harvesting, they actually retain more nutrients than fresh produce that has traveled for several days before arriving in the grocery store's produce section.

Chicken & Wild Rice

Mmm…great with fresh-baked bread and a green salad.

2 6.2-oz. pkgs. quick-cooking long-grain and wild rice with seasoning packets
4 boneless, skinless chicken breasts, cut into 1-inch cubes
10¾-oz. can cream of mushroom soup
1⅓ c. frozen mixed vegetables, thawed
3 c. water

Gently stir together all ingredients. Spread into an ungreased 13"x9" baking pan. Bake, uncovered, at 350 degrees until juices run clear when chicken is pierced with a fork, about 45 minutes, stirring occasionally. Serves 6 to 8.

Kimberly Lyons
Commerce, TX

Slow-Cooker Sweet & Sour Pork

This recipe is equally good with cubes of boneless chicken breast.

1½ lbs. boneless pork loin, cubed
1 green pepper, chopped
1 onion, chopped
14-oz. can pineapple chunks, drained
14½-oz. can chicken broth
10-oz. bottle sweet-and-sour sauce
hot cooked rice

Place pork cubes in a 4-quart slow cooker; top with remaining ingredients except rice. Cover and cook on low setting for 6 to 7 hours, or on high setting for 4 hours. Serve over hot cooked rice. Serves 6.

Janice Dorsey
San Antonio, TX

Chicken & Wild Rice

Pork Chops & Stuffing

Pork Chops & Stuffing

6 pork chops
1 T. shortening
1 t. salt, divided
1 c. celery, chopped
¾ c. onion, chopped
¼ c. butter, melted
¼ c. brown sugar, packed
5 c. bread, cubed
1 egg, beaten
1 t. dried sage
½ t. dried thyme
⅛ t. pepper
11-oz. can mandarin oranges, drained

Brown pork chops in shortening in a skillet; remove to a platter and season with ½ teaspoon salt. Lightly brown vegetables in butter in skillet; stir in brown sugar. Combine bread cubes, egg, sage, thyme, pepper and remaining ½ teaspoon salt; add to vegetables. Gently stir in oranges. Spoon stuffing into the center of an ungreased 3½-quart casserole dish. Place pork chops around the stuffing and cover with aluminum foil. Bake at 350 degrees for 30 minutes; uncover and bake 30 more minutes. Serves 6.

Barbara Schmeckpeper
Elwood, IL

I've been making this recipe for 28 years, and it's still one of my favorites! The mandarin oranges and brown sugar make it special. —Barbara

Apricot-Glazed Ham Steaks

When it's grilling season, heat the ham over hot coals and serve with grilled apricot halves...oh-so good!

¼ c. apricot preserves
1 T. mustard
1 t. lemon juice
⅛ t. cinnamon
4 ham steaks

Combine all ingredients except ham in a small saucepan. Cook and stir over low heat for 2 to 3 minutes. Place ham in a lightly greased 13"x9" baking pan. Pour sauce over ham. Bake, uncovered, at 350 degrees for 15 minutes, or until heated through. Serve ham topped with sauce from the pan. Serves 4.

Kelly Alderson
Erie, PA

sweet setting
Pretty vintage aprons can be found for a song at flea markets. Why not tie one on the back of each chair at the table? It's a sweet way to say, "Thanks for coming!"

Holiday Cranberry Pork Roast
Slow-Cooker Country Cornbread Dressing (page 197)

Holiday Cranberry Pork Roast

The cranberry sauce and juice impart a sweet flavor to this savory, slow-cooker pork roast...it's a delicious change from roast turkey during the holidays.

2½-lb. boneless pork loin roast
16-oz. can jellied cranberry sauce
½ c. cranberry juice cocktail
½ c. sugar
1 t. dry mustard
¼ t. ground cloves
2 T. cornstarch
2 T. cold water
1 t. salt

Place pork in a 5-quart oval slow cooker. Stir together cranberry sauce and cranberry juice cocktail, sugar, dry mustard and cloves. Pour cranberry mixture over pork. Cover and cook on high setting one hour; reduce heat to low setting and cook 4½ hours, or until pork is tender.

Skim fat from drippings in slow cooker. Measure drippings to equal 2 cups, adding water if necessary. Pour drippings into a medium saucepan; bring to a boil over medium-high heat. Stir together cornstarch and cold water until smooth; add to drippings and cook over medium-high heat, stirring constantly, 2 to 3 minutes, until thickened. Stir in salt. Serve gravy with sliced pork. Serves 4 to 6.

Patricia Wissler
Harrisburg, PA

Cube Steak in Savory Gravy

An easy meal that's perfect on a chilly evening. Serve with fluffy mashed potatoes and tender green beans.

1 lb. beef cube steak, cut into 4 serving-size pieces
¼ c. all-purpose flour
1 onion, chopped
1 T. oil
1 c. water
¼ c. catsup
1 T. Worcestershire sauce
1 t. beef bouillon granules
½ t. Italian seasoning
1 t. salt
¼ t. pepper

Coat beef pieces with flour; set aside. In a skillet over medium heat, sauté onion in oil until translucent. Add beef and brown on both sides; drain. Mix remaining ingredients in a small bowl; pour over beef mixture. Heat until boiling; reduce heat. Cover and simmer until beef is tender, about 1¼ to 1½ hours. Serves 4.

Deborah Burns
Lebanon, OR

cleanup's a breeze!

For quick cleanup, add a disposable slow-cooker liner before adding ingredients, or give the inside of the cooker a good coating of non-stick vegetable spray.

Shepherd's Pie

Stir in other veggies if you like…corn and baby lima beans are tasty additions.

2 lbs. ground beef
½ onion, chopped
garlic powder and seasoning salt to taste
¾-oz. pkg. brown gravy mix
2 10¾-oz. cans cream of mushroom soup
2½ c. water
1½ c. frozen sliced carrots, thawed
10-oz. pkg. frozen peas, thawed
salt and pepper to taste
2½ to 3 c. potatoes, peeled, cooked and mashed
paprika to taste

Brown beef and onion in a skillet; season to taste with garlic powder and seasoning salt. Drain; pour into a large bowl. Stir in gravy mix, soup, water, carrots and peas; mix well. Spoon into a greased 13"x9" baking pan or 4 to 6 individual baking dishes; sprinkle with salt and pepper. Spread mashed potatoes over top; bake, uncovered, at 350 degrees for 35 to 45 minutes, until bubbly and potatoes are browned. Sprinkle with paprika. Serves 4 to 6.

Kimberley Pfleiderer
Galion, OH

Shepherd's Pie

Slow-Cooker Pennsylvania Stuffed Peppers

The perfect comfort food...they taste even better the next day! Mashed potatoes are heavenly topped with some of the sauce from the peppers.

1½ lbs. ground beef
1 egg, beaten
1 c. orzo pasta or instant rice, uncooked
garlic salt and pepper to taste
6 green, yellow or red peppers, tops removed
2 10¾-oz. cans tomato soup
2½ c. water

Mix beef, egg, uncooked orzo or rice and seasonings in a bowl. Stuff peppers lightly with mixture. If any extra beef mixture remains, form into small meatballs. Blend together soup and water in a lightly greased 6-quart slow cooker. Arrange stuffed peppers in slow cooker; replace tops on peppers. Place meatballs around peppers. Lightly spoon some of soup mixture onto tops of peppers. Cover and cook on low setting for 8 to 10 hours. Serves 6.

Lora Burek
Irwin, PA

Lasagna Rolls

1 lb. ground mild or sage pork sausage,
    browned and drained
8-oz. pkg. plus 3 oz. cream cheese
1 bunch green onions, chopped
1 green pepper, diced
26-oz. jar spaghetti sauce
16 lasagna noodles, uncooked
1½ c. mozzarella cheese, shredded

Combine sausage and cream cheese in the skillet where sausage was browned. Cook over low heat until cream cheese melts. Stir in onions and green pepper; remove from heat. Spread half the spaghetti sauce in the bottom of an ungreased 13"x9" baking pan; set aside. Cook lasagna noodles according to package directions; remove from heat and leave in water. Lay one noodle flat on a cutting board and spoon one to 2 tablespoons of sausage mixture onto one end of the noodle. Roll up the noodle and place in pan. Repeat with remaining noodles. Pour reserved sauce over top of rolls; top with mozzarella. Bake, uncovered, at 350 degrees for 15 to 20 minutes, until cheese has melted. Serves 8.

Kelli Keeton
Delaware, OH

"When I was little, I remember standing on a chair next to my mom by the stove. I watched her roll these little bundles of noodles, meat and cheese, and I would beg her to let me roll up a few. She always let me try some, and even though they were nothing compared to hers, she made me feel like they were perfect. —Kelli

Lasagna Rolls

Stacie's Spaghetti Pie

Everyone loves this spaghetti! This baked version makes it ideal for toting to a potluck with friends.

8-oz. pkg. spaghetti, cooked
2 t. olive oil
1 c. pasta sauce
1 c. sliced mushrooms
½ c. green pepper, chopped
½ c. black olives, chopped
¼ lb. mozzarella cheese, cubed
2 t. garlic, minced
½ t. Italian seasoning
½ t. seasoning salt
¼ t. red pepper flakes
4 eggs
½ c. milk
¾ c. sliced pepperoni
½ c. grated Parmesan cheese

Toss cooked spaghetti with oil in a large bowl; add sauce, vegetables, mozzarella, garlic and seasonings. Mix well; spread in a lightly greased 13"x9" baking pan. Whisk together eggs and milk; pour over spaghetti mixture. Arrange pepperoni evenly on top; sprinkle with Parmesan cheese. Bake, uncovered, at 375 degrees for 25 to 30 minutes, until bubbly and golden. Let stand for 5 minutes; cut into squares. Serves 6 to 8.

Stacie Avner
Delaware, OH

Eggplant Parmigiana

Our favorite meatless meal! For a deliciously different serving suggestion, layer slices of warm baked eggplant on crusty Italian rolls for hero sandwiches.

2 eggplants, peeled and cut into ¼-inch-thick slices
1½ c. all-purpose flour
2 eggs, beaten
1½ c. dry bread crumbs
1½ t. salt, divided
¼ t. pepper, divided
1 clove garlic, halved
¾ c. olive oil, divided
28-oz. can diced tomatoes, undrained
⅓ c. tomato paste
2 T. fresh basil, minced
1 c. grated Parmesan cheese
½ lb. mozzarella cheese, thinly sliced and
    divided

Dip eggplant slices into flour, then eggs, then into bread crumbs seasoned with ½ teaspoon salt and ⅛ teaspoon pepper. Place slices on a baking sheet; refrigerate for 20 minutes. Sauté garlic in 2 tablespoons oil in a saucepan for one to 2 minutes. Remove and discard garlic from saucepan; add tomatoes, tomato paste, basil and remaining salt and pepper to pan. Cover; simmer over low heat for 30 minutes. Heat remaining oil in a skillet. Sauté eggplant on both sides until golden; drain on paper towels. Spread a thin layer of warm sauce mixture in a lightly greased 15"x10" jelly-roll pan. Alternately layer eggplant, remaining sauce, Parmesan and mozzarella cheeses. Bake, uncovered, at 350 degrees for 30 minutes. Serves 4 to 6.

Annette Mullan
North Arlington, NJ

Skinny Salsa Joes

The longer the beef simmers, the better these taste.

1 lb. ground beef, browned and drained
½ c. salsa
8-oz. can tomato sauce
1 T. brown sugar, packed
4 sandwich buns, split and toasted

Combine all ingredients except buns in a sauce-pan; bring to a boil. Reduce heat; simmer 10 to 15 minutes. Serve on buns. Makes 4.

Marcia Frahm
Urbandale, IA

Slow-Cooker Shredded Beef Sandwiches

I like to prepare these sandwiches for church get-togethers because they're so tasty.

11½-oz. jar sliced pepperoncini, undrained
4-lb. beef chuck roast
1¾ t. dried basil
1½ t. dried oregano
1½ t. garlic powder
1¼ t. salt
¼ t. pepper
¼ c. water
1 onion, sliced
10 to 12 sandwich buns, split and toasted

Pour pepperoncini into a 5 to 6-quart slow cooker; add roast. Mix together herbs, garlic powder, salt and pepper; sprinkle over meat. Add water and onion. Cover and cook on low setting for 8 to 9 hours, until meat is tender. Remove roast; shred using 2 forks. Return meat to slow cooker; mix well. Using a slotted spoon, place meat on buns. Makes 10 to 12 sandwiches.

Sharon Beach
Potosi, MO

Yummy Italian Sausage Sandwiches

I can't remember how long we've been making these sandwiches, but they are a favorite of my children... and those kids are grown-ups! Now they are making sausage sandwiches for their own children.

15-oz. can tomato sauce
½ t. dried basil
¼ t. red pepper flakes
¼ t. garlic powder
1 lb. ground Italian pork sausage, divided
    into 4 flat patties
1 loaf Italian bread, cut diagonally into 8 slices
4 slices mozzarella cheese
2 to 4 T. butter, softened

Stir together tomato sauce and seasonings in a small saucepan over low heat. Simmer until sauce thickens, about 8 to 10 minutes. Meanwhile, cook sausage patties in a skillet over medium heat until browned and cooked through; drain. Top each of 4 bread slices with a warm patty, a slice of cheese and another slice of bread. Spread butter over the outside top and bottom slices of each sandwich. Grill sandwiches on a griddle over medium-high heat, turning once, until golden and cheese is melted. Ladle sauce into bowls and serve as a dipping sauce with sandwiches. Makes 4 sandwiches.

Irene Putman
Canal Fulton, OH

Susan's Chicken Minis

I was trying to think of something a little different for lunch when I created these mini sandwiches. Now they're a favorite!

2 T. lemon juice
½ c. mayonnaise
salt to taste
1 t. pepper
3½ c. cooked chicken, finely diced
½ c. celery, finely diced
⅓ c. raisins
⅓ c. chopped walnuts
lettuce leaves
12 mini dinner rolls, split

Combine lemon juice, mayonnaise, salt and pepper. Toss with remaining ingredients except lettuce and rolls. Place lettuce on bottom halves of rolls; top with chicken mixture and top halves of rolls. Makes 12 mini sandwiches.

Susan Brzozowski
Ellicott City, MD

Susan's Chicken Minis

Classic Baked Macaroni & Cheese

Sweet Brown Rice

Add dried apricots, dates, figs or prune pieces for something a little different.

14-oz. pkg. instant brown rice, uncooked
½ c. dried cranberries
½ c. sunflower seeds
2 T. orange marmalade
1 T. spicy mustard
1½ t. prepared horseradish
1 T. honey

Prepare rice according to package directions; as it simmers add cranberries and sunflower seeds. Microwave marmalade in a microwave-safe dish on high for 10 seconds. Combine marmalade, mustard, horseradish and honey in a medium mixing bowl; toss with rice. Serves 9.

Natalie Holdren
Overland Park, KS

Classic Baked Macaroni & Cheese

It's worth shredding the cheese yourself for this classic dish. A sprinkle of cayenne pepper adds a surprise kick. For one-pot macaroni & cheese, prepare recipe as directed, stirring all shredded cheese into thickened milk mixture until melted. Stir in cooked pasta, salt and peppers, and serve immediately.

8-oz. pkg. elbow macaroni, uncooked
2 T. butter
2 T. all-purpose flour
2 c. milk
8-oz. block sharp Cheddar cheese,
    shredded and divided
1 t. salt
½ t. pepper
¼ t. cayenne pepper

Prepare macaroni according to package directions. Drain and keep warm. Melt butter in a large saucepan or Dutch oven over medium-low heat; whisk in flour until smooth. Cook, whisking constantly, 2 minutes. Gradually whisk in milk and cook, whisking constantly, 5 minutes, or until thickened. Remove from heat. Stir in one cup shredded cheese, salt, peppers and cooked macaroni. Spoon into 4 lightly greased 8-ounce oven-proof ramekins; top with remaining one cup cheese. Bake, uncovered, at 400 degrees for 15 minutes, or until bubbly. Let stand 10 minutes before serving. Serves 4.

Slow-Cooker Country Cornbread Dressing

You can purchase cornbread from your supermarket deli...just be sure that it's savory, not sweet. (Pictured on page 188)

6½ c. cornbread, crumbled
8 slices day-old bread, torn
4 eggs, beaten
1 onion, chopped
1 stalk celery, chopped
2½ c. chicken broth
2 10¾-oz. cans cream of chicken soup
1 T. dried sage
1 t. salt
¼ t. pepper
2 T. butter or margarine, sliced

Combine all ingredients except butter or margarine in a very large bowl; mix well. Spoon into a 5 to 6-quart slow cooker; dot with butter. Cover and cook on low setting 6 hours. Serves 8 to 10.

Tracy Chitwood
Van Buren, MO

The best dressing I've ever tasted...and so easy, too. —Tracy

Pineapple-Topped
Sweet Potatoes

Pineapple-Topped Sweet Potatoes

For individual servings, place sweet potato mixture into 6-ounce ungreased ramekins. Halve the Pineapple Topping, and sprinkle evenly on top of sweet potatoes; bake as directed below.

2 c. sweet potatoes, peeled, boiled and
    mashed
¼ t. salt
¼ c. butter or margarine, softened
1 c. sugar
2 eggs, beaten
¼ c. milk
1 t. vanilla extract

Combine all ingredients; spoon into an ungreased 2-quart casserole dish. Spoon Pineapple Topping over sweet potato mixture; bake, uncovered, at 350 degrees for 30 minutes. Serves 8.

Pineapple Topping:

¼ c. all-purpose flour
½ c. sugar
1 egg, beaten
¼ c. butter or margarine, softened
8-oz. can crushed pineapple, drained

Combine flour and sugar; stir in egg and butter or margarine. Fold in pineapple; mix well.

Linda Littlejohn
Greensboro, NC

My family won't eat sweet potatoes any other way! —Linda

Surprise Fries

My kids love these with burgers and brats.

2-lb. butternut squash, halved lengthwise,
    seeded and peeled
2 t. olive oil
salt to taste
½ t. ground cumin
½ t. chili powder
½ c. sour cream
2 T. maple syrup

Cut squash halves to resemble French fries; slice about ½-inch wide and 3 inches long. Add oil to a large bowl; add squash, tossing to coat. Line a baking sheet with aluminum foil; spray with non-stick vegetable spray. Arrange squash slices in a single layer on prepared baking sheet. Bake at 425 degrees for 35 minutes, or until tender. Combine salt, cumin and chili powder; sprinkle desired amount over fries. Blend together sour cream and syrup as a dipping sauce. Serves 4.

Teresa Podracky
Solon, OH

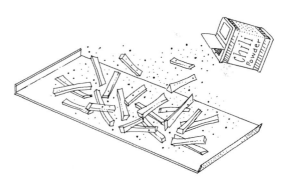

Escalloped Apples

Autumn Acorn Squash

A family fall favorite! This recipe started with one my mom used to make for us...I've added a few touches of my own.

2 acorn squash, halved and seeded
2 apples, peeled, cored and chopped
3 T. brown sugar, packed
3 T. chopped pecans
1 t. all-purpose flour
¼ t. cinnamon
2 T. butter, softened

Place acorn squash halves cut-side down in a greased 13"x9" baking pan. Bake at 350 degrees for 30 minutes. Combine remaining ingredients. Turn squash over and fill with apple mixture. Bake, uncovered, for 15 to 30 more minutes, until squash is soft when pierced with a fork. Serve squash as is, or scoop into a serving bowl. Serves 4.

Jenny Sarbacker
Madison, WI

Red Cabbage & Apple

My father used to fix this recipe, and it is really yummy! I prefer crisper cabbage, but for softer, old-fashioned cabbage, increase the cooking time to 25 to 30 minutes.

1 T. bacon drippings or oil
2 c. red cabbage, shredded
1 c. apple, cored and cubed
2 T. brown sugar, packed
2 T. white vinegar
2 T. water
¼ t. caraway seed
½ t. salt
⅛ t. pepper

Heat drippings or oil in a skillet over medium heat. Add remaining ingredients; cover tightly. Cook over low heat for about 15 minutes, stirring occasionally, to desired tenderness. Serves 4 to 6.

Peggy Frazier
Indianapolis, IN

Escalloped Apples

An old-fashioned dish that goes great with any meal!

½ c. butter
2 c. soft bread crumbs
5 tart apples, peeled, cored and sliced
½ c. sugar
½ t. cinnamon
¼ t. ground cloves

Melt butter in a saucepan over medium heat. Add bread crumbs and toast lightly for about 2 minutes; set aside. Toss apples with sugar, cinnamon and cloves. Layer half of apples and half of toasted bread crumbs in a greased 8"x8" baking pan. Repeat with remaining apples and bread crumbs. Bake, covered, at 325 degrees for 45 minutes, or until apples are tender. Bake, uncovered, 15 more minutes. Serves 6.

Rita's Wild Rice

This is one of my mom's favorite recipes. It makes a fabulous side dish for anything! We have it with our special meals...tastes even better the second day.

6-oz. pkg. long-grain and wild rice
½ c. onion, chopped
½ c. carrots, peeled and chopped
½ c. celery, chopped
½ c. radish, chopped
¾ c. Italian salad dressing

Prepare rice according to package directions; let cool. Toss rice with chopped vegetables. Stir in salad dressing to coat. Serve at room temperature or chilled. Serves 4 to 6.

Sharon Jones
Oklahoma City, OK

market fresh
While most farmers' markets are open on Saturday mornings, check to see if your area has a smaller midweek market on Wednesday or Thursday evenings. There are even fall and winter farmers' markets popping up in some towns.

Green Beans with Bacon & Garlic

Look for packages of ready-to-eat trimmed fresh green beans in your produce section. The beans can be microwaved right in their bags...a big time-saver. (Pictured on page 162)

6 slices bacon
¼ c. butter
2 t. garlic, minced
½ t. salt
¼ t. pepper
1 lb. green beans, cut into bite-size
    pieces and cooked

Cook bacon in a skillet over medium heat until crisp; drain. Crumble bacon and return to skillet. Add butter, garlic, salt and pepper to skillet; cook until butter is melted. Place beans in a serving bowl; toss with bacon mixture and serve immediately. Serves 4.

Diane Stout
Zeeland, MI

I invented this recipe so my daughter would enjoy eating green beans. It's good made with either fresh or frozen beans. —Diane

Simple Scalloped Tomatoes

This tangy-sweet side is delicious with fish and seafood.

1 onion, chopped
¼ c. butter
28-oz. can diced tomatoes, undrained
5 slices bread, lightly toasted and cubed
¼ c. brown sugar, packed
½ t. salt
¼ t. pepper

Cook onion in butter until just tender but not browned. Combine onion mixture with tomatoes in a bowl; add remaining ingredients, and mix well. Pour mixture into a greased 8"x8" baking pan. Bake, uncovered, at 350 degrees for 45 minutes. Serves 4 to 6.

Joan White
Malvern, PA

This is a scrumptious way to prepare canned tomatoes...don't be tempted to substitute fresh tomatoes! —Joan

Simple Scalloped Tomatoes

Chicken Taco Salad

Crispy tortilla cups jam-packed with yummy ingredients! Can't be beat!

8 6-inch flour tortillas
2 c. cooked chicken breast, shredded
1¼-oz. pkg. taco seasoning mix
¾ c. water
2 c. lettuce, shredded
15½-oz. can black beans, drained and rinsed
1½ c. shredded Cheddar cheese
2 tomatoes, chopped
½ c. green onion, sliced
15¼-oz. can corn, drained
2¼-oz. can sliced black olives, drained
1 avocado, peeled, pitted and cubed
Garnish: sour cream, salsa

Microwave tortillas on high for one minute, or until softened. Press each tortilla into an ungreased muffin cup to form a bowl shape. Bake at 350 degrees for 10 minutes; cool. Combine chicken, taco seasoning and water in a skillet over medium heat. Cook, stirring frequently, until blended, about 5 minutes. Divide lettuce among tortilla bowls. Top with chicken and remaining ingredients, garnishing with a dollop of sour cream and salsa. Serves 8.

Abby Snay
San Francisco, CA

Apple-Yogurt Coleslaw

The tart flavor of the apples, the sweetness of the pineapple and cranberries and the crunch of the nuts add a fresh twist to coleslaw.

1 c. plain or vanilla yogurt
¼ c. mayonnaise
8-oz. can crushed pineapple, undrained
4 Granny Smith apples, cored and chopped
½ head purple cabbage, shredded
½ head green cabbage, shredded
¼ c. red onion, finely chopped
1 carrot, peeled and shredded
1 stalk celery, diced
¼ c. sugar
½ t. salt
¼ t. pepper
1 t. mustard
¾ c. sweetened dried cranberries
¾ c. chopped walnuts
Garnish: cabbage leaves

Mix together yogurt, mayonnaise and pineapple in a large bowl. Stir apples into yogurt mixture, coating well. Add remaining ingredients except cranberries, walnuts and garnish; mix well. Cover and chill for at least one hour. Before serving, stir in cranberries and walnuts. Serve on whole cabbage leaves. Serves 8 to 10.

Lane McCloud
Siloam Springs, AR

Apple-Yogurt Coleslaw

Sweet Potato Salad

Sweet potatoes make this a nice change from traditional potato salad.

3 sweet potatoes, boiled and mashed
salt and pepper to taste
¼ c. green onion, chopped
¼ c. sugar
¼ c. vinegar
I egg, hard-boiled, peeled and sliced

Combine potatoes, salt, pepper, onion, sugar and vinegar in a large serving bowl. Top with egg slices. Chill before serving. Serves 4.

Gloria Robertson
Midland, TX

cute idea!
Shop flea market sales for vintage dollhouses. They're oh-so cute holding guests towels in the bathroom or tea towels in the kitchen. You can even use them to corral mail and desk supplies!

Yummy Carrot Cake

My grandma made this cake every Thanksgiving at her farm. Grandma has been gone more than 20 years now, and I honor her memory by making her carrot cake for my family's holiday. My husband always wants this cake for his birthday, too. This recipe is by far my most requested!

4 eggs, beaten
2 c. sugar
1¼ c. oil
3 c. carrots, peeled and grated
2 c. all-purpose flour
2 t. cinnamon
2 t. baking soda
I t. salt
Optional: chopped walnuts

Combine eggs, sugar, oil and carrots in a large bowl, beating well after adding each ingredient. Sift together remaining ingredients except walnuts in a separate bowl. Add flour mixture to egg mixture; beat well to make a thin batter. Pour into a greased and lightly floured Bundt® pan; bake at 325 degrees for 40 to 50 minutes, until a toothpick inserted near center comes out clean. A greased 13"x9" baking pan may also be used; bake at 325 degrees for 30 to 35 minutes, until a toothpick inserted near center comes out clean. Cool. Frost with Cream Cheese Frosting; sprinkle with walnuts, if desired. Serves 12 to 15.

Cream Cheese Frosting:
8-oz. pkg. cream cheese, softened
½ c. butter, softened
16-oz. pkg. powdered sugar

Blend all ingredients together until smooth.

Cindy Beach
Franklin, NY

Pumpkin Pie Ice Cream Fantasy

Two holiday dessert classics are swirled with caramel and pecans...what's not to love?

1 baked pumpkin pie
½ gal. vanilla ice cream
caramel topping
pecan halves, toasted

Place pie in freezer for one hour; remove pie from freezer and chop ¾ of pie into one-inch pieces. Allow ice cream to stand 8 to 10 minutes to slightly soften. Spoon ice cream into a large bowl. Gently fold in pie pieces until blended. To serve, scoop each serving into a wineglass or dessert bowl. Drizzle with caramel topping and top with pecans. Serves 12.

Pecan Tassies

Pecan Tassies

This is a family favorite that can be made ahead.

½ c. butter or margarine, softened
3-oz. pkg. cream cheese, softened
1 c. all-purpose flour
1½ c. brown sugar, packed
2 eggs, lightly beaten
2 T. butter or margarine, melted
1 t. vanilla extract
⅔ c. chopped pecans

Beat softened butter or margarine and cream cheese with an electric mixer at medium speed until creamy. Gradually add flour, beating well. Cover and chill 2 hours.

Shape dough into 30 one-inch balls; press balls into lightly greased miniature muffin pans. Set aside.

Combine brown sugar, eggs, butter and vanilla; stir well. Stir in pecans. Spoon one tablespoon pecan mixture into each pastry shell. Bake at 350 degrees for 25 minutes. Remove from pans immediately and cool completely on wire racks. Makes 2½ dozen.

Walnut Fudge Cake

For double fudgy deliciousness, I like to microwave some fudge frosting in a coffee mug for about 20 seconds and pour it over the cooled cake. Decorate the top with crushed walnuts...yum!

3 eggs, beaten
¼ c. oil
⅓ c. sour cream
½ c. brewed coffee, cooled
18½-oz. pkg. dark chocolate fudge cake mix
½ c. walnuts, ground
Optional: 1 to 3 T. milk

Mix eggs, oil, sour cream and coffee until well blended. Add dry cake mix and walnuts. If batter is too thick, stir in a little milk until a good consistency is reached. Pour into a greased Bundt® pan. Bake at 325 degrees for 45 minutes, or until cake pulls away from sides of pan and springs back to the touch. Cool cake in pan for 30 to 40 minutes before turning out onto a cake plate. Serves 10 to 12.

Wendy Lee Paffenroth
Pine Island, NY

stick around!

Keep most-used recipes at your fingertips! Tack them to self-stick cork tiles placed inside a kitchen cabinet door.

Peanut Butter-Oat Bars

For brownie-like bars, bake closer to 20 minutes; if you'd like them a bit crunchier, bake for 25 minutes.

½ c. whole-wheat flour
1 t. cinnamon
½ t. baking soda
⅛ t. sea salt
¾ c. crunchy peanut butter
¼ c. brown sugar, packed
⅓ c. honey
1 egg
2 egg whites
2 T. sunflower or olive oil
2 t. vanilla extract
2 c. long-cooking oats, uncooked
1 c. sweetened dried cranberries or raisins
½ c. sliced almonds
½ c. white or dark chocolate chips

Whisk together flour, cinnamon, baking soda and salt in a small bowl. Beat peanut butter, brown sugar and honey in a separate bowl with an electric mixer at medium speed. Beat egg and egg whites in a separate bowl; add to peanut butter mixture. Mix in oil and vanilla. Add flour mixture; stir in remaining ingredients. Spread into a greased 13"x9" baking pan. Bake at 350 degrees for 20 to 25 minutes. Cut into squares. Makes about 15 to 18 bars.

Jennifer Martineau
Delaware, OH

Turtle Pumpkin Pie

Turtle Pumpkin Pie

I made this wonderful pie during the holidays, and now it's a must at every Thanksgiving dinner! (Pictured on the cover)

1½ c. graham cracker crumbs
6 T. butter, melted
¼ c. plus 2 T. caramel ice-cream topping, divided
½ c. plus 2 T. pecan pieces, divided
1 c. milk
2 3.4-oz. pkgs. instant vanilla pudding mix
1 c. canned pumpkin
1 t. cinnamon
½ t. nutmeg
8-oz. container frozen whipped topping, thawed and divided

Combine crumbs and butter. Press into the bottom and up sides of a 9" pie plate. Bake at 350 degrees for 7 minutes. Pour ¼ cup caramel topping into crust; sprinkle with ½ cup nuts. Beat milk, dry pudding mix, pumpkin and spices with a whisk until blended. Stir in 1½ cups whipped topping; spread mixture into crust. Refrigerate at least one hour. Before serving, spread with remaining whipped topping, drizzle with remaining caramel topping and sprinkle with remaining pecans. Serves 10.

Tonya Lewis-Holm
Scottsburg, IN

Chocolate Bread Pudding

Just like Grandma's, but with a twist of cocoa to tempt your sweet tooth.

2 c. milk
6 slices white bread, crusts trimmed
½ c. sugar
⅓ c. baking cocoa
2 eggs, separated and divided
2 T. butter, melted
1 t. vanilla extract
½ c. semi-sweet chocolate chunks
Garnish: whipped cream, baking cocoa

Heat milk in a large saucepan just until tiny bubbles form; remove from heat. Cube bread and add to milk; stir until bread cubes are moistened. Add sugar, cocoa and egg yolks; stir until well blended. Add butter and vanilla; set aside. Beat egg whites until stiff peaks form; fold into mixture along with chocolate chunks. Pour into 6 lightly greased custard cups; set cups in a baking pan. Add one inch of hot water to the pan. Bake at 350 degrees for 40 minutes, or until firm. Garnish with whipped cream and baking cocoa; serve warm or cold. Serves 6.

Gail Bamford
Vienna, VA

Quick Apple Dumplings

Apple dumplings are a must during harvest season! If you can make a trip to the orchard, fresh-picked apples just can't be beat.

8-oz. tube refrigerated crescent rolls
2 Granny Smith apples, cored, peeled and
    quartered
⅛ t. cinnamon
½ c. butter
I c. sugar
I c. orange juice
I t. vanilla extract
½ c. pecans, very finely chopped
Optional: ice cream

Unroll and separate crescent roll dough into tri-angles. Wrap each piece of apple in a crescent roll. Arrange in a greased 8"x8" baking pan; sprinkle with cinnamon. Combine butter, sugar and orange juice in a medium saucepan. Bring to a boil; remove from heat and stir in vanilla. Pour mixture over dumplings; sprinkle pecans over top. Bake at 350 degrees for 30 minutes, or until crust is golden and sauce is beginning to bubble. To serve, spoon some of the syrup from the baking pan over dumplings. Serve with ice cream, if desired. Serves 8.

Ruth Miller
North Apollo, PA

Pears Extraordinaire

These pears are extraordinary because of their flavored cream cheese filling topped with gooey caramel sauce, whipped topping and pecans...a truly spectacular treat.

2 pears, halved and cored
¼ c. apple juice
2 T. cream cheese, softened
2 T. honey
2 t. brown sugar, packed
½ t. vanilla extract
4 t. caramel ice-cream topping
4 T. frozen whipped topping, thawed
4 t. chopped pecans

Arrange pear halves, cut-side down, in a microwave-safe dish. Drizzle with apple juice. Cover and microwave on high 5 minutes or until pears are tender; set aside.

Mix together cream cheese, honey, brown sugar and vanilla until creamy and smooth. Arrange pears, cut-side up, on 4 serving plates. Spoon one-quarter of cream cheese mixture into the center of each pear. Drizzle each serving with one teaspoon caramel topping, dollop with one tablespoon whipped topping and sprinkle with one teaspoon pecans. Serves 4.

Susan Metzger
Washougal, WA

Pears Extraordinaire

Peppermint Milkshakes (page 219)

Cranberry-Glazed Ham (page 242)

Jumbo Chocolate Cupcakes (page 259)

Twisty Rolls (page 227)

A FAMILY FEAST

Festive holiday recipes for Thanksgiving and Christmas

Holiday Stuffed
Mushrooms

Christmas Cheese Log

We enjoy this creamy spread at our house on Christmas Eve afternoon as we finish wrapping the last few presents.

¼ c. chopped pecans
8-oz. pkg. light cream cheese, softened
⅓ c. green onions, chopped
1 t. mustard
1 clove garlic, minced
¼ t. hot pepper sauce
1 c. shredded sharp Cheddar cheese
¼ c. fresh parsley, finely chopped
assorted crackers

Place pecans on an ungreased baking sheet. Bake at 350 degrees for 8 minutes, stirring twice; let cool. Place cream cheese, onions, mustard, garlic and hot pepper sauce in a bowl. Beat with an electric mixer at low speed for about 3 minutes. Stir in Cheddar cheese. Shape into a log and wrap in plastic wrap. Chill for about 15 to 20 minutes. Mix parsley with toasted pecans and spread on a baking sheet or wax paper. Unwrap log and roll in parsley mixture, covering completely. Wrap again in plastic wrap and store in refrigerator until ready to serve. Serve with crackers. Serves 6 to 8.

Jan Philips
Leola, PA

Holiday Stuffed Mushrooms

Start a memorable holiday tradition by making these mouthwatering mushroom tidbits.

8-oz. pkg. cream cheese, softened
1 T. dried, minced onion
2 t. Worcestershire sauce
1 lb. bacon, crisply cooked and crumbled
1½ lbs. mushrooms, stems removed

Beat together cream cheese, onion and Worcestershire sauce with an electric mixer at medium-high speed until thoroughly combined. Stir in bacon; fill mushroom caps with mixture. Arrange on an ungreased baking sheet. Bake at 375 degrees for 15 minutes, or until tops of mushrooms are golden. Serves 6 to 8.

Jennifer Apthorpe
Panama, NY

I started making this recipe as a newlywed, and it became a signature appetizer. My husband's grandfather especially enjoyed them. Now when I make these mushrooms, I think of Grandpa Morton. —Jennifer

Ruth's Swiss-Bacon-Onion Dip

A yummy hot appetizer to serve with crackers until dinner is ready.

8-oz. pkg. cream cheese, softened
1 c. shredded Swiss cheese
½ c. mayonnaise
2 T. green onions, chopped
8 slices bacon, crisply cooked and crumbled
1 c. round buttery crackers, crushed
assorted crackers

Mix together cheeses, mayonnaise and onions; spread in a greased 8"x8" baking pan. Top with bacon and cracker crumbs. Bake, uncovered, at 350 degrees for 15 to 20 minutes, until hot and bubbly. Serve with crackers. Makes about 4 cups.

Ruth Cooksey
Plainfield, IN

Chutney-Topped Brie

Chutney-Topped Brie

I was a little worried about trying Brie because I thought there was some mystery to it. To my surprise, I found an easy recipe, and it turned out great! We enjoyed this over the holidays and will definitely add it to our list of family favorites.

8-oz. round Brie cheese
¼ c. cranberry or apricot chutney
2 T. sliced almonds or walnuts
Garnish: fresh rosemary
assorted crackers
pear slices

Trim and discard rind from top of Brie round, leaving a ¼-inch border. Place Brie in an ungreased oven-proof casserole dish; top with chutney. Bake, uncovered, at 400 degrees for 10 minutes, or until cheese appears to be melted. Watch closely to ensure cheese doesn't seep out. Toast nuts in a small non-stick skillet over medium-low heat, stirring often, for 2 to 3 minutes. Sprinkle nuts over Brie. Garnish with rosemary and serve warm with assorted crackers and pear slices. Serves 8 to 10.

Kathy Harris
Valley Center, KS

Tiffani's Hot Spiced Cider

I've been making this delicious, soul-warming brew ever since my teenagers were babies…for church coffee hours, homeroom mom teas, PTO events, baby showers and just for fun. It smells so good when it's mulling in the slow cooker! We make a big pot and take it outside with us on Halloween while we're handing out candy. Any leftover cider heats up wonderfully.

1 gal. apple cider or apple juice
½ to ¾ c. brown sugar, packed
1 orange, unpeeled
15 to 20 whole cloves
2 to 3 4-inch cinnamon sticks

Pour cider into a 5-quart slow cooker. Stir in desired amount of brown sugar. Stud orange with cloves; add to cider along with cinnamon sticks. Cover and cook on low setting for 2 to 3 hours; do not boil. May be kept at serving temperature in slow cooker for several hours. Serves 16.

Tiffani Schulte
Wyandotte, MI

Peppermint Milkshakes

This yummy dessert drink appeals to all ages. Use less milk for really thick shakes. (Pictured on page 214)

8 c. vanilla ice cream, divided
2 c. milk, divided
1 c. peppermint candies (about 40 to
    50 candies), crushed and divided
8½-oz. can refrigerated instant whipped cream
Garnish: peppermint sticks

Process 4 cups ice cream, one cup milk and ½ cup crushed candies in a blender until smooth, stopping to scrape down sides as needed. Pour into small serving glasses; top with whipped cream and place a peppermint stick in each glass. Repeat with remaining ingredients. Serves 6 to 8.

Note: Process peppermint candies in a food processor for quick crushing.

Christmas Brew

Perfect for a Christmas Eve get-together.

½ c. sugar
⅓ c. water
¼ c. baking cocoa
¼ t. cinnamon
10 c. hot brewed coffee
Garnish: milk, sugar, whipped topping

Bring sugar, water, cocoa and cinnamon to a boil in a saucepan over medium heat. Boil for one minute, stirring frequently. Add to brewed coffee; stir and serve immediately with milk and sugar, dolloped with whipped topping. Serves 10.

Mary Ann Dell
Phoenixville, PA

Autumn Morning Casserole

I love the fall...it's my favorite time of year! It's the best when we're cuddled on the couch looking at the leaves and watching the birds prepare for the coming winter.

½ lb. maple-flavored ground pork
  breakfast sausage
1 onion, grated
2 cloves garlic, grated
salt and pepper to taste
¼ c. apple juice
6 slices bread, cubed
3 eggs, beaten
1 c. milk
1 T. mustard
1 t. hot pepper sauce
1½ c. shredded Cheddar cheese

Brown sausage in a skillet over medium-high heat; drain and stir in onion, garlic, salt and pepper. Pour apple juice into skillet; stir and cook over medium heat until juice evaporates. Arrange bread cubes in a lightly greased 9"x9" baking pan. Whisk together eggs, milk, mustard and hot sauce. Layer sausage mixture evenly over bread; top bread and sausage with egg mixture. Sprinkle with cheese. Bake, uncovered, at 350 degrees for 35 to 40 minutes, until eggs are set. Serves 4 to 6.

Laura Witham
Anchorage, AK

Holiday Quiche

Double the recipe. Freeze the second quiche, and you have a quick meal when time is short!

10-oz. pkg. frozen chopped spinach
2 c. shredded sharp Cheddar cheese
2 T. all-purpose flour
1 c. milk
2 eggs, beaten
3 slices bacon, crisply cooked and
  crumbled
⅛ t. pepper
9-inch pie crust
Garnish: tomato slices

Cook the spinach according to package directions; drain and cool. In a bowl, toss cheese with flour. Add spinach and remaining ingredients except crust and tomato slices; mix well. Pour into the pie crust and bake at 350 degrees for one hour. Cool for 10 minutes; slice into wedges. Garnish each wedge with tomato slices. Serves 6.

Holiday Quiche

Holiday Quiche

Sausage & Cherry Tart with Walnuts

This tart is perfect for brunches and teas. The combination of flavors is wonderful!

1 c. all-purpose flour
⅔ c. walnuts, ground
1 T. sugar
¼ t. salt
½ t. dry mustard
⅛ t. cayenne pepper
6 T. chilled butter, cubed
1 to 2 T. milk
½ lb. ground pork breakfast sausage
1 onion, finely diced
½ to 1 c. dried tart cherries or cranberries
½ c. chopped walnuts
¼ t. dried thyme
2 eggs, beaten
1 c. whipping cream
3-oz. pkg. crumbled Gorgonzola cheese

Combine flour, ground walnuts, sugar, salt, mustard, cayenne pepper and butter in a food processor. Pulse just until mixture resembles bread crumbs. Add one tablespoon milk; pulse until a dough forms. If dough is too crumbly, add more milk until it holds together. Shape dough into a ball and press evenly into a lightly greased 9" round tart pan. Freeze for 30 minutes. Bake crust at 350 degrees for 15 to 20 minutes, until golden. Remove from oven and set aside. Brown sausage and onion in a skillet over medium heat; drain well. Stir in cherries or cranberries, chopped walnuts and thyme. Set aside. Combine eggs and cream; whisk until smooth. Spoon sausage mixture into baked crust; sprinkle with cheese. Pour egg mixture over all. Bake at 350 degrees for 15 to 20 minutes, until golden and center tests done. Cool for 15 minutes before serving. Serves 8.

Sharon Demers
Dolores, CO

Cranberry Christmas Canes

My mother used this recipe for more than 40 years… she always made them for our Christmas breakfast. We really looked forward to munching on these sweet pastries while we opened our gifts!

1 c. plus 1 to 2 t. milk, divided
4 c. all-purpose flour
¼ c. sugar
1 t. salt
1 t. lemon zest
1 c. butter
1 env. active dry yeast
¼ c. warm water
2 eggs, beaten
½ c. powdered sugar
¼ t. vanilla extract

Heat one cup milk just to boiling; cool slightly. Combine flour, sugar, salt and lemon zest in a large bowl. Cut in butter with a pastry blender until mixture resembles coarse meal. Dissolve yeast in warm water, about 110 to 115 degrees. Add yeast mixture, milk and eggs to flour mixture; combine lightly. Refrigerate for 2 hours to 2 days. At baking time, prepare Cranberry Filling; divide dough into 2 parts. On a floured surface, roll out half of dough into an 18"x15" rectangle. Spread half of Cranberry Filling over dough. Fold rectangle into thirds, bringing both short edges over top of the center; press to seal. Slice rectangle into 15 strips. Holding both ends, twist each strip lightly in opposite directions; pinch ends. Place on a greased baking sheet; bend over tops to look like candy canes. Repeat with remaining dough and filling. Bake at 400 degrees for 10 to 15 minutes. Cool on wire racks. Mix powdered sugar with vanilla and remaining milk; frost pastries. Makes 2½ dozen.

Cranberry Filling:

1½ c. fresh cranberries, finely chopped
½ c. sugar
½ c. raisins
⅓ c. honey
⅓ c. chopped pecans
1½ t. orange zest

Combine all ingredients in a saucepan. Bring to a boil over medium heat. Cook for 5 minutes, stirring frequently. Cool.

Laura Flores
Middletown, CT

Cranberry Christmas Canes

Old-Fashioned Potato
Doughnuts

Old-Fashioned Potato Doughnuts

My mom was a wonderful cook, and her scrumptious homemade doughnuts were a family favorite.

1 c. buttermilk
1 c. cold mashed potatoes
4 c. all-purpose flour
1 c. sugar
3 eggs, beaten
1 T. butter, softened
4 t. baking powder
1 t. salt
1 t. nutmeg
½ t. mace
1 t. vanilla extract
peanut oil for deep frying
Garnish: sugar

Mix together buttermilk and remaining ingredients except oil and garnish in a large bowl. Turn out ⅓ of dough onto a floured surface. Roll out dough to a ½-inch thickness. Cut with a doughnut cutter. Repeat with remaining dough. Heat several inches of oil to 350 degrees in a deep fryer over high heat. Add doughnuts, a few at a time. Doughnuts will sink when put into the hot oil. When they rise to the top, turn doughnuts and cook until golden. When golden on both sides, remove with a slotted spoon. Drain on a brown paper bag or paper towels. Roll warm doughnuts in sugar. Makes 3 dozen.

Cathy Johnson
Oregon, WI

doughnut kabobs
Try this fun idea for a brunch buffet! Slide bite-size doughnuts onto wooden skewers and stand the skewers in a tall vase for easy serving.

Pecan Coffee Cake

Mom taught me how to make my dad's favorite coffee cake when I was young. I was always an early riser, and I started to get up extra early on Sunday mornings just to make coffee cake for Dad before he woke up. It always brings back wonderful memories!

1½ c. butter, softened and divided
1 c. sugar
2 eggs, beaten
1 t. vanilla extract
3 c. all-purpose flour
1 T. baking powder
½ t. salt
1 c. milk

Blend one cup butter and sugar in a large bowl. Stir in eggs and vanilla; set aside. Mix flour, baking powder and salt in a separate bowl. Add flour mixture and milk alternately to butter mixture; stir well. Pour half of batter into a lightly greased and floured 13"x9" baking pan. Sprinkle half of Pecan Filling over batter. Top with remaining batter and then remaining filling. Melt remaining butter; drizzle over top. Bake at 375 degrees for 20 to 30 minutes, until a toothpick inserted near center comes out clean. Serves 8 to 12.

Pecan Filling:
1½ c. brown sugar, packed
2 t. cinnamon
1 c. broken pecans

Mix together all ingredients in a small bowl.

Kelly Patrick
Ashburn, VA

Christmas Cranberry Muffins

These muffins create a wonderful aroma while baking, and they are so colorful, too!

2 c. all-purpose flour
1 c. sugar
1½ t. baking powder
½ t. baking soda
½ t. salt
2 T. shortening
juice and zest of 1 orange
water
1 egg, beaten
1 c. cranberries, halved

Combine flour, sugar, baking powder, baking soda and salt in a large bowl; blend in shortening. Add orange zest. Place juice from orange in a measuring cup and add enough water to equal ¾ cup; blend into flour mixture. Fold in egg and cranberries. Pour into greased muffin cups, filling ⅔ full. Bake at 350 degrees for 15 to 18 minutes. Remove from pan and cool on a wire rack. Makes about 1½ dozen.

Note: This can also be made into quick bread by pouring batter into a greased 9"x5" loaf pan and baking at 350 degrees for 50 to 60 minutes.

Christmas Cranberry
Muffins

Homemade Butter Rolls

These scrumptious rolls are a must for our family's holiday dinners. They go hand-in-hand with the ham we smoke here on our farm.

1 c. water
1 env. active dry yeast
½ c. sugar, divided
3 eggs, beaten
¾ t. salt
4½ c. all-purpose flour
½ c. butter, melted

Heat water until very warm, about 110 to 115 degrees. In a bowl, combine water, yeast and 2 tablespoons sugar. Stir; let stand 5 minutes. Stir in remaining sugar, eggs and salt. Gradually stir in enough flour to make a soft dough. Cover and let rise for about 1½ hours, until double in bulk. Punch down. Use the melted butter to coat hands generously; form dough into 2 dozen rolls. Place rolls into 2 greased 13"x9" baking pans. Cover and let rise again until double in bulk, about 2 hours. Bake at 400 degrees for 10 minutes, or until golden. Makes 2 dozen.

Deborah Goodrich
Smithfield, VA

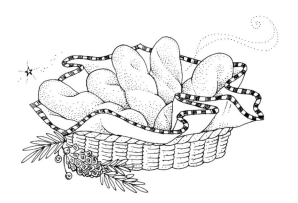

Twisty Rolls

I have been making these for years...but my dear Aunt Betty will always be the undisputed world champion Twisty Roll maker! (Pictured on page 214)

1 env. active dry yeast
3 T. sugar, divided
¼ c. warm water
1½ t. salt
4¼ c. all-purpose flour, divided
¼ c. butter, melted and cooled
¾ c. milk
1 egg, lightly beaten
1 T. water
1 egg, beaten
1 c. powdered sugar
2 T. milk

Dissolve yeast and one teaspoon sugar in warm water, 110 to 115 degrees; set aside. Mix remaining sugar, salt and 2 cups flour. Add yeast mixture, melted butter and milk. Stir until smooth. Beat in one egg. Add enough flour to make a soft dough. Knead in remaining flour until dough is smooth and elastic, about 5 minutes. Place in a greased bowl, cover and let rise in a warm place, until double in bulk, about 40 minutes. Punch down, and roll out to a ¼-inch thickness on a floured surface. Cut into ½"x 6" strips; braid 3 strips together to form a roll. Combine one tablespoon water and remaining egg. Place braids on a baking sheet; brush with egg mixture. Let rise 15 to 20 more minutes. Bake at 375 degrees for 10 to 12 minutes; let cool. Blend together powdered sugar and milk; drizzle over cooled rolls. Makes 14.

Debi Gilpin
Bluefield, WV

Christmas Tree
Pull-Apart Rolls

Christmas Tree Pull-Apart Rolls

Very yummy...so festive with dinner!

36 frozen dinner rolls
2 T. butter, melted
2 t. dried parsley, crumbled
garlic salt to taste
¼ c. shredded Romano cheese
Garnish: additional dried parsley

Arrange rolls on a baking sheet in a Christmas tree pattern. Bake according to package directions. Transfer to a platter. Combine butter, parsley and garlic salt; brush onto rolls. Sprinkle with cheese and garnish with dried parsley. Serve immediately. Makes 3 dozen.

Sour Cream Scones

Bake up some tender scones with ingredients you probably already have on hand. Serve with butter and jam...yum!

2 c. all-purpose flour
2 t. baking powder
½ t. baking soda
½ t. salt
¼ c. butter
2 eggs, beaten
½ c. sour cream

Combine flour, baking powder, baking soda and salt; beat in butter until mixture resembles coarse crumbs. Mix together eggs and sour cream in a separate bowl; stir into flour mixture until dough leaves the sides of the bowl. Knead for one minute. On a floured surface, roll out dough into a 9"x6" rectangle. Cut into six 3"x3" squares; cut each square diagonally. Arrange scones on an ungreased baking sheet, 2 inches apart. Bake at 400 degrees for 10 to 12 minutes. Makes one dozen.

Elaine Anderson
Aliquippa, PA

Pineapple Upside-Down Biscuits

My good friend Myrtie shared this recipe with me. So simple and delicious...we love it!

10-oz. can crushed pineapple, drained,
    juice reserved
½ c. brown sugar, packed
¼ c. butter, melted
¼ c. chopped pecans
10 maraschino cherries
10-oz. tube refrigerated buttermilk biscuits

Combine pineapple, sugar, butter and pecans; mix well. Place a cherry in the bottom of each of 10 lightly greased muffin cups. Divide pineapple mixture evenly among cups. Place one biscuit in each cup on top of pineapple mixture. Spoon one teaspoon of reserved pineapple juice over each biscuit. Bake at 350 degrees for 12 to 15 minutes, until golden. Cool for 2 minutes. Invert pan over a platter to release biscuits. Serve warm. Makes 10.

Billye Barrow
Cleveland, TX

French Onion Soup

This recipe was created at the college where I worked for many years.

1 T. butter
2 T. olive oil
4 onions, sliced
3 c. beef broth
3 to 4 bay leaves
salt and pepper to taste
6 slices French bread, toasted
¾ c. shredded Swiss cheese

Heat butter and oil in a stockpot over medium heat until butter melts. Add onions; cook for 20 to 30 minutes, until dark golden. Add broth, bay leaves, salt and pepper. Bring to a boil; reduce heat, cover and simmer for 30 minutes. Discard bay leaves. Ladle soup into 6 oven-safe soup bowls; top each with a slice of French bread, and sprinkle with cheese. Set bowls on a sturdy baking sheet. Broil until cheese is melted and golden. Serves 6.

Barbara Feist Stienstra
Goshen, NY

The best French onion soup you'll ever eat! —Barbara

Minestrone Soup

My aunt gave this recipe to me about 20 years ago. It's a wonderful main-dish soup, and it is very easy to prepare.

6 slices bacon, chopped
1 onion, chopped
1 c. celery, chopped
2 cloves garlic, minced
2 t. fresh basil, chopped
½ t. salt
3½ c. water
2 10¾-oz. cans bean & bacon soup
2 14½-oz. cans beef broth
2 14½-oz. cans stewed tomatoes, chopped, juice reserved
2 c. zucchini, peeled and chopped
2 c. cabbage, chopped
1 c. elbow macaroni, uncooked

Brown bacon, onion, celery and garlic in a large stockpot; drain. Add basil, salt, water, soup, broth, tomatoes with juice, zucchini, cabbage and macaroni. Boil until macaroni is tender, about 10 minutes. Serves 6 to 8.

Linda Newkirk
Central Point, OR

spice it up!

A vintage wooden soda crate makes a handy spice rack...enjoy it just as it is, or freshen it up with a coat of bright paint.

Minestrone Soup

Cincinnati-Style Chili

Living right on the border of Ohio, we've come to love Cincinnati-style chili. This is my husband's most requested recipe and a definite family favorite.

2 lbs. ground beef
4 c. water
8-oz. can tomato sauce
1 T. Worcestershire sauce
1 t. vinegar
1 onion, finely chopped
1 t. garlic, minced
3 T. chili powder
3 T. ground cumin
2 T. allspice
2 bay leaves
1 t. cinnamon
1 t. nutmeg
1 t. celery seed
1 t. salt
hot cooked spaghetti
Garnish: grated Cheddar cheese

Combine uncooked beef and water in a large pot. Add remaining ingredients except spaghetti and cheese. Simmer over medium heat for 3 hours, stirring often. Discard bay leaves. Serve over spaghetti; top with cheese. Serves 6.

Jennifer Oglesby
Brownsville, IN

Kathie's Beef & Barley Soup

You can substitute any favorite vegetable for the turnip if you'd prefer.

1 to 2-lb. beef shank
¼ c. celery, diced
2 T. fresh parsley, chopped
salt to taste
2 t. Worcestershire sauce
1 bay leaf
¼ t. dried thyme
8 c. water
½ c. pearled barley
1 c. turnip, peeled and diced
1 c. carrot, peeled and sliced
½ c. onion, chopped

Combine beef, celery, parsley, salt, sauce, bay leaf, thyme and water in a large stockpot over medium-high heat. Cover and bring to a boil; reduce heat and simmer 2 hours. Remove beef from broth; set aside. Strain broth and return to stockpot; stir in barley and simmer, covered, 30 minutes. When meat is cool enough to handle, cut off the bone and dice. Add beef and remaining vegetables to stockpot; simmer, uncovered until vegetables are tender, about 30 minutes. Serves 6 to 8.

Kathie Poritz
Burlington, WI

I make this soup ahead to have ready for the end of a shopping day. My grown daughters and I put our feet up and rest. When we're ready for dinner, all I have to do is reheat the soup. —Kathie

Christmas Luncheon Crabmeat Bisque

For a shrimp bisque, replace crab with 1½ cups cooked, peeled and cleaned shrimp.

6 T. butter, divided
¼ c. green pepper, finely chopped
¼ c. onion, finely chopped
1 green onion, chopped
1½ c. sliced mushrooms
2 T. fresh parsley, chopped
2 T. all-purpose flour
1 c. milk
1 t. salt
⅛ t. white pepper
⅛ t. hot pepper sauce
2 c. half-and-half
1½ c. cooked crabmeat, flaked
Optional: 3 T. dry sherry
Garnish: additional chopped green onion

Heat 4 tablespoons butter in a skillet over medium heat. Add vegetables and parsley; sauté until soft. Heat remaining 2 tablespoons butter in a saucepan; stir in flour. Add milk and cook, stirring constantly, until thickened and smooth. Stir in salt, pepper and hot pepper sauce. Add sautéed vegetables and half-and-half. Bring to a boil, stirring constantly; reduce heat. Add crabmeat and simmer, uncovered, for 5 minutes. If desired, stir in sherry just prior to serving. Top with additional green onion. Serves 4.

festive for fall

Bring out Mom's vintage Thanksgiving china early to get into the mood for fall. Use the bowls for soup suppers, the teacups for dessert get-togethers and layer sandwich fixin's on the turkey platter.

Christmas Luncheon
Crabmeat Bisque

Roast Turkey & Gravy

12 to 14-lb. turkey
1 T. salt, divided
2 t. pepper, divided
½ c. butter, softened
1 Golden Delicious apple, quartered
1 yellow onion, quartered
2 carrots, cut into 3-inch pieces
3 stalks celery with leaves, cut into 3-inch pieces
4 c. hot water
⅓ c. all-purpose flour
salt and pepper to taste

Remove giblets and neck from turkey; rinse and reserve for another use. Rinse turkey with cold water and pat dry. Sprinkle cavity with 1½ teaspoons salt and one teaspoon pepper. Rub skin of turkey with butter; sprinkle with remaining 1½ teaspoons salt and one teaspoon pepper.

Place apple, onion, carrot and celery in turkey cavity. Lift wing tips up and over back and tuck under bird. Place turkey, breast side up, on a lightly greased rack in a roasting pan. Tie ends of legs together with heavy string.

Bake at 425 degrees on lower oven rack 20 minutes. Reduce oven temperature to 325 degrees. Add hot water to pan; bake 2 to 2½ hours, until a meat thermometer inserted in turkey thigh registers 170 degrees, shielding turkey with aluminum foil after one hour and basting with pan juices every 20 minutes. Let stand 15 minutes. Transfer to a serving platter; reserve 2½ cups drippings.

Whisk together drippings and flour in a medium saucepan. Cook over medium heat, whisking constantly, 5 to 7 minutes, until thick and bubbly. Season gravy to taste. Serve gravy with turkey and Cornbread Dressing (page 247). Serves 12 to 14.

Penny's Turkey Enchiladas

Penny is my pen pal in Oklahoma; we've been friends since 1965 and often exchange recipes. A few years ago, I needed a good casserole to serve to a houseful of out-of-town guests, and she sent me this one. I doubled everything, made two of the casseroles and froze one for later on. It was a big hit…thanks, Penny!

8½-oz. jar green enchilada sauce
10¾-oz. can cream of chicken soup
2 c. cooked turkey, diced
1 c. onion, diced
2 c. shredded Cheddar or Monterey Jack
    cheese, divided
6 to 8 corn tortillas
oil for frying
Garnish: salsa, sour cream, guacamole

Stir together enchilada sauce and soup in a saucepan over medium-low heat; simmer until heated through. Mix together turkey, onion and one cup cheese in a separate bowl. Pour half of sauce mixture into turkey mixture; stir well and set aside. Fry tortillas in oil in a skillet over medium-high heat about 5 seconds each, until softened. Drain on paper towels. Spoon turkey mixture onto tortillas and roll up. Place enchiladas, seam-side down, in a lightly greased 2-quart casserole dish. Spoon remaining sauce mixture over top; sprinkle with remaining cheese. Bake, uncovered, at 350 degrees for 30 to 45 minutes, until hot and bubbly. Garnish as desired. Serves 6 to 8.

Sandra Smith
Lancaster, CA

Roast Turkey & Gravy

Two Herb-Roasted Turkey with Bourbon Gravy

This juicy bird is prepared with a traditional technique and has classic flavor. A bourbon-splashed gravy makes it extra special. Be sure to set aside half of the gravy for the kids before adding bourbon. (Pictured on the cover)

12 to 14-lb. fresh or frozen turkey, thawed
6 T. unsalted butter, softened
1½ T. fresh sage, minced, or 1½ t. dried sage
1½ T. fresh thyme leaves, or 1½ t. dried thyme
2 t. salt
1 t. pepper
1 onion, cut into wedges
2 stalks celery, coarsely chopped
3 cloves garlic, halved
Garnishes: fresh sage and fresh flat-leaf parsley

Remove giblets and neck from turkey; place in refrigerator for use in gravy. Rinse turkey with cold water; pat dry with paper towels. Lift wing tips up and over back and tuck under bird. Place turkey, breast side up, on a rack in a lightly greased roasting pan.

Combine butter and seasonings in a small bowl; rub 2 tablespoons seasoned butter inside turkey cavity. Place onion, celery and garlic inside turkey cavity. Rub remaining 4 tablespoons seasoned butter over outside of turkey. Tie ends of legs together with heavy string. Bake at 325 degrees, uncovered, for 2½ to 3 hours, until a meat thermometer inserted into the meaty part of thigh registers 170 degrees. Shield turkey with aluminum foil toward end of cooking, if necessary, to prevent overbrowning. Transfer turkey to a serving platter, reserving pan drippings for Bourbon Gravy. Let turkey stand, covered with foil, for at least 15 minutes before carving. Garnish platter, if desired. Serve turkey with Bourbon Gravy. Serves 12 to 14.

Bourbon Gravy:

Giblets and neck reserved from turkey
3 cups water
pan drippings from turkey
½ c. all-purpose flour
½ c. water
½ t. garlic powder
2 T. bourbon

Combine giblets, neck and water in a saucepan. Bring to a boil; cover, reduce heat, and simmer 45 minutes to one hour, until giblets are tender. Strain, reserving broth. Discard turkey neck. Coarsely chop giblets; set aside. Add 2 cups reserved broth to turkey pan drippings; stir until browned bits are loosened from bottom of roasting pan. Continue cooking in roasting pan placed over 2 burners on the stovetop. Stir in chopped giblets. Bring to a boil; reduce heat and simmer, uncovered, 3 to 5 minutes. Combine flour and ½ cup water, stirring until blended; gradually stir into gravy. Bring to a boil; boil one minute or until thickened. Set aside some plain gravy, if desired. Stir garlic powder and bourbon into remaining gravy. Serve hot. Makes about 3 cups.

Note: Substitute canned chicken broth instead of making homemade broth, if desired.

turkey trot

Start a new Thanksgiving tradition! Instead of snoozing after savoring a big dinner together, lead everyone on a brisk walk. Enjoy the fresh crisp air and the last fallen leaves or the first snowflakes...you'll be ready to sample all those scrumptious pies afterward!

Curried Harvest Chicken

My family loves meat combined with fruit, so this savory dish is a favorite. I can toss it in the slow cooker in the morning and then forget about it until it's time for dinner. Tasty and convenient!

21-oz. can apple pie filling
2 10¾-oz. cans cream of mushroom soup
2 to 3 T. curry powder
1 t. salt
6 boneless, skinless chicken breasts
12-oz. pkg. frozen mixed vegetables

Combine pie filling, soup, curry powder and salt in a 5-quart slow cooker; stir in chicken and vegetables. Cover and cook on low setting for 6 hours, or until chicken juices run clear when pierced. Serves 6.

Jill Ball
Highland, UT

Sweet & Sour Brisket

This is a great alternative to the traditional Sunday pot roast. It tastes even better the next day, sliced and made into sandwiches! This brisket can easily be prepared in a slow cooker, if you prefer. Cook it on low setting for 6 to 8 hours.

2 T. oil
4-lb. beef brisket
28-oz. can crushed tomatoes
1 c. catsup
¾ c. brown sugar, packed
½ c. balsamic vinegar
1.35-oz. pkg. onion soup mix

Heat oil in a large oven-proof saucepan over medium heat. Add brisket, and brown on both sides; drain. Mix together remaining ingredients; pour mixture over brisket. If necessary, add a little water so that brisket is half covered by liquid. Cover and bake at 350 degrees for 3 to 4 hours, until tender. Serves 6 to 8.

Beth Shaeffer
Greenwood, IN

Feliz Navidad Casserole

More than 20 years ago, my husband and I were newlyweds attending college in Lubbock, Texas. I clipped the original recipe for this casserole out of the local newspaper. I've changed it over the years to include our family's favorite ingredients. It's a real winner!

1½ lbs. ground beef
1 onion, chopped
10¾-oz. can cream of chicken soup
10-oz. can red enchilada sauce
4-oz. can diced green chiles
2 t. ground cumin
½ t. salt
½ t. pepper
3 c. shredded Mexican-blend or Monterey Jack cheese, divided
10 8-inch flour tortillas
Garnish: chopped tomatoes, sliced green onions

Brown beef and onion in a large skillet over medium heat; drain. Stir in cream of chicken soup, enchilada sauce, green chilies, cumin, salt and pepper; simmer for 10 minutes. Spread ⅓ of meat sauce in a greased 13"x9" baking pan. Sprinkle with one cup of cheese. Add a layer of tortillas, tearing tortillas to fit pan and completely covering the beef mixture and cheese. Repeat layers, ending with remaining beef mixture and cheese. Bake, uncovered, at 350 degrees for 20 minutes, or until bubbly and cheese is melted. Garnish with tomatoes and onions. Serves 8.

Tracee Cummins
Amarillo, TX

Feliz Navidad Casserole

Special Baked Lasagna

My mother-in-law has made this recipe for years, and it is always so delicious. At my husband's request, she's even served it alongside the roast turkey on Christmas Day!

1 lb. ground beef, browned and drained
14½-oz. can diced tomatoes
2 6-oz. cans tomato paste
1 c. water
1 clove garlic, pressed
1 T. dried basil
3 T. dried parsley, divided
2½ t. salt, divided
3 c. cottage cheese
½ c. grated Parmesan cheese
2 eggs, beaten
½ t. pepper
16-oz. pkg. lasagna noodles, uncooked
2 8-oz. pkgs. shredded mozzarella cheese

Combine beef, tomatoes, tomato paste, water, garlic, basil, one tablespoon parsley and 1½ teaspoons salt in a large bowl; set aside. In a separate bowl, stir together cottage cheese, Parmesan cheese, eggs, pepper and remaining parsley and salt. Spoon ⅓ of beef mixture into an ungreased, deep 13"x9" baking pan. Layer with half each of uncooked noodles, beef mixture, cheese mixture and mozzarella; repeat layers. Make sure noodles are completely covered by sauce. Cover pan with aluminum foil. Bake at 375 degrees for 45 minutes. Uncover; bake an additional 15 minutes, or until bubbly and heated through. Serves 12.

Gretchen Brown
Forest Grove, OR

Filet Mignon with Mushrooms

A terrific choice for a special meal.

4 6-oz. filet mignon steaks
½ t. salt
½ t. pepper
½ t. garlic powder
8-oz. pkg. sliced mushrooms
4 cloves garlic, chopped
¼ c. plus 2 T. Marsala wine

Sprinkle each steak with salt, pepper and garlic powder; set aside. Coat a large skillet with non-stick vegetable spray and heat to medium-high. Add mushrooms and garlic; cook, stirring frequently, for 5 minutes, or until mushrooms are golden. Remove from heat and set aside. Arrange steaks on a broiler pan about 4 inches below the heat source. Broil for about 4 minutes on each side or to desired doneness. Reheat mushroom mixture in skillet over medium-high heat. Add wine to mixture and bring to a boil; cook for about 2 minutes, or until wine is reduced. Place each steak on a serving plate, and top with mushroom mixture. Serves 4.

Teresa Beal
Bowling Green, KY

gift for grandma

Wouldn't doting grandparents love to receive a grandchild's best artwork in a sweet frame? Paint a simple frame in a color that goes well with the picture and then glue on wooden alphabet tiles to spell out the child's name. It's a gift that's sure to be cherished!

Filet Mignon with
Mushrooms

Grandmother's Scalloped Oysters

This casserole reheats well in the microwave.

½ c. round buttery crackers, crumbled
½ c. saltine crackers, crumbled
I pt. fresh oysters, drained, liquid reserved
½ t. pepper, divided
½ c. butter, sliced and divided
I to I ½ c. whipping cream

Mix together cracker crumbs. Place ⅓ of crumbs in a buttered, shallow 1½-quart casserole dish. Spread half of oysters over crumbs; sprinkle with half of pepper and dot with half of butter. Repeat layers, starting with crumbs; top with remaining crumbs. Combine reserved oyster liquid and cream; pour over casserole. With a knife, pierce the top several times to allow the liquid to flow all through the dish. Bake, uncovered, at 400 degrees for 25 to 30 minutes, until heated through and golden on top. Serves 8.

Kay Neubauer
Taylorsville, NC

My grandmother always served this dish at Thanksgiving and Christmas. When my son-in-law joined our family, it quickly became a favorite of his, too. —Kay

mix it up
Hosting lots of guests for Thanksgiving dinner? Feel free to mix & match plates and glasses for a whimsical look that's more fun than carefully matched china.

Maple-Marinated Salmon

The flavors of ginger and maple combine to bring out the best in the salmon.

¾ c. maple syrup
2 T. fresh ginger, peeled and grated
2 T. lemon juice
2 T. lite soy sauce
½ t. pepper
¼ t. salt
2¼ lbs. skin-on salmon fillets

Stir together all ingredients except salmon in a greased 13"x9" baking pan. Place salmon, skin-side up, in pan. Cover and refrigerate 15 minutes. Turn; marinate an additional 15 minutes. Line another 13"x9" baking pan with parchment paper. Place salmon on parchment, skin-side down; brush with marinade. Bake at 400 degrees for 10 minutes. Brush with remaining marinade and return to oven for 10 to 15 minutes, until fish flakes easily with a fork. Discard skin before serving. Serves 6.

Joan White
Malvern, PA

Honey-Roasted Pork Loin

A wonderful, old-fashioned main dish when served with homemade stuffing or noodles.

2 to 3-lb. boneless pork loin roast
¼ c. honey
2 T. Dijon mustard
2 T. mixed or black peppercorns, crushed
½ t. dried thyme
½ t. salt
Garnish: fresh thyme sprigs

Place roast on a lightly greased rack in a shallow roasting pan. In a bowl, combine honey and remaining ingredients except thyme sprigs; brush half of mixture over roast. Bake at 325 degrees for one hour; brush with remaining honey mixture. Bake 20 more minutes, or until thermometer inserted in thickest portion registers 160 degrees. Garnish with fresh thyme sprigs and serve with Harvest Dressing (page 245). Serves 8.

Honey-Roasted Pork Loin and Harvest Dressing (page 245)

Cranberry-Glazed Ham

Cranberry-Glazed Ham

Serve slices topped with a generous spoonful of the brown sugar-cranberry glaze…wonderful!

5 to 6-lb. ham
16-oz. can jellied cranberry sauce
1 c. brown sugar, packed
¼ c. orange juice
½ t. ground cloves
¼ t. cinnamon
¼ t. allspice
Garnish: fresh sage, fresh thyme, orange wedges,
    cherries

Bake ham at 350 degrees for 18 to 20 minutes per pound, until meat thermometer registers 160 degrees. While ham is baking, combine remaining ingredients except garnishes in a saucepan; heat slowly, whisking until smooth. Spoon half the glaze mixture over the ham 30 minutes before removing it from the oven; continue baking for 30 minutes. Serve with remaining glaze. Garnish, if desired. Serves 8 to 10.

Beverly Smith
Malin, OR

Jambalaya in a Jiff

Add a little more hot pepper sauce if you like it spicy!

2 T. butter
7-oz. pkg. chicken-flavored rice
    vermicelli mix
2¾ c. water
¼ t. pepper
¼ t. hot pepper sauce
1 T. dried, minced onion
¼ c. celery, diced
¼ c. green pepper, diced
2 c. cooked ham, diced
1 lb. cooked medium shrimp

   Melt butter in a large saucepan over medium heat. Add rice vermicelli mix and sauté just until golden. Stir in remaining ingredients; reduce heat, cover and simmer for 15 minutes. Serves 4 to 6.

Patricia Perkins
Shenandoah, IA

Country-Style Scalloped Potatoes

Old-fashioned flavor…slow-cooker convenience!

6 russet potatoes, thinly sliced
1½ lbs. ham steak, cubed
10¾-oz. can cream of mushroom soup
1¼ c. water
1 c. shredded Cheddar cheese
grill seasoning to taste

   Layer potatoes and ham in a lightly greased 4-quart slow cooker. Combine remaining ingredients; pour over potatoes and ham. Cover and cook on high setting for 3½ hours, or until potatoes are fork-tender. Turn slow cooker to low setting; continue cooking for about one hour. Serves 4 to 6.

Eleanor Paternoster
Bridgeport, CT

Harriet's Potato Pancakes

These are so good. I passed this recipe along to our niece who owns a cafe, and it is one of her breakfast hits.

1 c. all-purpose flour
2 t. baking powder
Optional: 1 t. salt
2 eggs, beaten
1 c. milk
2 T. onion, grated
¼ c. butter, melted
3 c. potatoes, peeled and finely grated
additional butter for frying

   Mix together flour, baking powder and salt, if desired, in a small bowl; set aside. Combine remaining ingredients, except butter for frying, in a medium bowl. Stir flour mixture into potato mixture until well blended. Drop by tablespoonfuls onto a buttered frying pan or griddle. Cook on both sides until golden. Serves 6.

Harriet Hughes
Wurtsboro, NY

Holiday Sweet Potatoes

Holiday Sweet Potatoes

This dish combines sweet potatoes and cranberry sauce into one scoop. For individual casseroles, spoon sweet potato filling into small baking dishes or ramekins. Top evenly with cranberry mixture and brown sugar syrup. Bake at 350 degrees for 10 minutes, or until thoroughly heated.

2 29-oz. cans cut sweet potatoes in syrup, drained
⅔ c. brown sugar, packed
¼ t. salt
2 c. fresh cranberries
1 apple, cored, peeled and chopped
⅓ c. sugar
¼ c. plus 2 T. water, divided
1 c. chopped walnuts
½ c. brown sugar, packed
2 T. butter

Combine sweet potatoes, ⅔ cup brown sugar and salt in a bowl. Mash until smooth. Spoon into a lightly greased 11"x7" baking pan; set aside. Stir together cranberries, apple, sugar and ¼ cup water in a saucepan. Cook over medium heat for 8 to 10 minutes, until cranberries burst. Add walnuts; stir well. Spoon over sweet potatoes in dish.

Combine ½ cup brown sugar, remaining 2 tablespoons water and butter in a small saucepan. Bring to a boil; boil, stirring constantly, for 2 minutes. Pour over cranberries and sweet potatoes. Bake, uncovered, at 350 degrees for 15 minutes, or just until heated through. Serves 8.

sweet potato fries

Sweet potato fries are deliciously different! Slice sweet potatoes into strips or wedges, toss with olive oil and place on a baking sheet. Bake at 400 degrees for 20 to 40 minutes, until tender, turning once. Sprinkle with a little cinnamon sugar for added sweetness or chili powder for a spicy kick.

Harvest Dressing

Not your ordinary dressing...delicious with pork or poultry! (Pictured on page 241)

2 apples, cored and chopped
½ c. golden raisins
3 T. butter
½ c. walnuts or pecans, coarsely chopped
¼ c. brown sugar, packed
2 c. whole-wheat bread, cubed
½ c. apple juice or cider

Sauté apples and raisins in butter; add nuts, brown sugar and bread cubes. Add enough juice or cider to moisten to desired texture. Bake, uncovered, in a 1½-quart casserole dish at 400 degrees for 18 minutes. Serves 4.

Mini Cheddar Soufflés

3 T. butter
3 T. all-purpose flour
¾ c. milk
¾ c. shredded Cheddar cheese
1 T. Dijon mustard
4 slices bacon, crisply cooked and crumbled
4 eggs, separated
Optional: fresh parsley or chives, chopped

Melt butter in a saucepan over medium heat. Stir in flour; cook and stir for one minute. Gradually add milk; stir until well blended. Cook and stir until mixture comes to a boil. Remove from heat; stir in cheese until melted. Mix in mustard and bacon. Cool slightly. Stir in egg yolks one at a time; set aside. Beat egg whites until stiff but not dry, about 5 minutes, with an electric mixer at medium speed. Gently fold into cheese mixture. Spoon into 12 lightly greased non-stick muffin cups. Bake at 350 degrees for about 25 minutes, until puffed and set. Serve warm; sprinkle with parsley or chives, if desired. Serves 12.

Zoe Bennett
Columbia, SC

Merry Christmas Rice

Yorkshire Pudding

This is especially good when the pan is greased with drippings from roast beef.

1½ c. all-purpose flour
¾ t. salt
1½ c. milk
3 eggs, beaten
½ c. currants

Mix together flour, salt, milk and eggs in a bowl. Beat well with a wire whisk. Fold in currants. Pour into a greased 8"x8" baking pan. Bake, uncovered, at 450 degrees for 25 to 30 minutes. Serves 6 to 8.

Margaret Hoehler
Littleton, CO

Merry Christmas Rice

This quick & easy recipe was my daughter Kim's very first dish on the holiday table.

½ c. onion, finely chopped
3 stalks celery, finely chopped
1 red pepper, chopped
1 green pepper, chopped
1 T. butter, softened
2 c. chicken broth
2 c. instant rice, uncooked
Optional: ½ t. salt
¼ t. pepper

Sauté onion, celery and peppers in butter in a skillet over medium heat for 2 minutes, or until crisp-tender. Remove from heat; set aside. Bring broth to a boil in a saucepan over medium-high heat. Remove from heat. Quickly stir in rice, onion mixture, salt, if desired, and pepper. Cover and let stand for 6 to 7 minutes. Stir before serving. Serves 6.

Kerry Mayer
Denham Springs, LA

Cornbread Dressing

This Southern classic is a Thanksgiving favorite. This version is quite moist; if you prefer a firmer dressing, use only four cans of broth.

1 c. butter, divided
3 c. white cornmeal
1 c. all-purpose flour
2 T. sugar
2 t. baking powder
1½ t. salt
1 t. baking soda
7 eggs, divided
3 c. buttermilk
3 c. soft bread crumbs
3 c. celery, finely chopped
2 c. onion, finely chopped
½ c. fresh sage, finely chopped, or 1 T. dried
    rubbed sage
5 10½-oz. cans condensed chicken broth
1 T. pepper

Place ½ cup butter in a 13"x9" baking pan; heat in oven at 425 degrees for 4 minutes.

Combine cornmeal, flour, sugar, baking powder, salt and baking soda; whisk in 3 eggs and buttermilk. Pour hot butter from pan into batter, stirring until blended. Pour batter into pan. Bake at 425 degrees for 30 minutes, or until golden. Cool.

Crumble cornbread into a large bowl; stir in bread crumbs and set aside.

Melt remaining ½ cup butter in a large skillet over medium heat; add celery and onion and sauté until tender. Stir in sage and sauté one more minute.

Stir vegetables, remaining 4 eggs, chicken broth and pepper into cornbread mixture; spoon into one lightly greased 13"x9" baking pan and one lightly greased 8"x8" baking pan. Cover and chill 8 hours, if desired.

Bake dressing, uncovered, at 375 degrees for 35 to 40 minutes, until golden. Serves 16 to 18.

Roasted Brussels Sprouts with Pancetta

This just happens to be a newer and easier version of an older recipe. Canadian bacon can be substituted for the pancetta, if you prefer.

2 lbs. Brussels sprouts, halved
6-oz. pkg. pancetta, chopped
¼ c. olive oil
kosher salt and pepper to taste

Combine Brussels sprouts, pancetta and oil in a large bowl. Toss well to coat; season with salt and pepper. Spread mixture in one layer on an ungreased 15"x10" jelly-roll pan. Bake at 425 degrees for 25 to 30 minutes, until Brussels sprouts are crisp-tender. Serves 4 to 6.

Denise Piccirilli
Huber Heights, OH

pumpkin patch

Be sure to stop at roadside stands along the country roads. You'll find fun pumpkin names, such as Cinderella, Big Max and Baby Boo, alongside gooseneck and apple gourds.

Homestyle Green Beans

This is a tasty way to serve fresh green beans.

2 lbs. green beans, trimmed
2 c. water
1¼ t. salt, divided
⅓ c. butter or margarine
1½ T. sugar
1 t. dried basil
½ t. garlic powder
¼ t. pepper
2 c. cherry or grape tomatoes, halved

Place beans in a Dutch oven; add water and one teaspoon salt. Bring to a boil; cover, reduce heat and simmer 15 minutes, or until tender. Drain; keep warm.

Melt butter or margarine in a saucepan over medium heat; stir in sugar, basil, garlic powder, remaining ¼ teaspoon salt and pepper. Add tomatoes and cook, stirring gently, until thoroughly heated. Pour tomato mixture over beans and toss gently. Serve hot. Serves 8.

Slow-Cooker Baked Apples

Delectable as either a side or a dessert!

8 Jonathan or Granny Smith apples, cored
⅓ c. raisins
⅓ c. chopped nuts
⅓ c. brown sugar, packed
1½ t. apple pie spice
2 T. butter or margarine, sliced
½ c. apple cider
1 T. lemon juice

Remove peel from top ⅓ of each apple. Mix together raisins, nuts and brown sugar; spoon evenly into apples. Arrange apples in a greased 6-quart slow cooker. Sprinkle with apple pie spice; dot with butter or margarine. Mix cider and lemon juice and drizzle over apples. Cover and cook on low setting for 8 hours. Serves 8.

Homestyle Green Beans

Cranberry Relish

Cranberry Relish

An easy make-ahead dish!

8-oz. can crushed pineapple
4 c. mini marshmallows
2 c. fresh cranberries, ground
1 c. sugar
2 c. whipped cream

Pour crushed pineapple over marshmallows; let stand overnight. Mix cranberries and sugar; let stand overnight. In the morning, combine mixtures and fold in whipped cream. Serves 6.

Sweet Ambrosia

16-oz. container low-fat frozen whipped
    topping, thawed
15-oz. can pineapple tidbits, drained
15-oz. can fruit cocktail, drained
10-oz. jar maraschino cherries, drained
8-oz. can mandarin oranges, drained
2 c. chopped walnuts
10½-oz. pkg. mini marshmallows
1 c. sweetened flaked coconut

Spoon whipped topping into a large serving bowl. Add remaining ingredients and mix well. Cover and refrigerate at least one hour before serving. Serves 10 to 15.

Sammie Warwick
Gulf Shores, AL

My mother-in-law shared the recipe for this old favorite with me. My husband enjoys it so much, I have to set aside a bowl just for him to enjoy later! It is a fast, easy dish that everyone likes. —Sammie

Old-Time Pickled Peaches

A simple and delicious recipe that's a tradition in our house. My family has served these for generations... they're a "must" year-round at holiday dinners and summer cookouts.

2 15¼-oz. cans peach halves, drained and
    juice reserved
3 to 6 4-inch cinnamon sticks, broken in half
1 t. whole cloves
2 T. white vinegar
½ c. sugar

Pour reserved juice into a large saucepan over medium heat. Heat to boiling; add remaining ingredients except peaches. Simmer 5 minutes. Add peaches; simmer an additional 5 minutes. Remove from heat and allow to cool. Discard spices. Chill before serving. Serves 6 to 8.

Lisa Sett
Thousand Oaks, CA

organize with style

Vintage carryalls are terrific for corralling clutter. Pick up a few to use in the kitchen, organize a craft room or display on a buffet table.

Tart Apple Salad

Tart Apple Salad

My husband really likes this nice fall salad. I always serve it at Thanksgiving.

6 tart crisp apples, cored and chopped
1½ c. red grapes, halved and seeded
1 c. celery, finely chopped
½ c. chopped walnuts
¼ c. sugar
1 T. mayonnaise-type salad dressing
1 c. whipping cream, whipped
¼ c. dried cranberries

Toss together apples, grapes, celery and walnuts in a large serving bowl; sprinkle with sugar. Stir in salad dressing; mix well. Cover and chill until serving time. Fold in whipped cream and cranberries just before serving. Serves 10 to 12.

Leona Krivda
Belle Vernon, PA

Tossed Salad & Cider Dressing

With three kinds of apple flavor, the creamy dressing makes this salad perfect for a chilly-weather dinner.

2 c. fresh spinach, torn
2 c. romaine lettuce, torn
1 c. iceberg lettuce, torn

Toss together spinach and lettuces in a salad bowl. Drizzle with Cider Dressing; toss well and serve immediately. Serves 6.

Cider Dressing:

¼ c. frozen apple juice concentrate, thawed
3 T. sour cream
3 T. water
2 T. cider vinegar
2 T. fresh parsley, chopped
2 T. apple, cored, peeled and finely shredded
1 T. Dijon mustard
¼ t. salt
⅛ t. pepper

Whisk together all ingredients. Keep refrigerated; shake well before using.

Tina Wright
Atlanta, GA

Bûche de Noël

1 c. all-purpose flour
1 t. baking powder
¼ t. salt
4 eggs, separated
¾ c. sugar, divided
⅓ cup water
1 t. vanilla extract
3 T. powdered sugar
Garnish: fresh mint and fresh cranberries

Combine flour, baking powder and salt; set aside. Beat egg whites with an electric mixer at high speed until foamy. Gradually add ¼ cup sugar, one tablespoon at a time, beating until stiff peaks form and sugar dissolves, about 2 to 4 minutes; set aside. Beat egg yolks in a large mixing bowl with an electric mixer at high speed, gradually adding ½ cup sugar; beat 5 minutes, or until thick and pale. Add water and vanilla; beat well. Add flour mixture; beat just until blended. Fold in about ⅓ of egg white mixture. Gently fold in remaining egg white mixture.

Grease bottom and sides of a 15"x10" jelly-roll pan. Line with wax paper; grease and flour paper. Spread batter evenly into pan. Bake at 375 degrees for 10 minutes, or until top springs back when lightly touched. Sift powdered sugar in a 15"x10" rectangle on a clean cloth. When cake is done, immediately loosen from sides of pan; turn out onto cloth. Peel off wax paper. Starting at narrow end, roll up cake and cloth together; cool completely on a wire rack, seam side down.

Unroll cake and remove cloth. Spread half of Chocolate Frosting onto cake; carefully reroll. Cut a one-inch-thick diagonal slice from one end of cake roll. Place cake roll on a serving plate, seam side down. Position slice against side of cake roll to resemble knot; use frosting to "glue" in place. Spread remaining frosting over cake and knot. If frosting is soft, chill cake before serving. Garnish with fresh mint and fresh cranberries. Serves 8 to 10.

Chocolate Frosting:

3¾ c. sifted powdered sugar
½ c. baking cocoa
6 T. milk
6 T. butter, softened

Combine powdered sugar and cocoa in a large bowl. Add milk and butter to sugar mixture; beat with an electric mixer at medium speed until smooth.

Red Velvet Bars

The bars are easy to prepare...plus they're tasty and pretty!

18½-oz. pkg. red velvet cake mix
2 T. brown sugar, packed
1 t. baking cocoa
2 eggs, beaten
½ c. oil
½ t. vanilla extract
2 T. water
1 c. white chocolate chips
½ c. chopped pecans
Optional: whipped topping, additional
    chopped pecans

Combine dry cake mix, brown sugar and cocoa in a large bowl. Stir in eggs, oil, vanilla and water. Mix in chocolate chips and pecans. Spread batter into a lightly greased 13"x9" baking pan. Bake at 350 degrees for 18 to 20 minutes. Cool and spread with whipped topping and additional pecans, if desired. Cut into bars. Makes 20.

Judy Jones
Chinquapin, NC

Kris Kringle Cake

Kris Kringle Cake

A special cake for a special time of year.

1¼ c. butter or margarine, softened and divided
1½ c. brown sugar, packed
3 eggs
1 c. sour cream
½ c. plus 3 T. milk, divided
2 c. all-purpose flour
2 t. cinnamon
1½ t. baking soda
1 t. baking powder
½ t. ground cloves
½ t. nutmeg
½ t. salt
6 c. powdered sugar
¾ c. shortening
1 T. vanilla extract
brown and red paste food coloring
red candied cherry, halved
4 large marshmallows

For cake, beat ½ cup butter or margarine and brown sugar in a large bowl until fluffy. Add eggs, one at a time, beating well after each addition. Add sour cream and ½ cup milk; stir until well blended. Sift together flour, cinnamon, baking soda, baking powder, cloves, nutmeg and salt in a medium bowl. Add dry ingredients to butter mixture, stirring until well blended. Spoon batter into a greased and floured 12½"-wide star-shaped baking pan. Bake at 350 degrees for 35 to 40 minutes, until a toothpick inserted near the center comes out clean. Cool in pan 10 minutes. Remove cake from pan and cool completely on a wire rack.

For frosting, combine powdered sugar, shortening, remaining ¾ cup butter, 3 tablespoons milk and vanilla in a large bowl; beat until smooth. Spoon 1½ cups frosting into a pastry bag; cover end of bag with plastic wrap and set aside. Spoon ¼ cup frosting into small bowl; tint brown. Spoon brown frosting into a pastry bag; cover end of bag with plastic wrap and set aside. Spoon one cup frosting into another small bowl; tint red.

Spread remaining white frosting on sides of cake, on top of 4 tips of cake for hands and feet and on top of cake for face. Spread red frosting on top of cake for hat and suit. Use a table knife or small metal spatula dipped in water to smooth frosting.

Using white frosting and a basket weave tip with smooth side of tip facing up, pipe stripes on pants and trim on shirt and hat. Using brown frosting and a basket weave tip with smooth side of tip facing up, pipe belt and trim on top of boots. Using brown frosting and a small round tip, pipe eyes and laces on boots. Using white frosting and a grass tip, pipe beard.

Place one cherry half on cake for nose. Reserve other cherry half for another use. Cut one marshmallow in half crosswise. Place one marshmallow half on top of hat for pom-pom. Draw and cut out patterns for mustache and eyebrows. Use a rolling pin to roll out remaining marshmallows to ⅛-inch thickness. Place patterns on marshmallow pieces and use small sharp knife to cut out 2 mustache pieces and 2 eyebrows; place on cake. Store in an airtight container in refrigerator. Serves 16.

Creamy Rice Pudding

9 c. milk
1 c. long-cooking rice, uncooked
⅛ t. salt
1 c. plus 1 t. sugar, divided
3 eggs
1 T. vanilla extract
Optional: 1 c. cooked raisins
Garnish: cinnamon

Combine milk, rice and salt in a 3½ to 4-quart slow cooker. Cover and cook on high setting for 2½ to 3 hours, stirring every hour. After rice is cooked, stir in one cup sugar. Beat together eggs, remaining sugar and vanilla in a bowl. Add to slow cooker. Cover and cook an additional 5 to 10 minutes, until heated through. Fold in raisins, if desired. Sprinkle cinnamon on top. Serves 6 to 8.

Darlene Brown
Herndon, PA

Peppermint Candy Cheesecake

Peppermint Candy Cheesecake

1 c. graham cracker crumbs
¾ c. sugar, divided
6 T. butter, melted and divided
1½ c. sour cream
2 eggs
1 T. all-purpose flour
2 t. vanilla extract
2 8-oz. pkgs. cream cheese, softened
¼ c. peppermint candies, coarsely crushed
Optional: frozen whipped topping, thawed; crushed
    peppermint candies; mini candy canes

Blend crumbs, ¼ cup sugar and ¼ cup melted butter in bottom of an ungreased 8" round springform pan; press evenly over bottom. Blend sour cream, remaining sugar, eggs, flour and vanilla in a blender or food processor until smooth, stopping to scrape sides. Add cream cheese and blend; stir in remaining 2 tablespoons melted butter until completely smooth. Fold in crushed candies and pour over crust. Bake at 325 degrees for 45 minutes. Remove from oven and run a knife around edge of pan. Cool; refrigerate overnight. Loosen pan sides and remove springform; garnish with whipped topping, crushed candies and candy canes, if desired. Serves 12.

Bobbi Carney
Hobart, IN

Drizzle strawberry syrup on each slice right before serving for a merry little touch. —Bobbi

Apple Crumble

This recipe uses a cake mix, making it super simple!

½ c. butter, softened
18½-oz. pkg. yellow cake mix
½ c. sweetened flaked coconut
3 c. apples, peeled, cored and thinly sliced
½ c. sugar
1 t. cinnamon
1 egg, beaten
1½ t. vanilla extract
1 c. sour cream
Garnish: whipped cream

Combine butter and cake mix in a bowl. Cut in butter with a pastry blender or 2 knives until mixture resembles coarse crumbs; stir in coconut. Pat mixture into the bottom of an ungreased 13"x9" baking pan. Bake at 350 degrees for 8 to 10 minutes, until golden. Arrange apple slices in rows over warm crust. Stir together sugar and cinnamon; sprinkle over apple slices. Blend egg and vanilla into sour cream; drizzle over apples. Return to oven and bake for an additional 25 minutes, or until apples are tender. Serve warm with dollops of whipped cream. Serves 6 to 8.

Wendy Lee Paffenroth
Pine Island, NY

Jumbo Chocolate Cupcakes

(Pictured on page 214)

1 c. butter, softened
½ c. sugar
1 c. brown sugar, packed
4 eggs
3 1-oz. sqs. unsweetened baking chocolate, melted
3 1-oz. sqs. semi-sweet baking chocolate, melted
1 t. vanilla extract
2 c. all-purpose flour
1 t. baking soda
½ t. salt
1 c. buttermilk
12 Christmas-themed cupcake toppers

Beat butter with an electric mixer at medium speed until creamy. Gradually add sugars, beating well. Add eggs, one at a time, beating after each addition. Add melted chocolates and vanilla, beating well.

Combine flour, baking soda and salt; add to batter alternately with buttermilk, beginning and ending with flour mixture. Beat at low speed after each addition until blended. Spoon batter into paper-lined jumbo muffin cups, filling ¾ full. Bake at 350 degrees for 30 minutes, or until a toothpick inserted near center comes out clean. Cool in pans on wire racks 5 minutes. Remove from pans and cool completely on wire racks 45 minutes. Spread with Thick Chocolate Frosting. Insert one topper into top of each cupcake. Makes one dozen.

Thick Chocolate Frosting:
½ c. butter, softened
16-oz. pkg. powdered sugar
1 c. semi-sweet chocolate chips, melted
½ c. whipping cream
2 t. vanilla extract
⅛ t. salt

Beat butter with an electric mixer at medium speed until creamy; gradually add powdered sugar alternately with melted chocolate and whipping cream. Beat at low speed after each addition until blended. Stir in vanilla and salt. Makes 3½ cups.

White Chocolate Cranberry Cookies

This is a family favorite…no one can resist eating one of these mouthwatering cookies!

½ c. butter-flavored shortening
¼ c. sugar
1 c. light brown sugar, packed
3.4-oz pkg. instant French vanilla pudding mix
½ t. baking soda
1½ t. vanilla extract
2½ c. all-purpose flour
1½ c. white chocolate chips
½ c. macadamia nuts, crushed
1 c. dried cranberries

Blend together shortening, sugars, dry pudding mix, baking soda, vanilla and flour in a large bowl. Fold in remaining ingredients. Drop by tablespoonfuls onto parchment paper-lined baking sheets. Bake at 375 degrees for 8 minutes. Makes about 3½ dozen.

Lea Burwell
Charlestown, WV

Good Neighbor Sugar Cookies

3 c. all-purpose flour
1 t. cream of tartar
1 t. baking soda
1 t. salt
1 c. shortening
2 eggs, beaten
1 c. sugar
1 t. vanilla extract
Optional: drinking straw
assorted candies and sprinkles

Mix together flour, cream of tartar, baking soda and salt in a bowl. In a separate bowl, whisk together shortening and next 3 ingredients with a fork. Stir shortening mixture into flour mixture. Wrap dough in plastic wrap; refrigerate for 30 minutes. On a floured surface, roll out dough ⅛ inch thick; cut into shapes with cookie cutters, as desired (for cookie ornaments, before baking, use the straw to make a hole in each cookie for hanging). Arrange on lightly greased baking sheets. Bake at 375 degrees for 5 to 6 minutes, until golden; cool completely. Decorate with Sugar Cookie Frosting, candies and sprinkles. Makes about 4 dozen.

Sugar Cookie Frosting:
5 c. powdered sugar
5½ to 6½ T. water
1½ t. almond extract
paste food coloring

Combine powdered sugar, water and almond extract in a medium bowl; beat until smooth. Transfer frosting into small bowls and tint with food coloring. Spread onto cooled cookies.

Dianna Hamilton
Beaverton, OR

Good Neighbor
Sugar Cookies

Walnut Rugelach

The most popular Christmas cookies on my holiday trays! I have made them for weddings, showers and parties...they always sell out at our church bake sale too. Taste them and you'll find out why!

1½ c. butter, divided
8-oz. pkg. cream cheese, softened
2 c. all-purpose flour
1½ c. sugar
1½ T. cinnamon
6 T. walnuts, finely chopped and divided

Place one cup softened butter and cream cheese in a large bowl. Beat with an electric mixer at low speed until smooth. Beat in flour. Divide dough into 4 portions; form each into a disk. Wrap in plastic wrap; chill until firm, about one hour. Combine sugar and cinnamon; set aside. Roll one disk into a 10-inch circle on a floured surface. Brush with one tablespoon melted butter; sprinkle evenly with 2½ tablespoons cinnamon-sugar and one tablespoon nuts. Cut circle into 12 wedges with a pizza cutter. Roll up wedges from wide end to point. Place on ungreased baking sheets, 2 inches apart. Bend into crescent shapes. Repeat with remaining dough. Bake at 350 degrees for 28 minutes, or until golden. Let cool slightly. While still warm, lightly brush with remaining butter; sprinkle with remaining cinnamon-sugar and nuts. Remove to wire racks to cool. Makes 4 dozen.

Karen Sampson
Waymart, PA

Pecan Pie Bars

Wonderful little pecan pie bars you can't stop eating! Great for a church social or holiday cookie exchange.

1¼ c. all-purpose flour
½ c. plus 3 T. brown sugar, packed and divided
½ c. plus 2 T. butter, divided
2 eggs
½ c. light corn syrup
1 t. vanilla extract
½ c. chopped pecans

Combine flour with 3 tablespoons brown sugar; cut in ½ cup butter until mixture resembles coarse crumbs. Press into a lightly greased 11"x7" baking pan. Bake at 375 degrees for 20 minutes. Meanwhile, beat eggs in a large bowl and add remaining brown sugar, remaining melted butter, corn syrup and vanilla. Blend in pecans and pour mixture into hot crust. Bake for 15 to 20 minutes. Cool and cut into bars. Makes 2 dozen.

wrap it up
A vintage holiday tea towel is a quick & easy way to wrap small gifts. Place the gift in the center and bring the corners together. Secure with a length of ribbon and voilà! You're done!

Pecan Pie Bars

Cheery Cherry Punch (page 270)

Chicken-Corn Tortilla Soup (page 283)

Easy Cheesy Lasagna (page 286)
Tuscan Salad (page 300)

Miss Lizzie's Pound Cake (page 307)

GATHERING TOGETHER

Homestyle favorites for celebrating throughout the year

Toasted Ravioli

Such fun to eat! Choose either cheese or meat-filled ravioli…it's up to you!

2 T. milk
1 egg
¾ c. Italian-seasoned dry bread crumbs
½ t. salt
24 frozen meat- or cheese-filled ravioli,
    thawed
oil for deep frying
1 T. grated Parmesan cheese
Garnish: marinara sauce, warmed

Whisk together milk and egg in a small bowl. Place bread crumbs and salt in a separate small bowl. Dip ravioli into milk mixture; roll in crumbs to coat. Pour 2 inches of oil into a large heavy saucepan. Heat oil to 375 degrees until a cube of bread sizzles and turns brown. Add ravioli, a few at a time, frying for one minute on each side, or until golden. Drain on paper towels; sprinkle with Parmesan cheese. Serve warm with sauce for dipping. Makes 2 dozen.

Brenda Smith
Delaware, OH

Chinese Chicken Wings

This recipe can also be made with chicken drummies. Serve them with ranch dressing for dipping and celery stalks for a cool crunch.

½ c. soy sauce
½ c. brown sugar, packed
½ c. butter
¼ c. water
½ t. dry mustard
4 lbs. chicken wings

Combine all ingredients except wings in a saucepan; cook for 5 minutes over medium heat. Place wings on an ungreased large shallow baking pan; brush with sauce. Bake at 350 degrees for one hour, turning occasionally and brushing with remaining sauce. Makes about 20 wings.

Trisha Donley
Pinedale, WY

"This is a very easy recipe, a quick go-to that's so yummy." —Trisha

grandma's stain remover
Grandma knew how to remove stains from a favorite tablecloth. Combine ½ teaspoon salt with a tablespoon of water. Wet the stain with the mixture and then lay the tablecloth in the sun. After an hour, gently rinse the tablecloth with cold water.

Chinese Chicken Wings

7-Layer Mexican Dip

Make your own tortilla chips! Cut corn tortillas into wedges and bake at 350 degrees for five minutes, or until crisp. Add salt to taste…terrific!

16-oz. can refried beans
2 c. sour cream
1¼-oz. pkg. taco seasoning mix
2 avocados, pitted, peeled and mashed
2 t. lemon juice
3 cloves garlic, minced
2 c. shredded Cheddar cheese
4 green onions, chopped
¼ c. black olives, sliced
1 tomato, diced
tortilla chips

Spread beans in the bottom of a 10" round or square clear glass dish; set aside. Combine sour cream and seasoning mix; spread over beans. Mix avocados, lemon juice and garlic; layer over sour cream mixture. Sprinkle with cheese; top with onions, olives and tomato. Serve with tortilla chips. Serves 8.

Renee Purdy
Mount Vernon, OH

Halloween Party Mix

I put this mix into bags, tie with pretty Halloween ribbon and give to trick-or-treaters.

2 c. candy-coated peanut butter-filled
   candies
2 c. doughnut-shaped oat cereal
2 c. candy corn
2 c. bite-size honey-flavored corn cereal
2 c. salted peanuts
2 c. bagel chips
2 c. bite-size crispy rice cereal squares

Toss all ingredients together. Store in an airtight container. Makes 14 cups.

Brenda Huey
Geneva, IN

Reuben Appetizers

Put these mini Reubens together in minutes, and they'll be gone in seconds.

1 loaf sliced party rye
½ c. Thousand Island salad dressing
¾ lb. sliced corned beef
14-oz. can sauerkraut, drained
1½ c. shredded Swiss cheese

Spread bread with dressing; set aside. Slice corned beef to fit bread; place 2 slices beef on each bread slice. Top with one to 2 teaspoons sauerkraut; sprinkle with cheese. Arrange on an ungreased baking sheet; bake at 350 degrees for 10 minutes, or until cheese melts. Serves 12.

Carol Hickman
Kingsport, TN

Reuben Appetizers

Celebration Fruit Salsa

While planning our youngest son's wedding reception, I was looking for just the right recipes. My aunt, who is a terrific cook, shared this one with me. It was a hit from the get-go. I don't know how many times I shared the recipe while I was on the dance floor…everyone just kept asking for it!

1 c. strawberries, hulled and chopped
1 orange, peeled and finely chopped
2 kiwi, peeled and finely chopped
½ fresh pineapple, peeled and finely chopped, or 8-oz. can crushed pineapple, drained
¼ c. green onion, thinly sliced
¼ c. green or yellow pepper, finely chopped
1 T. lime or lemon juice
1 jalapeño pepper, seeded and chopped
Garnish: fresh parsley, whole strawberries or cantaloupe slices
tortilla chips

Combine all ingredients except garnish and tortilla chips in a bowl; stir well. Refrigerate until chilled. Garnish as desired. Serve with tortilla chips. Makes 3 cups.

Lavonda Wingfield
Boaz, AL

Cinnamon-Sugar Crisp Strips

When my mother taught me to make this recipe, we used wonton wrappers. I modified it slightly and now use flour tortillas, but both taste great. In fact, once you taste these you'll have trouble walking away from them! Try dipping these crispy strips in warm cinnamon-apple pie filling…yummy!

1 T. cinnamon
1 c. sugar
oil for deep frying
8 10-inch flour tortillas, cut into 1-inch strips

Combine cinnamon and sugar in a bowl; set aside. Heat 2 inches of oil in a heavy skillet over medium-high heat. Add 5 to 7 tortilla strips at a time; cook for 20 to 40 seconds on each side, until crisp. Drain on a paper towel–lined plate for 5 minutes; sprinkle with cinnamon-sugar mixture. Place strips and remaining cinnamon-sugar mixture into a paper bag. Gently toss to coat well. Remove from bag and arrange on a serving plate. Serves 6 to 8.

Melissa Fraser
Valencia, CA

Cheery Cherry Punch

The sweet-tart flavors of cherry, apple, pineapple and lemon combine in this fruity concoction…along with a fizzy splash of ginger ale.

3-oz. pkg. cherry gelatin mix
1 c. hot water
46-oz. can pineapple juice, chilled
4 c. apple juice, chilled
¾ c. lemon juice
1 ltr. ginger ale, chilled
Optional: maraschino cherries, lemon wedges

Stir together gelatin mix and hot water in a small bowl until gelatin dissolves. Pour into a large pitcher and stir in juices; chill. When ready to serve, add ginger ale to pitcher, stirring gently to combine. Garnish each serving with a sliced cherry and lemon wedge, if desired. Makes 3 quarts.

Beth Bundy
Long Prairie, MN

Cheery Cherry Punch

Summertime Citrus Tea

Watermelon Lemonade

My family loves melon, and this is a wonderful way to serve it on hot summer days. The purée freezes well, so this can be enjoyed in the winter months when you're missing summer.

4 c. watermelon, chopped
1 c. sugar
1½ c. lemon juice
6 c. cold water

Place watermelon in a blender; process until smooth and set aside. Combine sugar and lemon juice in a large pitcher; stir until sugar is dissolved. Stir in water. Add watermelon; mix well. Serve very cold; stir well before serving. Serves 8 to 10.

Sherry Calloway
Spencer, IN

Summertime Citrus Tea

Try herbal teabags if you like.

4 c. water
6 teabags
1½ c. sugar
6-oz. can frozen orange juice concentrate,
    thawed
6-oz. can frozen lemonade concentrate,
    thawed
10 c. cold water
ice
Garnish: lemon slices, mint sprigs

Bring water to a boil in a saucepan. Remove from heat and add teabags; steep overnight. Discard teabags. Pour into a large pitcher; add remaining ingredients except garnishes. Serve in tall glasses over ice. Serve with lemon slices and mint sprigs. Serves 6.

Susan Wilson
Johnson City, TN

Italian Hot Chocolate

Not your ordinary hot chocolate...share it with someone special!

1⅓ c. milk
2 T. sugar
1½ t. cornstarch
4 1-oz. sqs. semi-sweet baking chocolate,
    chopped
Optional: whipped cream

Whisk together milk, sugar and cornstarch in a saucepan. Stir in chocolate; cook over medium heat, stirring constantly, until mixture comes to a boil. Simmer for 30 seconds, stirring constantly. Remove from heat. Ladle into mugs; serve with a dollop of whipped cream, if desired. Serve immediately. Serves 2.

Arlene Smulski
Lyons, IL

French Toast Berry Bake

French Toast Berry Bake

Our family loves to share this French toast bake for special family occasions, such as my son's birthday breakfast and when my sister's family visits from out of town. Both fresh and frozen berries are scrumptious, so you can enjoy this treat year-round.

12 slices French bread, sliced 1-inch thick
5 eggs
2½ c. milk
1¾ c. brown sugar, packed and divided
1½ t. vanilla extract
1¼ t. cinnamon
Optional: ½ t. nutmeg
Optional: ¼ t. ground cloves
Optional: 1 c. chopped pecans
½ c. butter, melted
2 c. blueberries, strawberries, raspberries
 and/or blackberries
powdered sugar

Arrange bread slices in a greased 13"x9" baking pan; set aside. Combine eggs, milk, one cup brown sugar, vanilla, cinnamon and desired spices in a bowl. Whisk until blended; pour over bread. Cover and refrigerate 8 hours to overnight. Let stand at room temperature for 30 minutes before baking. Sprinkle with pecans, if using. Combine melted butter and remaining brown sugar; drizzle over top. Bake, uncovered, at 400 degrees for 40 minutes, or until a fork comes out clean. Sprinkle with berries and powdered sugar just before serving. Serves 12.

Suzanne Vella
Babylon, NY

Tex-Mex Egg Puff

I experimented with this recipe until it was just right! Mix, bake and serve...how easy is that?

1 doz. eggs, beaten
2 4.5-oz. cans chopped mild green chiles
16-oz. pkg. shredded Monterey Jack cheese
16-oz. container small-curd cream-style
 cottage cheese
½ c. butter, melted, cooled slightly
½ c. all-purpose flour
1 t. baking powder
½ t. salt

Mix all ingredients together in a large bowl. Pour into a greased 13"x9" glass baking pan. Bake, uncovered, at 350 degrees for 35 to 40 minutes, until set. Cut into squares. Serves 8 to 10.

Carol Creed
Battlefield, MO

easy substitute
Non-stick vegetable spray can usually be used instead of shortening to prepare baking sheets and baking dishes.

Honey Ham Quiche

Try proscuitto or peppered ham for a different flavor.

2 c. all-purpose flour
1 t. salt
½ c. shortening
7 T. cold water
⅓ c. onion, chopped
1 red pepper, chopped
2 T. butter
7 eggs
⅓ c. sour cream
⅓ c. milk
3 T. parsley, chopped
4 oz. cooked honey ham, chopped
14-oz. can artichoke hearts, drained, chopped and
    squeezed dry
4 oz. Swiss cheese, shredded

Combine flour and salt in a large bowl. Blend in shortening until mixture is crumbly. Sprinkle with water, one tablespoon at a time, until dough comes together. Roll dough out thinly and place in a 9" deep-dish pie plate. Bake at 450 degrees for 10 minutes. Remove from oven and reduce oven temperature to 325 degrees. Sauté onion and red pepper in butter in a skillet until tender. Beat eggs, sour cream and milk in a mixing bowl. Add onion mixture, parsley, ham and artichoke hearts. Pour over crust and sprinkle cheese over top. Bake until filling is firm, about 25 to 30 minutes. Allow to stand 5 minutes; cut into wedges. Serves 6 to 8.

Farm-Style Cinnamon Rolls

There's nothing like waking up to the aroma of baking cinnamon rolls.

16-oz. pkg. frozen bread dough, thawed
¼ c. butter, melted and divided
¼ c. sugar
¼ c. brown sugar, packed
1 t. cinnamon

Place dough in a well-oiled bowl, and let rise until almost double in bulk. Roll out dough on a floured surface into a 14"x10" rectangle. Brush with 2 tablespoons butter; sprinkle with sugars and cinnamon. Starting on one long side, roll up jelly-roll style. Pinch seam together. Cut rolled dough into 12 slices. Coat a 9"x9" baking pan with one tablespoon butter. Arrange rolls in baking pan; brush with remaining butter. Cover and let rise in a warm place for 45 minutes to one hour. Uncover and bake at 375 degrees for 20 to 25 minutes, until lightly golden. Makes one dozen.

Cindy Adams
Winona Lake, IN

recipe keeper
Keep all your favorite fall recipes right at your fingertips. Keep recipe cards organized in a retro tin lunchbox...how fun!

Farm-Style Cinnamon Rolls

Anytime Cheesy Biscuits

Parmesan Cheesy Twists

Buttery good, oh-so tasty, quick & easy!

2 eggs, beaten
2 T. water
½ c. grated Parmesan cheese
2 T. fresh parsley, chopped
1 t. dried oregano
17.3-oz. pkg. frozen puff pastry sheets,
    thawed

Whisk together eggs and water. Combine cheese and herbs in a separate bowl; set aside. Unfold one pastry sheet on a lightly floured surface. Roll out into a 14"x10" rectangle; cut in half lengthwise. Brush one piece with half of egg mixture; sprinkle with half of cheese mixture. Top with the other piece. Cut into ½-inch-wide strips; twist strips and place on a lightly greased baking sheet. Repeat with second pastry sheet. Bake at 400 degrees for 10 to 12 minutes, until golden. Makes 5 dozen.

Rhonda Reeder
Ellicott City, MD

Anytime Cheesy Biscuits

So easy…you can whip them up in minutes!

2 c. biscuit baking mix
½ c. shredded Cheddar cheese
⅔ c. milk
¼ c. butter, melted
¼ t. garlic powder

Mix together baking mix, cheese and milk until a soft dough forms; beat vigorously for 30 seconds. Drop by rounded tablespoonfuls onto an ungreased baking sheet. Bake at 450 degrees for 8 to 10 minutes, until golden. Whisk together butter and garlic powder; spread over warm biscuits. Makes about 1½ dozen.

Naomi Cooper
Delaware, OH

Spoon Bread

This is wonderful…it brings back memories of my childhood when my Granny Hudson made "Morning Bread" for our breakfast. I use fresh cornmeal that is ground at a local grist mill.

1 c. cornmeal
3 c. milk, divided
3 eggs, beaten
2 t. baking powder
1 T. butter, melted
2 t. salt

Combine cornmeal and 2 cups milk in a saucepan over medium heat; bring to a boil, stirring constantly. Add remaining milk, eggs, baking powder, butter and salt. Pour into a greased one-quart casserole dish. Bake at 400 degrees for about 35 minutes, until a knife inserted near the center comes out clean. Serve warm. Serves 4 to 6.

Tina Goodpasture
Meadowview, VA

everyday enamelware

Enamelware dishpans are so useful in the kitchen…don't pass them by at barn sales! They're perfect for mixing up company-size batches of bread dough, cookies, tossed salad, turkey dressing…or for serving popcorn on family movie night!

Chilled Melon Soup

This delicious and beautiful recipe is perfect for summer get-togethers with friends.

3 c. cantaloupe, peeled, seeded and
    chopped
2 T. sugar, divided
¼ c. orange juice, divided
⅛ t. salt, divided
3 c. honeydew, peeled, seeded and
    chopped
Garnish: fresh mint sprigs or orange slices

Process cantaloupe, half the sugar, half the juice and half the salt in a blender until smooth. Cover and refrigerate. Repeat with honeydew and remaining ingredients except garnish. Refrigerate, covered, in a separate container. To serve, pour equal amounts of each mixture at the same time on opposite sides of individual soup bowls. Garnish as desired. Serves 4 to 6.

Janice Woods
Northern Cambria, PA

"souper" soup!

Here's a handy way to pour two flavors of chilled soup into a bowl at the same time. Fill two small cream pitchers with each flavor of soup and then pour. The pitcher's small size makes pouring so easy!

White Bean-Chicken Chili

Add crusty rolls and a fresh salad for a hearty meal.

3 15.8-oz. cans Great Northern beans
4 boneless, skinless chicken breasts, cooked
    and cubed
16-oz. jar salsa
8-oz. pkg. shredded Monterey Jack cheese
8-oz. pkg. jalapeño cheese, shredded

Add all ingredients to a stockpot; heat over low heat until cheeses melt. Stir in up to one cup water for desired consistency; heat until warmed through. Serves 4 to 6.

Kristie Matry
Ada, MI

Crawfish-Corn Chowder

My family loves this chowder!

12-oz. pkg. bacon, crisply cooked and
    crumbled, drippings reserved
2 c. potatoes, peeled and diced
1 c. onion, diced
2 T. butter
2 pts. half-and-half
2 16-oz. cans creamed corn
1 T. Creole seasoning
Optional: 1 t. hot pepper sauce
1 lb. frozen crawfish tails or uncooked
    medium shrimp, peeled

Place 4 tablespoons reserved drippings in a soup pot. Sauté potatoes and onion in drippings for about 15 minutes, until golden. Stir in butter, half-and-half, corn, Creole seasoning and hot sauce, if using. Add crumbled bacon. Cook over medium heat until potatoes are tender, 20 to 30 minutes. Add crawfish or shrimp and simmer for another 15 to 20 minutes; do not overcook. Serves 6 to 8.

Becky Garrett
Richardson, TX

White Bean-Chicken Chili

Cheesy Chicken & Noodle Soup

Spice up this classic by topping it with shredded Pepper Jack cheese.

2 to 3 c. chicken, cooked and shredded
10¾-oz. can Cheddar cheese soup
4 to 6 c. chicken broth
8-oz. pkg. fine egg noodles, uncooked
1 c. milk
Optional: shredded Cheddar cheese

Combine all ingredients except milk and cheese in a large stockpot; bring to a boil over medium heat. Reduce heat; simmer until noodles are soft. Stir in milk. Spoon into bowls; sprinkle with cheese, if desired. Serves 6 to 8.

Christi Perry
Denton, TX

Cheesy Chicken &
Noodle Soup

Creamy Asparagus Soup

Asparagus is plentiful in our garden in the spring, and this is a family favorite...it tastes even better the next day.

1 to 1½ lbs. asparagus, trimmed and
    chopped
14-oz. can chicken broth
1 T. onion, minced
1 t. salt
¼ t. white pepper
½ to ¾ c. half-and-half

Set aside asparagus tips for garnish. Combine remaining ingredients except half-and-half in a soup pot over medium heat. Bring to a boil; reduce heat and simmer 5 to 7 minutes, until asparagus is tender. Working in small batches, ladle asparagus mixture into a blender. Add half-and-half to taste and purée. Return mixture to soup pot and heat through without boiling. Steam or microwave reserved asparagus tips just until tender; use to garnish soup. Serves 4.

Elaine Slabinksi
Monroe Township, NJ

Chicken-Corn Tortilla Soup

Yummy soup that's ready in a flash! (Pictured on page 264)

3 12½-oz. cans white-meat chicken,
    undrained
4 c. low-sodium, fat-free chicken broth
1 c. salsa
1 c. corn tortilla chips, crushed
½ c. fresh cilantro, chopped
2 t. lime juice
¼ t. pepper
Garnish: shredded Cheddar cheese,
    sour cream

Shred chicken, using 2 forks, in a large saucepan. Add broth and salsa; bring to a boil over medium-high heat. Add tortilla chips; reduce heat and simmer for 10 minutes. Stir in cilantro, lime juice and pepper. Garnish; serve immediately. Serves 8.

Trick-or-Treaters' Taco Soup

We always make this quick, yummy soup for Halloween dinner before trick-or-treating. It keeps our tummies warm as we're out & about visiting family & friends.

1 lb. ground beef
½ c. onion, chopped
14½-oz. can diced tomatoes
15¼-oz. can corn
16-oz. can kidney beans
15-oz. can tomato sauce
1¼-oz. pkg. taco seasoning mix
Garnish: shredded Cheddar cheese, sour cream,
    sliced olives, corn chips

Brown beef and onion in a large stockpot over medium heat. Drain; stir in undrained vegetables, tomato sauce and seasoning mix. Simmer, uncovered, for 20 minutes, stirring often. Garnish bowls of soup as desired. Serves 6.

Olivia Gust
Independence, OR

---

next-day soup

Here's a super-simple tip for scrumptious soup! Make soup ahead of time and refrigerate for one to two days to let the flavors blend; then reheat and serve.

Lime & Cilantro Cornish Game Hens

My mom used to make this every year when I came home from summer camp as my welcome-home dinner. The aroma was so nice to come home to! This recipe will always remind me of those summer days and my sweet mom, who was happily waiting for me at home with my favorite meal.

4 Cornish game hens or 4 boneless,
   skinless chicken breasts
12 limes
1 bunch fresh cilantro, chopped
salt and pepper to taste
cooked white rice

Place each hen into a one-gallon plastic zipping bag. Squeeze juice of 3 limes into each bag; add ¼ of cilantro to each bag. Add salt and pepper. (If using chicken breasts, place all pieces, limes, cilantro and salt and pepper into a one-gallon plastic zipping bag.) Refrigerate overnight. Remove hens or chicken breasts from bags; discard marinade. Bake at 350 degrees for one hour, or until juices run clear. If using chicken breasts, bake for 20 to 25 minutes. Serve over rice. Serves 4.

Jaime Hughes
Yucca Valley, CA

decorate for summer
Think flea market fresh when decorating the kitchen for summer. An enamelware colander filled with soil can hold a collection of herbs or pretty pansies, while a vintage child-size watering can is perfect for just-picked garden blooms.

Sunday Baked Chicken

3 lbs. chicken
1 T. all-purpose flour
¼ c. water
¼ c. brown sugar, packed
¼ c. catsup
2 T. white vinegar
2 T. lemon juice
2 T. Worcestershire sauce
1 onion, chopped
1 t. mustard
1 t. paprika
1 t. chili powder
salt and pepper to taste
Optional: lemon wedges

Arrange chicken pieces in a lightly greased 13"x9" baking pan; set aside. Whisk together flour and water in a small saucepan until smooth; add brown sugar, catsup, vinegar, lemon juice and Worcestershire. Cook and stir over medium heat until beginning to boil. Continue cooking and stirring for 2 minutes, or until thick. Add remaining ingredients except lemon wedges; mix well. Pour over chicken; cover and refrigerate for 2 to 4 hours. Remove from refrigerator 30 minutes before baking. Bake, uncovered, at 350 degrees for 35 to 45 minutes, until juices run clear. Garnish with lemon wedges. Serves 4 to 6.

Linda Behling
Cecil, PA

Every Sunday when I was a child, we would have a large noontime meal of pasta and meatballs with grandparents, aunts, uncles and cousins that included accordion playing. After that meal, Dad would say he couldn't eat another bite that day...but when Mom made this chicken for the evening meal, he was the first one at the table. –Linda

Sunday Baked Chicken

Hot & Spicy Ginger Chicken

Serve the remaining marinade as a sauce for dipping.

½ c. water
5 slices fresh ginger
2 dried chili peppers, crumbled
½ c. onion, chopped
¼ c. white vinegar
1 T. hot pepper sauce
1 t. dried thyme
½ t. ground allspice
½ t. ground black pepper
1½ lbs. boneless, skinless chicken breasts,
    cubed

Purée all ingredients except chicken in a blender. Pour marinade into a large mixing bowl; add chicken, tossing gently to cover. Refrigerate 4 hours. Remove chicken from mixing bowl, reserving marinade. Bring marinade to a boil in a small saucepan; cook 5 minutes and then transfer to a serving bowl to be used for dipping. Skewer chicken and grill 5 minutes on each side. Serves 4.

Gingered Broccoli Beef

The list of ingredients may look long, but this one-dish meal goes together very quickly. Try it with boneless chicken or pork, too.

1 bunch broccoli, cut into flowerets
1 lb. beef tenderloin, sliced into thin strips
1 T. fresh ginger, peeled and grated
3 cloves garlic, pressed
¼ t. red pepper flakes
1 to 2 t. olive oil
¾ c. chicken broth
3 T. soy sauce
1 T. cornstarch
½ t. sesame oil

Cover broccoli with water in a saucepan. Bring to a boil and cook until crisp-tender, about 3 to 5 minutes. Drain; set aside and cover to keep warm. Toss beef with ginger, garlic and red pepper flakes. Add oil to a skillet over medium-high heat. Add beef mixture and cook for 2 to 3 minutes, stirring constantly, until beef is lightly browned. Whisk together remaining ingredients and add to skillet; heat to boiling. Cook and stir for one minute, or until sauce thickens slightly. Add broccoli and toss to coat. Serves 4.

Regina Wickline
Pebble Beach, CA

Easy Cheesy Lasagna

No layering of ingredients for this lasagna. You get the great flavor of a more complicated dish but exert none of the effort.

1 lb. ground beef
26-oz. jar spaghetti sauce
8-oz. pkg. wide egg noodles, cooked
8-oz. pkg. shredded mozzarella cheese
1 c. cottage cheese
1 c. grated Parmesan cheese

Brown ground beef in a saucepan; drain. Stir sauce into beef; simmer 5 minutes. Add noodles, mozzarella cheese and cottage cheese; mix well. Place in a greased 2-quart casserole dish. Sprinkle with Parmesan cheese; bake, uncovered, at 350 degrees for 30 minutes. Serves 4 to 6.

Amy Blanchard
Hazel Park, MI

Easy Cheesy Lasagna
Tuscan Salad (page 300)

Ham with Bourbon,
Cola & Cherry Glaze

Ham with Bourbon, Cola & Cherry Glaze

This holiday ham sizzles with comfort! Pick a ham with an intact fat layer that will crisp up when baked and show off its pepper-and-clove crust.

12 to 14-lb. fully cooked, bone-in ham
1 T. black peppercorns
30 whole cloves
12-oz. can cola, divided
Optional: ¼ c. bourbon, divided
6 T. brown sugar, packed and divided
13-oz. jar cherry preserves, divided
Optional: kumquats, cherries

Remove skin from ham; trim fat to ¼-inch thickness. Make shallow cuts in fat one inch apart in a diamond pattern. Place peppercorns in a small plastic zipping bag. Tap peppercorns with a meat mallet or small heavy skillet until coarsely crushed. Rub peppercorns over surface of ham; insert cloves in centers of diamonds. Insert a meat thermometer into ham, making sure it does not touch fat or bone. Place ham in a lightly greased 13"x9" baking pan; set aside.

Combine ¼ cup cola, 2 tablespoons bourbon, if desired, and 2 tablespoons brown sugar; set aside. Combine remaining cola, bourbon, if desired, and brown sugar; pour over ham. Bake at 350 degrees for 2 hours, basting with cola mixture every 15 minutes. Remove ham from oven; leave oven on. Meanwhile, combine reserved cola mixture and ⅔ cup cherry preserves in a medium saucepan. Cook over medium heat 3 minutes or until glaze is hot and sugar dissolves; brush ham with glaze. Return ham to oven; bake at 350 degrees for an additional one hour and 45 minutes, or until thermometer registers 140 degrees. (Cover ham with aluminum foil during the last hour, if necessary, to prevent excessive browning.) Let ham stand one hour before carving.

Transfer baked ham to a serving platter; cover with foil. Remove fat from drippings in pan. Whisk remaining cherry preserves into drippings in pan. Transfer mixture to a saucepan, if desired, or continue cooking in roasting pan placed over 2 burners on the stovetop. Bring to a boil; reduce heat and simmer until slightly thickened (8 to 10 minutes). Serve glaze with ham. Garnish with kumquats and cherries, if desired. Serves 12 to 14.

Vickie
Gooseberry Patch

Sweet & Saucy Slow-Cooker Spareribs

These scrumptious ribs are equally at home at a summer picnic or at a lucky New Year's Day dinner.

2 lbs. pork spareribs, sliced into serving-size portions
10¾-oz. can tomato soup
1 onion, chopped
3 cloves garlic, minced
1 T. brown sugar, packed
1 T. Worcestershire sauce
2 T. soy sauce
¼ c. cold water
1 t. cornstarch

Place ribs in a stockpot and add water to cover. Bring to a boil; reduce heat and simmer for 15 minutes. Drain; arrange ribs in a 5 to 6-quart slow cooker. Mix together remaining ingredients except cold water and cornstarch; pour over ribs. Cover and cook on low setting for 6 to 8 hours. When ribs are tender, place on a serving platter; cover to keep warm. Pour sauce from slow cooker into a saucepan over medium-high heat. Stir together cold water and cornstarch; stir into sauce and bring to a boil. Cook and stir until sauce has reached desired thickness. Serve ribs with sauce. Serves 4.

Susie Backus
Gooseberry Patch

Pork Crown Roast
with Fruit Glaze

Pork Crown Roast with Fruit Glaze

The crowning glory of your holiday table.

1½ t. fennel seed, crushed
1½ t. onion powder
2 t. salt
1 t. pepper
8-lb. pork crown roast
vegetable oil

Combine seasonings in a small bowl. Rub mixture on all sides of roast; cover and refrigerate overnight. Brush roast lightly with oil and insert a meat thermometer. Cover the bone ends with foil and place roast on a lightly greased rack in a roasting pan. Bake at 425 degrees for 30 minutes; reduce oven temperature to 325 degrees and bake 1½ more hours, or until meat thermometer reads 165 degrees. Allow to stand for 10 minutes before carving. Garnish with Fruit Glaze. Serves 8 to 10.

Fruit Glaze:
½ c. dried apricot halves
½ c. dried peach halves
¾ c. apple juice, divided
¼ t. cardamom or nutmeg
2 t. cornstarch
1 c. seedless green grapes
1 c. seedless red grapes

Combine fruit, ½ cup apple juice and cardamom or nutmeg in a 1½-quart casserole dish. Cover casserole dish and microwave on high for 6 minutes, or until fruit begins to fill out. In a separate bowl, combine cornstarch and remaining apple juice, stirring well. Add to fruit mixture and microwave on high for 2 minutes, or until thick. Add grapes and stir gently.

BBQ Roasted Salmon

By far, this is my favorite salmon recipe. It has great flavor, and I always have the spices on hand.

2 T. brown sugar, packed
4 t. chili powder
¾ t. ground cumin
½ t. salt
¼ t. cinnamon
4 salmon fillets

Combine sugar and spices in a shallow dish. Dredge fillets in sugar mixture. Arrange fillets in a lightly greased 11"x7" baking pan. Bake, uncovered, at 400 degrees for 12 minutes, or until fish flakes easily with a fork. Serves 4.

Tara Horton
Delaware, OH

Sea Scallops

So tender when grilled!

2 T. lime juice
1 T. canola oil
1 garlic clove, crushed
½ t. ground cumin
⅛ t. cayenne pepper
1 lb. sea scallops
2 c. cherry tomatoes

Combine lime juice, oil, garlic, cumin and cayenne pepper in a medium mixing bowl. Whisk thoroughly. Alternately thread scallops and tomatoes on metal skewers, and brush with marinade. Place skewers on a platter; cover and refrigerate 30 minutes. Grill scallops 5 to 7 minutes, basting with marinade. Serves 4.

Penne Pasta with
Tomatoes

Penne Pasta with Tomatoes

6 T. olive oil, divided
1½ c. onion, chopped
1 t. garlic, minced
3 28-oz. cans Italian plum tomatoes, drained
2 t. fresh basil, chopped
1½ t. red pepper flakes
2 c. chicken broth
1 t. salt
1 t. pepper
16-oz. pkg. penne pasta, uncooked
2½ c. Havarti cheese, grated
½ c. Kalamata olives, sliced
½ c. grated Parmesan cheese
Garnish: ¼ c. fresh basil, chopped

Heat 3 tablespoons oil in a Dutch oven over medium-high heat. Sauté onion and garlic in oil for 5 minutes. Add tomatoes, basil and red pepper flakes; bring to a boil. Mash tomatoes with the back of a spoon; add broth. Reduce heat and simmer one hour. Add salt and pepper; set aside. Cook pasta according to package directions; drain. Toss with remaining 3 tablespoons oil and combine with tomato sauce. Stir in Havarti cheese. Pour into an ungreased 13"x9" casserole dish. Top with olives and then Parmesan cheese. Bake, uncovered, at 375 degrees for 30 minutes. Sprinkle with fresh basil before serving. Serves 6 to 8.

Dana Stewart
Webster Groves, MO

I love this pasta dish in the winter when practically everything is out of season and I'm bored with all my 'family standards.' –Dana

Cucumber Tea Sandwiches

I like to think I'm a good cook, but this simple recipe is the one people always request! These dainty sandwiches are one of the few things that my 89-year-old mother still has an appetite for.

2 cucumbers, peeled and thinly sliced
1 c. sour cream
½ c. mayonnaise
1 t. dill weed
½ t. onion powder
½ t. seasoned salt
¼ t. garlic powder
⅛ t. kosher salt
20 slices white bread

Place cucumber slices between paper towels; allow to dry for 5 minutes. Mix together remaining ingredients except bread. Spread sour cream mixture over one side of each bread slice. Cover 10 slices with cucumbers; top with remaining bread slices. Quarter each sandwich; arrange on a serving plate. Cover and refrigerate; serve within 6 hours. Makes 40 mini sandwiches.

Celeste Pierce
Overland Park, KS

Green Chile Rice

Green Chile Rice

Sprinkle with sliced jalapeños for an extra kick!

4 c. hot cooked rice
8-oz. pkg. shredded mozzarella cheese
2 c. sour cream
4-oz. can diced green chiles, drained
Optional: sliced jalapeño peppers

Combine all ingredients except garnish in a bowl and mix well. Pour into an ungreased 2-quart casserole dish. Bake, uncovered, at 400 degrees until bubbly, about 20 minutes. Garnish, if desired. Serves 6.

Debbie Wilson
Weatherford, TX

rice done right
For extra-fluffy rice, just add a teaspoon of white vinegar to the cooking water.

Slow-Cooker Country Corn Pudding

With four kinds of corn, this new twist on an old favorite is scrumptious!

16-oz. pkg. frozen corn
2 11-oz. cans sweet corn & diced peppers
14¾-oz. can creamed corn
6½-oz. pkg. corn muffin mix
¾ c. water
¼ c. butter, melted
1 t. salt

Mix all ingredients well; pour into a 3 to 4-quart slow cooker. Cover and cook on low setting for 5 to 6 hours, stirring after 3 hours. Serves 8.

Angela Lively
Baxter, TN

Lemon-Chive Potatoes

These are our favorite potatoes...they're really delicious!

1 T. olive oil
1 lb. redskin potatoes, cubed
salt and pepper to taste
½ c. water
3 chives, thinly sliced
1 t. lemon juice

Heat oil in a large pot over medium-high heat. Add potatoes; sprinkle with salt and pepper. Cook, stirring occasionally, until golden, about 10 to 15 minutes, adding a little more oil if needed. Add water, stir and cover. Cook until potatoes are tender and liquid has evaporated, about 5 minutes. Transfer to a serving bowl; toss potatoes with chives and lemon juice. Serves 4.

Stefanie St. Pierre
North Chatham, MA

heavenly home fries
Leftover potatoes make great home fries! In a heavy skillet, heat one to 2 tablespoons oil until sizzling. Add 3 cups cubed cooked potatoes and ½ cup chopped onion. Cook for 5 minutes. Turn potatoes over and season with salt, pepper and paprika. Cook 5 to 10 more minutes, to desired crispness.

Savory Stuffed Potatoes

Savory Stuffed Potatoes

My father-in-law used to make these potatoes in the oven and serve them with London broil. When my husband started grilling them for summer picnics, they quickly became a must-have.

6 baking potatoes
1 red onion, sliced
6 slices bacon, crisply cooked and crumbled
6 to 7 mushrooms, sliced
½ c. butter, thinly sliced
salt, pepper and garlic powder to taste
Garnish: shredded Cheddar cheese, sliced green
    onions

With a knife, make 4 to 5 cuts across each potato without cutting through. Place onion slices, bacon and mushrooms into slits of potatoes. Place butter slices in slits; sprinkle with salt, pepper and garlic powder. Wrap each potato with aluminum foil; seal tightly. Place on a hot grill; cook about 45 minutes, or until potatoes are tender. Garnish with cheese and green onions. Serves 6.

Betsy Ferris
Fultonville, NY

Minted Baby Carrots

Mint is so easy to grow…keep some growing in a sunny spot by the kitchen door and you can whip up these yummy carrots anytime.

½ lb. baby carrots
2 T. butter
salt and pepper to taste
1 T. lemon zest, minced
1 T. brown sugar, packed
2 t. fresh mint, minced

Cook carrots in a stockpot of boiling water for 5 minutes. Remove from heat and drain. Melt butter in a skillet over medium-high heat. Stir in carrots; cook until crisp-tender. Season with salt and pepper. Combine remaining ingredients and sprinkle over individual servings. Serves 4.

Tori Willis
Champaign, IL

Summertime Feta & Tomatoes

We love to change up the spices and vinegars in this recipe each time we make it. If you eat all the tomatoes and still have dressing left, pour it over your next salad or dip some crusty bread in it!

6 to 7 roma tomatoes, chopped
4-oz. pkg. crumbled feta cheese
¼ c. olive oil
½ c. red wine vinegar
2 t. Italian seasoning
¼ t. seasoned salt

Combine all ingredients; toss. Refrigerate for 30 minutes to allow flavors to blend. Serves 6 to 8.

Rebecca Pickett
Houston, TX

---

simple stir-fry

Whip up a veggie stir-fry in a flash. Combine 2 tablespoons cornstarch, 2 tablespoons sugar and ½ teaspoon ground ginger. Blend in one cup orange juice and ¼ cup soy sauce. Toss any of your favorite veggies in a skillet with a bit of oil and cook for about 4 to 5 minutes. Add the orange juice mixture; cook and stir until thickened.

Hearty Black-Eyed Peas

Hearty Black-Eyed Peas

Serve these slow-simmered peas plain or with rice and cornbread.

3 c. water
3 c. low-sodium chicken broth
1 onion, chopped
1 smoked ham hock
1 bay leaf
½ t. pepper
Optional: 4 whole jalapeño peppers
16-oz. pkg. dried black-eyed peas
1 t. salt, divided

Bring water, broth, onion, ham hock, bay leaf, pepper and jalapeños, if desired, to a boil in a Dutch oven; cover, reduce heat and simmer 30 minutes.

Rinse and sort peas according to package directions. Add peas and ½ teaspoon salt to Dutch oven; cook, covered, one hour or until peas are tender. If desired, remove meat from ham hock, finely chop and return to Dutch oven. Season with remaining salt. Remove and discard bay leaf. Serves 4 to 6.

lucky year
Good luck is said to be the reward for eating black-eyed peas on New Year's Day. Try this tasty recipe to bring your family good fortune!

Asparagus & Savory Cream Sauce

1½ lbs. fresh asparagus
1 T. butter
1 T. all-purpose flour
1 c. half-and-half
½ c. Swiss cheese, shredded
2 T. round buttery crackers, crushed

Cook asparagus in a little water in a non-stick skillet until just tender. Drain and place in a greased 2-quart casserole dish. Melt butter in a saucepan, add flour and cook one minute. Pour in half-and-half, whisking to blend with flour. Bring to a boil and cook 2 minutes, stirring constantly. Remove from heat and add cheese. Blend until cheese is melted; pour over asparagus. Sprinkle cracker crumbs over top. Place under broiler for 3 minutes, or until very lightly golden. Serves 4.

Grandma's Swiss String Beans

My grandmother always made this bean dish for special holidays. When she could no longer do the cooking, my aunt took over, then my mother, then me. Now my children enjoy it, too. You can use fresh, canned or frozen green beans.

¼ c. plus 2 T. butter, divided
½ c. dry bread crumbs
2 T. all-purpose flour
1 T. onion, minced
1 t. sugar
1 t. salt
¼ t. pepper
1 c. sour cream
4 c. green beans, trimmed and thinly
    sliced lengthwise
2 c. shredded Swiss cheese

Toss 2 tablespoons butter with bread crumbs; set aside for topping. Melt remaining butter in a large saucepan over low heat. Blend flour, onion, sugar, salt and pepper into butter in saucepan. Add sour cream and stir until smooth. Increase heat to medium; cook and stir until thick and bubbly. Fold in beans; transfer to a greased 13"x9" baking pan. Sprinkle with cheese and bread crumb mixture. Bake, uncovered, at 400 degrees for 20 to 25 minutes. Serves 6.

Audrey Zukowski
Clintondale, NY

Easy Layered Salad

Packed full of tasty ingredients, this salad is always a hit at potlucks and family gatherings.

12-oz. pkg. salad mix with iceberg lettuce
    and carrots
15-oz. can green peas, drained
8-oz. can sliced water chestnuts, drained
1 red pepper, diced
8-oz. pkg. shredded Cheddar cheese
1½ c. mayonnaise
1 t. sugar
3-oz. pkg. bacon bits
½ c. shredded Parmesan cheese

Layer ingredients in a large serving bowl in the following order: salad mix, peas, water chestnuts, red pepper and Cheddar cheese. Mix together mayonnaise and sugar; spread over layers. Sprinkle bacon bits and Parmesan cheese over top. Cover and chill before serving. Serves 10 to 12.

Debbie Worthington
Bainbridge, GA

beautiful bowls

A large, clear glass bowl is a must-have for entertaining family & friends. Serve up a layered salad, a pasta dish or a sweet dessert trifle...or fill it with water and floating candles for a pretty centerpiece.

Tuscan Salad

This salad bursts with color and flavor from the freshest ingredients available, including fresh mozzarella cheese. Don't be tempted to substitute regular mozzarella cheese; it's drier and stringier than mild, delicate fresh mozzarella. (Pictured on page 287)

1 lb. red and yellow tomatoes, sliced
    ¼-inch thick
1 red onion, diced
4 oranges, peeled and sectioned
1 bunch fresh basil, thinly sliced
1 t. salt
½ t. pepper
16-oz. pkg. fresh mozzarella cheese, diced

Combine all ingredients except cheese in a large salad bowl; add Vinaigrette Dressing, tossing gently to coat. Top with mozzarella and serve at room temperature. Serves 6 to 8.

Vinaigrette Dressing:

¼ c. olive oil
1 T. balsamic vinegar
1 T. sugar
¼ t. Dijon mustard
¼ t. salt
¼ t. garlic, minced
2 T. water

Combine all ingredients in a blender or food processor; process 30 seconds or until smooth.

Helen Eads
Memphis, TN

fresh from the farm

Farmers' market foods taste so fresh because they're all grown and picked in season at the peak of flavor...lettuce, asparagus and strawberries in the springtime; tomatoes, peppers and sweet corn in the summer; squash and greens in the fall and winter.

BLT Salad with Basil Dressing

My daughter and I like to go to our local farmers' market each Saturday morning. Together we buy fresh, ripe tomatoes, lettuce and basil for this salad and then go home and make it...enjoy!

1 lb. romaine lettuce, torn
1 pt. cherry tomatoes, halved
½ lb. bacon, crisply cooked and crumbled,
   2 T. drippings reserved
½ c. mayonnaise
2 T. red wine vinegar
¼ c. fresh basil, chopped
pepper

  Combine lettuce, tomatoes and crumbled bacon in a large salad bowl; set aside. Whisk together reserved drippings, mayonnaise, vinegar and basil in a small bowl. Drizzle dressing over salad and toss well. Top with Homemade Croutons, sprinkle with pepper and serve immediately. Serves 4.

Homemade Croutons:

4 slices French bread, cubed
1 t. salt
1 t. pepper
1 T. olive oil

  Toss bread cubes with salt and pepper in a skillet over medium heat. Drizzle with oil; toss and cook until golden.

Nancy Willis
Farmington Hills, MI

BLT Salad with Basil Dressing

Chili-Cornbread Salad

Down-South Creamy Coleslaw

We all love this cool, refreshing coleslaw. It's great as a side for your favorite barbecue ribs or pulled pork.

¾ c. mayonnaise
1 T. cider vinegar
1 T. sweet onion, grated, juice reserved
2 to 3 T. sugar
½ t. salt
¼ t. pepper
¼ t. celery seed
4 c. cabbage, shredded
1 c. carrot, peeled and shredded

Whisk together all ingredients except cabbage and carrot in a large bowl. Add cabbage and carrot; toss to mix. Chill for at least 2 hours, stirring once or twice while coleslaw chills. Stir well again at serving time. Serves 6 to 8.

Staci Meyers
Montezuma, GA

Chili-Cornbread Salad

I've been making this recipe for five years. I get so many requests for it, and I've never heard anyone say they don't like it. I also like to use my own frozen corn and shred the cheese myself for more flavor.

8½-oz. pkg. cornbread muffin mix
⅛ t. ground cumin
⅛ t. dried oregano
⅛ t. dried sage
1 c. mayonnaise
1 c. sour cream
1-oz. env. ranch salad dressing mix
4½-oz. can chopped green chiles
2 15-oz. cans pinto beans, drained and rinsed
2 15½-oz. cans corn, drained
1 c. green pepper, chopped
1 c. onion, chopped
10 slices bacon, crisply cooked and crumbled
2 c. shredded Cheddar cheese
3 tomatoes, chopped

Prepare cornbread batter according to package directions; stir in seasonings. Spread in a greased 8"x8" baking pan. Bake at 400 degrees for 20 to 25 minutes, until a toothpick inserted near center comes out clean; set aside to cool. Combine mayonnaise, sour cream and ranch dressing mix in a small bowl; set aside. Crumble half of the cornbread into a lightly greased 13"x9" baking pan or 3-quart serving dish. Layer with chiles, half each of beans, mayonnaise mixture, corn, green pepper, onion, bacon, cheese and tomatoes. Repeat layers. Cover and refrigerate for 2 hours. Serves 12.

Rachel Keim
Millersburg, OH

Heavenly Chicken Salad

My girlfriend Glinda and I made this for our church bazaar luncheon. We've served this as a salad and on a croissant as a sandwich. Now it's been requested for four years in a row!

8 c. cooked chicken, chopped
2 c. seedless grapes, quartered
2 c. celery, chopped
1 c. chopped pecans
1 c. mayonnaise
1½ t. salt
¾ t. pepper

Combine all ingredients; refrigerate until ready to serve. Serves 18 as a salad, 20 to 30 as a sandwich spread on croissants.

Patricia King
Portsmouth, VA

Patriotic Cupcakes

Patriotic Cupcakes

2 c. sugar
1 c. butter, softened
2 eggs
2 t. lemon juice
1 t. vanilla extract
2½ c. cake flour
½ t. baking soda
1 c. buttermilk
24 mini American flags

Beat sugar and butter with an electric mixer at medium speed until creamy. Add eggs, one at a time, beating well after each addition. Beat in lemon juice and vanilla.

Combine flour and baking soda in a small bowl; add to sugar mixture alternately with buttermilk, beginning and ending with flour mixture. Beat at medium speed just until blended after each addition.

Spoon batter into paper-lined muffin cups, filling ⅔ full. Bake at 350 degrees for 18 to 22 minutes, until a toothpick inserted near center comes out clean. Cool in pans on a wire rack 10 minutes. Remove cupcakes from pans to wire rack; cool 45 minutes, or until completely cool.

Spoon 5-Cup Cream Cheese Frosting into a plastic zipping bag (do not seal). Snip one corner of bag to make a hole (about one inch in diameter). Pipe frosting in little loops onto tops of cupcakes as desired. Insert one flag into top of each cupcake. Makes 2 dozen.

egg advice
Eggs work best in baking recipes when they're brought to room temperature first. If time is short, just slip the eggs carefully into a bowl of lukewarm water and let stand for 15 minutes...they'll warm right up.

5-Cup Cream Cheese Frosting:

2 8-oz. pkgs. cream cheese, softened
½ c. butter, softened
2 16-oz. pkgs. powdered sugar
2 t. vanilla extract

Beat cream cheese and butter with an electric mixer at medium speed until creamy. Gradually add powdered sugar, beating until fluffy. Stir in vanilla. Makes about 5 cups.

Note: To make ahead, bake and cool cupcakes as directed. Do not frost and decorate. Double-wrap cupcakes in plastic wrap and heavy-duty aluminum foil or place in airtight containers; freeze up to one month.

Black Kitty Kat Cupcakes

Don't be afraid of these black cats...they are devilishly good!

18½-oz. pkg. devil's food cake mix
16-oz. can dark chocolate frosting
12 chocolate sandwich cookies, quartered
48 yellow or green jellybeans
24 black jellybeans
24 pieces black rope licorice

Prepare and bake cake according to package directions for cupcakes using paper liners. Cool in pans for 10 minutes; remove to wire racks to cool completely. Frost tops of cupcakes with chocolate frosting; insert 2 cookie pieces for ears and lightly frost each. Arrange yellow or green jellybeans for eyes and a black jellybean for the nose. Cut each piece of black licorice into thirds and then in half. Place 3 halves on each side of the nose for whiskers. Makes 2 dozen.

Mildred Biggin
Lyons, IL

Holly's Chocolate Silk Pie

The rich filling is as smooth as silk!

¾ c. brown sugar, packed
¼ c. butter, softened
3 eggs
1¼ c. semi-sweet chocolate chips, melted
1½ t. instant coffee granules
½ t. almond extract
1 c. almonds, toasted and chopped
¼ c. all-purpose flour
9-inch pie crust
½ c. whole almonds

Beat brown sugar and butter in a mixing bowl until fluffy. Beat in eggs, one at a time. Mix in chocolate chips, coffee and almond extract. Add chopped nuts and flour; mix well. Pour filling into pie crust. Decorate top with whole almonds. Bake at 375 degrees for 30 minutes on lower rack in oven; cool. Serves 6 to 8.

Holly's Chocolate Silk Pie

Berry-Lemon Trifle

This was a big hit when I made it for a summer gathering...there was nothing left to take home!

14-oz. can sweetened condensed milk
8-oz. container lemon yogurt
⅓ c. lemon juice
2 t. lemon zest
8-oz. container frozen whipped topping, thawed
1 angel food cake, cut into 1-inch cubes
1 c. strawberries, hulled and sliced
1 c. blueberries
1 c. peaches, pitted, peeled and sliced
Garnish: additional whipped topping,
   1 c. raspberries

Combine condensed milk, yogurt, lemon juice and zest in a large bowl; fold in whipped topping. Layer ⅓ each of cake cubes, lemon mixture and one cup strawberries in a 3-quart clear glass trifle dish. Repeat with ⅓ each of cake, lemon mixture and 1 cup blueberries. Layer remaining cake, lemon mixture and peaches. Top with additional whipped topping; sprinkle with raspberries. Cover and refrigerate for at least 4 hours. Serves 16.

Brenda Huey
Geneva, IN

Miss Lizzie's Pound Cake

A yummy caramel frosting paired with a moist & delicious pound cake makes for an irresistible dessert. (Pictured on page 264)

1 c. butter, softened
½ c. shortening
3 c. sugar
¼ t. salt
6 eggs
1 c. milk
1 t. imitation vanilla butter & nut flavoring
3 c. all-purpose flour

Beat together butter and shortening in a large mixing bowl with an electric mixer at medium speed; gradually add sugar and salt. Add eggs, one at a time, beating well after each addition; set aside. Combine milk and flavoring; add to butter mixture alternately with flour. Spread into a greased and floured 10" tube pan. Bake at 325 degrees for one hour, or until a toothpick inserted near center comes out clean. Remove from pan; cool completely. Frost with Caramel Frosting. Serves 8 to 10.

Caramel Frosting:

1½ c. brown sugar, packed
½ c. sugar
½ c. butter
5-oz. can evaporated milk
1 t. vanilla extract

Combine all ingredients except vanilla in a saucepan over medium heat. Cook 15 minutes, stirring constantly. Remove from heat; stir in vanilla. Immediately spread over cooled cake.

Jody Brandes
Hartfield, VA

"This recipe came from my grandfather's neighbor back in the 1950s. I've been making it for 45 years and topping it with my mom's caramel frosting. I think you'll love it as much as I do." —Jody

Peanut Butter Pound Cake

Delicious without the frosting, too!

1 c. butter, softened
2 c. sugar
1 c. brown sugar, packed
½ c. creamy peanut butter
5 eggs
1 T. vanilla extract
3 c. cake flour
½ t. baking powder
½ t. salt
¼ t. baking soda
1 c. whipping cream or whole milk

Beat butter and sugar in a bowl until fluffy. Add brown sugar and peanut butter; beat thoroughly. Add eggs, one at a time, beating well after each addition; stir in vanilla. Sift together the dry ingredients and add alternately with whipping cream or milk. Pour into a lightly greased and floured 10" tube pan. Bake at 325 degrees for one hour, or until a toothpick inserted near center comes out clean. Frost with Peanut Butter Frosting, if desired. Serves 10 to 12.

Peanut Butter Frosting:

¼ c. butter, softened
⅛ t. salt
5 to 6 T. milk
⅓ c. creamy peanut butter
16-oz. pkg. powdered sugar

Combine all ingredients and beat until smooth.

Charlotte Wolfe
Fort Lauderdale, FL

Peanut Butter
Pound Cake

Big Yellow Sheet Cake

A terrific cake for large family get-togethers and potlucks!

18½-oz. pkg. yellow cake mix, divided
4 eggs, divided
½ c. butter or margarine, softened
1½ c. water
½ c. brown sugar, packed
1½ c. corn syrup
Optional: chopped nuts
Garnish: favorite frosting

Mix together 1⅔ cups dry cake mix, one egg, butter or margarine and water in a large bowl. Pour into a greased 13"x9" baking pan. Bake at 325 degrees for 15 minutes. Mix together remaining cake mix, remaining eggs, brown sugar, corn syrup and nuts, if desired. Pour into center of partially baked cake. Return to oven; bake at 325 degrees for about one hour. Cool; frost as desired. Serves 12 to 15.

Claire Boucher
Ocean Springs, MS

fast frosting

Whip up a chocolatey homemade frosting in no time. Beat together 6 tablespoons butter, 2⅔ cups powdered sugar, ½ cup baking cocoa, 4 to 6 tablespoons milk and one teaspoon vanilla extract. This makes about 2 cups of the yummiest buttercream frosting for spreading on cupcakes or cookies.

Best-Ever Bakery Frosting

We love the taste of this frosting! A lady in Nunda, New York, gave me this recipe when we stopped in her little bakery many years ago.

2 16-oz. pkgs. powdered sugar
1 c. shortening
1 t. clear vanilla extract
½ to ¾ c. milk

Mix together all ingredients in a large bowl until just moistened, adding milk as needed. Do not overbeat. Makes about 3 cups, enough to frost 6 dozen cookies or 2 large cakes.

Renee Shock
Beaver Dams, NY

Hannah's Lemon Bars

My family just loves these sweet-tart lemon bars, especially my daughter, Hannah. When she's having an extra-busy day of college and work, I'll make a batch for her...they perk her right up!

1½ c. plus 3 T. all-purpose flour, divided
1 c. powdered sugar, divided
¾ c. butter, softened
3 eggs, beaten
1½ c. sugar
¼ c. lemon juice

Combine 1½ cups flour, ⅔ cup powdered sugar and butter in a large bowl. Mix well; pat into a greased 13"x9" baking pan. Bake at 350 degrees for 20 minutes; remove from oven. Whisk together eggs, sugar, remaining flour and lemon juice until frothy; pour over hot crust. Bake at 350 degrees for 20 to 25 minutes, until light golden. Cool in pan on a wire rack. Dust with remaining powdered sugar. Cut into bars. Makes 3 to 4 dozen.

Tina George
El Dorado, AR

Friendship Peppermint Mud Pie

Friendship Peppermint Mud Pie

Minty chocolate ice cream cake with hot fudge topping...oh, my!

14-oz. pkg. chocolate sandwich cookies, crushed
　and divided
6 T. butter, melted
½ gal. peppermint ice cream
16-oz. jar hot fudge ice cream topping
8-oz. container frozen whipped topping, thawed

Set aside ¼ cup cookie crumbs. Combine remaining cookie crumbs and melted butter in a large bowl. Toss to coat. Transfer to a greased 13"x9" baking pan; press crumbs firmly to cover bottom of pan. Spread ice cream over crumb crust. Top with fudge topping. Freeze until firm. At serving time, spread whipped topping to edges. Garnish with reserved cookie crumbs. Serves 12.

Lori Vincent
Alpine, UT

Each Christmas, I get together with four dear friends for brunch. It's great for us to have 'girl time.' We traditionally eat pie, so whenever I make this recipe, I always think of my best friends! —Lori

Frosted Mango-Banana Bars

I entered this tropical treat in a contest at the state fair and won first place!

½ c. butter, softened
1½ c. sugar
2 eggs, at room temperature
8-oz. container plain yogurt
1½ t. vanilla extract
2 c. all-purpose flour
1 t. baking soda
¼ t. salt
1 ripe mango, peeled, pitted and mashed
2 ripe bananas, mashed
½ c. sweetened flaked coconut
Optional: toasted coconut

Blend butter and sugar in a large bowl; add eggs, yogurt and vanilla. Sift together flour, baking soda and salt; gradually add to butter mixture. Stir in mango, bananas and coconut. Spread into a lightly greased 15"x10" jelly-roll pan. Bake at 350 degrees for 20 to 25 minutes, until a toothpick inserted near center comes out clean. Cool completely. Spread Frosting over top; sprinkle with toasted coconut, if desired. Store in refrigerator. Cut into bars to serve. Makes 3 dozen.

Frosting:
8-oz. pkg. cream cheese, softened
½ c. butter, softened
2 t. vanilla extract
3¾ c. powdered sugar
½ c. sweetened flaked coconut

Beat cream cheese, butter and vanilla together in a large bowl. Gradually beat in powdered sugar to a smooth consistency. Stir in coconut.

Lane McLoud
Siloam Springs, AR

Crunchy Biscotti

In the afternoon or after dinner, you'll crave these treats with your next cup of coffee. (Pictured on page 360)

3⅓ c. all-purpose flour
2½ t. baking powder
½ t. salt
¼ c. oil
1¼ c. sugar
2 eggs, beaten
2 egg whites, beaten
Optional: melted white chocolate

Mix flour, baking powder and salt in a large bowl. Whisk together remaining ingredients except white chocolate in a separate bowl. Blend flour mixture into egg mixture. Divide dough into 3 portions; knead each portion 5 to 6 times and shape into a ball. Place dough balls on a parchment paper–lined 17"x11" baking sheet. Shape into 9-inch logs; flatten slightly. Bake at 375 degrees for 25 minutes. Remove from oven; place logs on a cutting board. Using a serrated bread knife, cut ½-inch-thick slices on a slight diagonal. Return slices to baking sheet, cut-sides up. Bake for an additional 10 minutes. Turn slices over; continue baking for 5 to 7 minutes. Let cool and drizzle with white chocolate, if desired; store in an airtight container. Makes about 3 dozen cookies.

Jo Ann
Gooseberry Patch

I like to dress up these cookies with a drizzle of white chocolate! –Jo Ann

Caramel Apples

Caramel apples are the stuff of fall festivals and Halloween carnivals! With each messy bite, they bring out the child in us all.

6 Granny Smith apples
6 wooden craft sticks
14-oz. pkg. caramels, unwrapped
1 T. vanilla extract
1 T. water
2 c. chopped pecans or peanuts, toasted
Optional: 12-oz. bag semi-sweet chocolate
     chips, pecan halves

Wash and dry apples; remove stems. Insert a craft stick into stem end of each apple; set aside.
Combine caramels, vanilla and water in a microwave-safe bowl. Microwave on high 90 seconds or until melted, stirring twice.
Dip each apple into the caramel mixture quickly, allowing excess caramel to drip off. Roll in chopped nuts; place apples on lightly greased wax paper. Chill at least 15 minutes.
If desired, to make chocolate-dipped caramel apples, microwave chocolate chips on high 90 seconds, or until melted, stirring twice; cool 5 minutes. Pour chocolate where craft sticks and apples meet, allowing chocolate to drip down sides of apples. Press pecan halves onto chocolate, if desired. Chill 15 minutes or until set. Makes 6 apples.

fall treats
After wrapping each apple in cellophane, nestle it inside a small orange gift sack. Add a pumpkin face to the sack using a black permanent marker; then gather the sack around the stick and tie with green curling ribbon.

Caramel Apples

Marinated Greek Olives
(page 354)

Nutty Popcorn Snack Mix
(page 317)

Holiday Pretzel Rods (page 330)

Mom's Secret Spaghetti
Seasoning Mix (page 348)

CHRISTMAS PANTRY

Handcrafted goodies made for sharing

Comet's White Chocolate Crunch

Comet's White Chocolate Crunch

A favorite of children and reindeer everywhere!

10-oz. pkg. mini pretzels
5 c. doughnut-shaped oat cereal
5 c. bite-size crispy corn cereal squares
2 c. peanuts
16-oz. pkg. candy-coated chocolates
2 12-oz. pkgs. white chocolate chips
3 T. oil

Combine all ingredients except chocolate chips and oil in a very large bowl; set aside. Melt chocolate chips with oil in a double boiler; stir until smooth. Pour over cereal mixture; mix well. Spread mixture equally onto 3 wax paper-lined baking sheets; allow to cool. Break into bite-size pieces; store in airtight containers. Makes 5 quarts.

Honey-Rum Pretzels

If you prefer, you can eliminate the rum extract and double the maple extract.

½ c. brown sugar, packed
¼ c. butter, sliced
1 T. honey
¼ t. salt
¼ t. baking soda
⅛ t. rum extract
⅛ t. maple extract
6 c. mini pretzel twists

Combine brown sugar, butter and honey in a large microwave-safe bowl. Microwave on high for 45 seconds to one minute, until butter melts. Stir; microwave about 30 seconds longer, until mixture boils. Immediately stir in salt, baking soda and extracts. Stir in pretzels. Microwave for 20 to 30 seconds. Stir until well coated. Spread on wax paper. Cool before serving. Makes 6 to 8 cups.

Rebekah Tank
Mount Calvary, WI

Nutty Popcorn Snack Mix

If you're using microwave popcorn, simply pop two 3½-oz. packages. (Pictured on page 314)

16 c. popped popcorn
5 c. mini pretzel twists
1 c. dry-roasted peanuts
2 c. brown sugar, packed
½ c. butter or margarine
½ c. dark corn syrup
¼ t. salt
1 t. vanilla extract
½ t. baking soda
1½ c. mini candy-coated chocolates

Combine popcorn, pretzels and peanuts in a large roasting pan; set aside.

Combine brown sugar, butter or margarine, corn syrup and salt in a heavy medium saucepan. Cook over medium heat for 12 to 14 minutes, stirring occasionally, until mixture comes to a boil. Continue cooking and stirring until mixture reaches the soft-ball stage, or 234 to 243 degrees on a candy thermometer. Remove from heat; stir in vanilla and baking soda. Pour over popcorn mixture in roasting pan; stir until mixture is well coated.

Bake at 250 degrees for 45 minutes, stirring every 15 minutes. Immediately spoon onto wax paper; let cool 10 minutes and sprinkle with chocolates. Cool completely; break into pieces. Store in an airtight container. Makes about 24 cups.

Red-Hot Crackers

At the school where I work, our Home Ec teacher made these and placed them in the teachers' lounge. They were gobbled up!

16-oz. pkg. saltine crackers
0.4-oz. pkg. ranch salad dressing mix
2½ T. red pepper flakes
1½ c. canola oil

   Arrange crackers in a single layer on ungreased baking sheets. Mix together remaining ingredients; drizzle over crackers. Let stand 2 to 3 hours. Break crackers apart and store in an airtight container. Serves 30.

Lori Comer
Kernersville, NC

Cheese Straws

This is my Aunt Sister's famous signature recipe. She passed away several years ago, yet she is still remembered as being an awesome cook.

16-oz. pkg. shredded sharp Cheddar cheese,
   at room temperature
1¼ c. butter or margarine, softened
3 c. all-purpose flour
1 t. cayenne pepper
1 t. salt

   Combine all ingredients in a large bowl. Mix well, using your hands. Spoon dough into a cookie press with a star tip. Press dough in strips onto ungreased baking sheets; cut strips 3 inches long. Bake at 350 degrees for 12 to 15 minutes, until cookies are orange on bottom and around edges. Cool on wire racks; store in an airtight container. Makes 3 to 4 dozen.

Cindy McKinnon
El Dorado, AR

Seeded Tortilla Crisps

They're a pleasing change from ordinary chips… serve with spreads, salads and soups. They bake up in a jiffy!

¼ c. butter, melted
8 10-inch flour tortillas
¾ c. grated Parmesan cheese
1 egg white, beaten
Garnish: sesame, poppy and/or caraway seed;
   onion powder; cayenne pepper or
   dried cumin to taste

   Brush butter lightly over one side of each tortilla; sprinkle evenly with cheese and press down lightly. Carefully turn tortillas over. Brush other side with egg white and sprinkle with desired seeds and seasonings. Cut each tortilla into 4 strips with a pastry cutter or knife. Place strips cheese-side down on a lightly greased baking sheet. Bake on middle rack of oven at 400 degrees for 8 to 10 minutes, until crisp and golden. Cool on a wire rack. Makes about 2½ dozen.

Jewel Grindley
Lindenhurst, IL

Cheddar Shortbread

2 c. shredded sharp Cheddar cheese
1½ c. all-purpose flour
¾ t. dry mustard
¼ t. salt
¼ t. cayenne pepper
¼ c. sun-dried tomatoes, chopped
2 cloves garlic, minced
½ c. butter, melted
Optional: 1 to 2 T. water

Toss together all ingredients except butter and water; mix in butter. Mix with your hands to form a dough. Add water if dough feels too dry. On a floured surface, roll out half the dough to a ¼-inch thickness. Cut with a 2½-inch star-shaped cookie cutter and place on an ungreased baking sheet. Re-roll scraps and repeat with the remaining dough. Bake at 375 degrees for 10 to 12 minutes. Remove to a rack to cool. Makes 2½ dozen.

Cheddar
Shortbread

Mini Bacon-Cheese Balls

These tasty bite-size appetizers are sure to be a hit at your next picnic, potluck or pitch-in dinner!

8-oz. container chive & onion cream cheese
   spread, softened
8-oz. pkg. shredded mozzarella cheese
4 slices bacon, crisply cooked and crumbled
½ t. Italian seasoning
½ t. garlic powder
½ c. walnuts, toasted and ground or finely chopped

Mix cheeses until well blended; stir in bacon and seasonings. Shape mixture into balls by level teaspoonfuls. Roll each ball in walnuts. Place in a serving dish; cover with plastic wrap. Refrigerate at least 2 hours before serving. Makes about 4½ dozen.

Ruby Dorosh
Shippensburg, PA

Mini Bacon-Cheese Balls

Cream Cheese Terrine

My family & friends all call this my $20 dip...it looks (and tastes!) like it's from a gourmet store.

4 8-oz. pkgs. cream cheese, softened
    and divided
2 cloves garlic, chopped
Optional: 2 t. herbes de Provence
⅛ t. dried basil
7-oz. pkg. sun-dried tomatoes, sliced
3 T. green onions, sliced
⅛ t. dried parsley
4-oz. pkg. crumbled blue cheese
½ c. sliced almonds
7-oz. jar basil pesto sauce
assorted crackers

Blend one package cream cheese with garlic and herbes de Provence, if desired; spread into a plastic wrap–lined 8"x4" loaf pan. Sprinkle with basil; chill for 15 minutes. Mix second package cream cheese with tomatoes and onions; spread over first layer. Sprinkle with parsley; chill for 15 minutes. Blend third package cream cheese with blue cheese and almonds; spread over tomato layer. Chill for 15 minutes. Combine remaining package cream cheese with pesto; spread over blue cheese layer. Cover and chill for at least one hour. To serve, gently pull up on plastic wrap; invert onto a serving platter and peel away plastic wrap. Serve with crackers. Serves 12.

Amy Palsrock
Silverdale, WA

Best-Ever Breakfast Bars

My husband won't eat cereal for breakfast but loves these bars! This is a quick & easy, versatile recipe... if your family doesn't like nuts, use chocolate chips or coconut instead. I like using a combination of walnuts and almonds, but you can use peanuts, cashews or pecans. For dried fruit, try raisins, apples, cherries, pineapple, mango or a combination of several.

1 c. granola
1 c. quick-cooking oats, uncooked
½ c. all-purpose flour
⅛ t. cinnamon
¼ c. brown sugar, packed
1 c. nuts, coarsely chopped
½ c. dried fruit, chopped into small pieces
2 T. ground whole flaxseed meal
⅓ c. canola oil
⅓ c. honey
½ t. vanilla extract
1 egg, beaten

Combine granola, oats, flour, cinnamon, brown sugar, nuts, fruit and flaxseed meal in a large bowl. Whisk together oil, honey and vanilla; stir into granola mixture. Add beaten egg; stir to blend. Press mixture into a parchment paper–lined 8"x8" baking pan. Bake at 325 degrees for 30 to 35 minutes, until lightly golden around the edges. Remove from oven and cool for 30 minutes to one hour. Slice into bars. Serves 8 to 12.

Mary Ann Lewis
Olive Branch, MS

Festive Cranberry Salsa

Festive Cranberry Salsa

Serve this fresh-tasting salsa with white corn tortilla chips or spoon it over baked chicken...scrumptious!

½ c. cranberry juice cocktail
1½ c. diced tomatoes, drained
1 c. fresh cranberries, finely chopped
½ c. crushed pineapple, drained
½ c. green onions, thinly sliced
¼ c. avocado, pitted, peeled and diced
¼ c. jalapeño pepper, finely chopped
2 T. lemon juice
2 cloves garlic, pressed

Pour cranberry juice into a medium saucepan; bring to a boil over medium-high heat. Boil for about 5 minutes, until juice is reduced to one tablespoon. Add remaining ingredients. Return to a boil; stir until well mixed. Cover and chill before serving. Serves 8.

Vickie
Gooseberry Patch

Snackin' Pumpkin Seeds

Every Halloween we carve pumpkins...I can't resist doing something yummy with all those seeds!

2 c. pumpkin seeds
3 T. butter, melted
1¼ t. salt
½ t. Worcestershire sauce

Combine all ingredients in an ungreased shallow baking pan; stir to mix. Bake at 250 degrees for about 2 hours, stirring occasionally, until seeds are crisp, dry and golden. Cool completely; store in an airtight container. Makes 2 cups.

Suzanne Bayorgeon
Norfolk, NY

Chili-Lime Pecans

These spicy nuts for nibbling are very easy to make and are enjoyed at all kinds of get-togethers. I usually double this recipe to make sure I'll have enough!

2 T. lime juice
1 T. olive oil
1 t. paprika
1 t. sea salt
1 t. chili powder
½ t. cayenne pepper
3 c. pecan halves

Stir together all ingredients except pecans in a bowl. Add pecans and toss to coat well. Spread pecans in an aluminum foil–lined, lightly greased 15"x10" jelly-roll pan. Bake at 350 degrees for 12 to 14 minutes, until pecans are toasted and dry, stirring occasionally. Cool completely; store in an airtight container. Makes 3 cups.

Sharon Jones
Oklahoma City, OK

Chili-Lime Pecans

Savory Garlic Almonds

So quick, so easy...so tasty!

1 T. butter
2 T. soy sauce
2 t. hot pepper sauce
3 cloves garlic, pressed
1 lb. blanched whole almonds
3 t. pepper
1 T. seasoned salt
¼ t. red pepper flakes

Coat a 15"x10" jelly-roll pan with butter; set aside. Combine soy sauce, hot pepper sauce and garlic in a mixing bowl; add almonds, stirring until well coated. Pour mixture in a single layer. Bake at 350 degrees for 10 minutes. Sprinkle almonds with remaining ingredients. Bake for 15 minutes; cool in pan. Store in an airtight container. Makes about one pound.

plant a portable herb garden!

Tuck several herb plants inside a vintage tin picnic basket...so easy to carry to the kitchen when it's time to snip fresh herbs. Try easy-to-grow herbs such as parsley, chives, oregano and basil, just to name a few, that will add delicious flavor to any meal.

Grandma Weiser's English Toffee

This recipe will become a family favorite.

1 c. butter
1 c. sugar
1 T. light corn syrup
2 T. water
1 c. chocolate chips
1 c. almonds, sliced

Combine all ingredients except chocolate chips and almonds in a heavy saucepan. Cook over medium heat, stirring constantly, until a candy thermometer reads 300 degrees, or until candy is thick and golden. Spread on a greased baking sheet and then sprinkle with chocolate chips. Spread chips evenly until melted and top is completely covered. Sprinkle with almond slices and refrigerate to set. Break into pieces before serving. Makes about one pound.

Sunflower Seed Brittle

I'm from Kansas, the Sunflower State, so I had to try this deliciously different recipe for homemade brittle!

1 T. butter
1 c. dry-roasted sunflower kernels
¼ t. salt
1 c. sugar

Melt butter in a small saucepan over low heat. Add sunflower kernels and salt; mix well and cover to keep warm. Carefully melt sugar in a heavy skillet over medium heat, stirring constantly. Sugar will be extremely hot. When sugar is golden, quickly stir in warm sunflower kernel mixture. Pour out onto a buttered baking sheet. Using a wooden spoon, quickly spread into a 10"x10" square. Let cool until firm; break into bite-size pieces. Store in an airtight container. Makes about ¾ pound.

Angie Venable
Gooseberry Patch

Grandma Weiser's English Toffee

Peanut Brittle Candy Bars
Peppermint-White Chocolate Candy Bars
Hello Dolly Candy Bars

TO:

Peppermint-White Chocolate Candy Bars

24 red and green hard round peppermint candies
2 12-oz. pkgs. white chocolate chips
1 t. peppermint extract

Line three 9"x5" loaf pans with plastic wrap; set aside. Place candies in a plastic zipping bag. Coarsely crush candies using a rolling pin. Set aside crushed candies, reserving 3 tablespoons for topping.

Microwave white chocolate chips in a large microwave-safe bowl at 70% power one minute and 15 seconds. (Chips will not look melted.) Stir chips until melted. Microwave again in 15-second intervals, if necessary. Add peppermint extract and the larger portion of crushed candies to melted chocolate, stirring until evenly distributed.

Quickly spread melted white chocolate evenly in prepared pans; sprinkle with reserved 3 tablespoons candies, pressing gently with fingertips. Let stand one hour or until firm. Makes 3 bars.

Peanut Brittle Candy Bars:

Melt white chocolate as directed in recipe above, gently folding in 1½ cups crushed store-bought peanut brittle and ½ cup creamy peanut butter; spread evenly in prepared loaf pans. Dollop one tablespoon creamy peanut butter over candy mixture in each loaf pan; swirl with a knife. Sprinkle ½ cup crushed peanut brittle evenly over candy in pans, pressing gently with fingertips. Makes 3 bars.

Hello Dolly Candy Bars:

Measure and combine ⅔ cup each mini semi-sweet chocolate chips, toasted flaked coconut, chopped pecans, and chopped graham crackers; set aside ½ cup of this mix for topping. Melt white chocolate as directed in recipe above, gently folding in combined ingredients; spread evenly in prepared loaf pans. Sprinkle reserved ½ cup topping mixture over candy in pans, pressing gently with fingertips. Makes 3 bars.

Licorice Caramels

Growing up, Dad would buy us licorice toffee. I got this recipe from my sister, and it's as close as I can get to that original toffee taste. It's always a part of our Christmas celebration.

2 c. sugar
1½ c. light corn syrup
1 c. butter
14-oz. can sweetened condensed milk
2½ t. licorice or anise extract
½ t. black food coloring

Combine sugar, corn syrup, butter and condensed milk in a large heavy saucepan. Cook over medium heat stirring constantly to soft-ball stage, or 234 to 243 degrees on a candy thermometer. Remove from heat; stir in extract and food coloring. Line a 13"x9" baking pan with parchment paper; coat with butter. Pour mixture into pan. Cool at least 4 hours to overnight. Remove from pan and cut into ½-inch squares; wrap pieces in wax paper or paper candy wrappers. Makes 2½ pounds.

Angie Whitmore
Farmington, UT

> **tried & true tip**
> An old-fashioned candy-making hint...a cold, sunny winter day is perfect for making candy. Don't try to prepare homemade candy on a rainy or humid day, as it may not set properly.

Easy Cream Cheese Truffles

Easy Cream Cheese Truffles

It's fun rolling these in the different coatings.

8-oz. pkg. cream cheese, softened
4¼ c. powdered sugar, divided
5 1-oz. sqs. unsweetened baking chocolate,
    melted and cooled
¼ c. baking cocoa
¼ c. almonds, toasted and finely chopped
¼ c. sweetened flaked coconut, toasted

Beat cream cheese until fluffy. Slowly add 4 cups powdered sugar. Beat until smooth. Add melted chocolate and beat until blended. Chill for about one hour. Shape chilled mixture into one-inch balls. Roll some in ¼ cup powdered sugar, some in cocoa, some in almonds and some in coconut. Store in an airtight container in the refrigerator for up to 2 weeks. Makes 6½ dozen.

Chocolate-Covered Raisin Fudge

Cut fudge into both small and large pieces to please appetites of all sizes.

1½ c. sugar
⅔ c. evaporated milk
2 T. butter
¼ t. salt
2 c. mini marshmallows
1½ c. semi-sweet chocolate chips
2 c. chocolate-covered raisins, divided
1 t. vanilla extract
½ c. chopped nuts

Combine sugar, milk, butter and salt in a heavy saucepan; bring to a boil over medium heat, stirring constantly. Boil for 4 to 5 minutes and remove from heat. Stir in marshmallows, chocolate chips, one cup raisins, vanilla and nuts. Stir continuously for one minute, or until marshmallows are melted. Pour into an 8"x8" baking pan lined with foil; cool

for one minute. Sprinkle remaining raisins on top, pressing in slightly. Chill for 2 hours, or until firm. Lift from pan and remove foil. Cut into squares. Makes 2½ pounds.

Penuche

A rich-tasting fudge recipe that's made in the microwave...what could be easier?

2 c. brown sugar, packed
5-oz. can evaporated milk
½ c. butter, cut up
2 c. powdered sugar
1 t. vanilla extract

Combine brown sugar, evaporated milk and butter in a microwave-safe container. Microwave on high for 9 minutes, stirring every 3 minutes. Let stand for 5 minutes. Add powdered sugar and vanilla; stir until almost set. Pour into a lightly greased 9"x9" baking pan. Cool; cut into squares. Makes 1¾ pounds.

Jo Ann
Gooseberry Patch

share your sweet tooth
Who wouldn't want to receive her very own little pot of fudge? Pour hot fudge into a shallow plastic food-storage container with a snap-on lid and chill. Be sure to tuck in a small plastic knife so that the lucky recipient can indulge right away.

Holiday Pretzel Rods

Roll the rods in colored sprinkles to match any holiday throughout the year. When December arrives, use red and green for Christmas and blue and white for Hanukkah. A tall mug or plastic cup is perfect for melting the coating. (Pictured on page 314)

1½ c. semi-sweet chocolate chips
½ c. creamy peanut butter
10-oz. pkg. large pretzel rods
Garnish: chopped walnuts, colored or
    chocolate sprinkles

Microwave chocolate chips in a tall, narrow, microwave-safe container on high until melted, about 1½ minutes. Add peanut butter and stir until combined. One at a time, dip each pretzel rod ⅔ of the way into chocolate mixture; gently tap against side of container to remove excess. Immediately roll rod in desired garnish. Place on baking sheets lined with wax paper; let stand until completely set. Makes about 2½ dozen.

Louise Beveridge
Philipsburg, PA

Twice-Cooked Divinity

This is a childhood favorite of mine...Grandmother would make this for every holiday.

2 c. sugar
⅓ c. water
⅛ t. salt
½ c. light corn syrup
2 egg whites, stiffly beaten
Optional: ½ c. chopped pecans

Stir sugar, water, salt and corn syrup in a heavy saucepan over medium heat until sugar dissolves. Boil until mixture reaches the soft-ball stage, or 234 to 243 degrees on a candy thermometer. Remove from heat. Gradually pour ⅓ of syrup mixture over egg whites and beat together. Cook remaining syrup mixture to hard-ball stage, or 250 to 269 degrees. Beat egg white mixture into hot syrup mixture until it holds shape. Stir in nuts, if using. Drop by teaspoonfuls onto wax paper. Store in an airtight container. Makes 4 dozen.

Patty Fosnight
Childress, TX

Gingerbread Babies

Tuck them into a little box and leave on someone's doorstep...surely you know someone who will give them a good home at Christmas!

¾ c. butter, softened
¾ c. brown sugar, packed
1 egg
½ c. dark molasses
2⅔ c. all-purpose flour
2 t. ground ginger
½ t. nutmeg
½ t. cinnamon
½ t. allspice
¼ t. salt

Blend butter and brown sugar in a large bowl until fluffy. Add egg and molasses. Combine remaining ingredients in a separate bowl; gradually stir into butter mixture. Turn dough out onto a well-floured surface; roll out to a ⅛-inch thickness. Cut dough with a 2-inch gingerbread man cookie cutter. Place on greased baking sheets. Bake at 350 degrees for 9 to 10 minutes, until firm. Makes 12 dozen.

Gingerbread Babies

Old-Time Molasses Cookies

Whenever we stopped to visit my Grandma Hoak, she had a plate of molasses cookies ready to serve along with a glass of milk or a cup of tea. These days she doesn't bake much anymore, but I can still remember the sweet scent of these cookies in her cozy home, along with her welcoming hugs.

¾ c. shortening
2 c. powdered sugar
1 c. molasses
1 egg, beaten
4 c. all-purpose flour
2 t. baking soda
1 t. salt
1 t. cinnamon
2 t. ground ginger
1 t. vanilla extract
Garnish: powdered sugar

Blend together shortening, powdered sugar, molasses and egg in a large bowl. Add remaining ingredients except garnish; stir until blended. Roll into one-inch balls and place on ungreased baking sheets. Bake at 350 degrees for 10 to 12 minutes, until cookies crack. Cool; dip tops in powdered sugar. Makes 5 dozen.

Alysson Marshall
Newark, NY

Double Chocolate Mint Brownies

These fantastic brownies are rich and chocolatey with a yummy layer of mint.

1 c. all-purpose flour
1 c. sugar
1 c. plus 6 T. butter, softened and divided
4 eggs, beaten
16-oz. can chocolate syrup
2 c. powdered sugar
1 T. water
½ t. mint extract
3 drops green food coloring
1 c. semi-sweet chocolate chips

Beat flour, sugar, ½ cup butter, eggs and syrup in a large bowl until smooth; pour into a greased 13"x9" baking pan. Bake at 350 degrees for 25 to 30 minutes, until top springs back when lightly touched. Cool completely in pan. Combine powdered sugar, ½ cup butter, water, mint extract and food coloring in a bowl; beat until smooth. Spread over brownies; chill. Melt chocolate chips and remaining butter in a double boiler; stir until smooth. Pour over chilled mint layer; cover and chill until set. Cut into small squares to serve. Makes about 4 dozen.

Amy Gitter
Fond du Lac, WI

Double Chocolate
Mint Brownies

to: Kate
from: Emily

Cookie Dough Brownies

You will definitely get your chocolate fix with this one...it's simply decadent!

2 c. sugar
½ c. baking cocoa
1 c. oil
2 t. vanilla extract
1½ c. all-purpose flour
½ t. salt
4 eggs, beaten
Optional: ½ c. chopped walnuts
1 c. semi-sweet chocolate chips
1 T. shortening
Garnish: ¼ c. chopped walnuts

Mix together all ingredients except chocolate chips, shortening and garnish. Pour into a greased 13"x9" baking pan and bake at 350 degrees for 30 minutes. Cool completely. Prepare Cookie Dough and spread over cooled brownies. Add chocolate chips to a microwave-safe bowl and microwave on low to melt. Add shortening, stirring to blend. Drizzle over brownies. Garnish with nuts. Refrigerate until glaze is firm. Serves 8 to 12.

Cookie Dough:
½ c. butter, softened
¼ c. sugar
1 t. vanilla extract
½ c. brown sugar, packed
2 T. milk
1 c. all-purpose flour

Mix together all ingredients in a small bowl.

Linda Vogt
Las Vegas, NV

Salted Nut Roll Bars

Salty, sweet, crunchy and gooey...every bite satisfies!

18½-oz. pkg. yellow cake mix
1 egg, beaten
¼ c. butter, melted and slightly cooled
3 c. mini marshmallows
10-oz. pkg. peanut butter chips
½ c. light corn syrup
½ c. butter, softened
1 t. vanilla extract
2 c. salted peanuts
2 c. crispy rice cereal

Combine dry cake mix, egg and melted butter; press into a greased 13"x9" baking pan. Bake at 350 degrees for 10 to 12 minutes. Sprinkle marshmallows over baked crust; return to oven and bake for 3 additional minutes, or until marshmallows are melted. Melt peanut butter chips, corn syrup, butter and vanilla in a saucepan over medium heat. Stir in peanuts and cereal. Spread mixture over marshmallow layer. Chill until firm; cut into squares. Makes 2½ dozen.

Sandy Groezinger
Stockton, IL

Grandma Mary's Shortbread

I received this wonderful recipe 20 years ago from a dear friend who was like a grandmother to me.

1 c. butter, softened
2 c. all-purpose flour
½ c. superfine sugar
2 T. cornstarch

Combine all ingredients in a medium bowl and knead to form a smooth dough. Roll out on a floured surface to a ¼-inch thickness. Cut out with a cookie or biscuit cutter. Transfer to ungreased baking sheets. Bake at 275 degrees for 45 minutes; cool. Frost with Cream Cheese Frosting. Refrigerate until set or ready to serve. Makes about 3 dozen.

Cream Cheese Frosting:

4 oz. cream cheese, softened
¼ c. butter, softened
1 t. vanilla extract
2¼ c. powdered sugar

Beat cream cheese and butter with an electric mixer at medium speed until blended. Add vanilla and mix well. Add powdered sugar and mix at low speed until combined. Beat on high speed for one minute.

Kerry McNeil
Anacortes, WA

Grandma Mary's
Shortbread

Big Crunchy Sugar Cookies

Big Crunchy Sugar Cookies

These goodies get their name from a crunchy coating of coarse sugar.

1 c. butter, softened
1 c. sugar
1 egg
1½ t. vanilla extract
2 c. all-purpose flour
½ t. baking powder
¼ t. salt
assorted coarse decorating sugars

Beat butter with an electric mixer at medium speed until creamy. Gradually add sugar, beating until smooth. Add egg and vanilla, beating until blended.

Combine flour, baking powder and salt; gradually add to butter mixture, beating just until blended. Shape dough into a ball; cover and chill 2 hours.

Divide dough into 3 portions. Work with one portion at a time, storing remaining dough in refrigerator. Shape dough into 1½-inch balls; roll each ball in decorating sugar. Place 2 inches apart on parchment paper–lined baking sheets. Gently press and flatten each ball to ¾-inch thickness. Bake at 375 degrees for 13 to 15 minutes, until edges of cookies are lightly golden. Cool 5 minutes on baking sheets; remove to wire racks to cool. Makes 1½ dozen.

giftable goodies

Grandma always said, "Never return a dish empty." Gather up cookie tins, pie plates and casserole dishes that have been left behind, fill them with home-baked goodies and return them to their owners...they'll be pleasantly surprised!

Spumoni Cookie Squares

Just as yummy as the ice cream!

1 c. butter
1½ c. powdered sugar
1 egg
2 t. vanilla extract
2½ c. all-purpose flour
½ c. mini semi-sweet chocolate chips, divided
2 drops green food coloring
½ c. pistachios, chopped
1 drop red food coloring
¼ c. candied cherries, finely chopped

Beat together butter and sugar; beat in egg and vanilla. Gradually beat in flour until just blended. Shape dough into a brick and cut into three equal parts. Melt 2½ tablespoons chocolate chips; cool. Flatten one portion of dough, smooth melted chocolate over top and carefully knead until blended. Knead in remaining chips; roll dough into a 24-inch rope and flatten to a ½-inch thickness. Flatten second dough portion; add green food coloring and knead to blend. Knead in chopped pistachios. Roll dough into a 24-inch rope, flatten and place on chocolate layer. Repeat with third dough portion, kneading in red food coloring and then cherries. Roll dough into a 24-inch rope, flatten and place on pistachio layer. Cut into two 12-inch blocks, squaring off sides as much as possible. Wrap and chill until firm. Cut dough crosswise in ¼-inch-thick slices. Place on ungreased baking sheets. Bake at 375 degrees for 8 minutes or until puffed. Remove to wire rack to cool. Makes 5 dozen.

Santa Claus Cookie Pops

Put one at each place setting for a festive touch.

1 c. sugar
½ c. shortening
2 T. milk
1 egg
1½ t. vanilla extract, divided
2 c. all-purpose flour
1 t. baking powder
½ t. baking soda
½ t. salt
16 wooden craft sticks
sugar
1½ c. powdered sugar
2 to 3 T. water
¼ c. red decorating sugar
1 c. sweetened flaked coconut
16 miniature marshmallows
32 raisins
16 red cinnamon candies

Beat together sugar and shortening. Beat in milk, egg and one teaspoon vanilla. Stir in flour, baking powder, baking soda and salt. Shape dough into 1¼-inch balls. Place balls 2 inches apart on a baking sheet. Insert a stick into the side of each dough ball and flatten with the bottom of a glass dipped in sugar. Bake at 350 degrees for 8 to 10 minutes, until cookies are golden. Let cool on baking sheet 2 minutes. Remove from baking sheet and cool on a wire rack.

Combine powdered sugar and remaining ½ teaspoon vanilla in a small bowl; add water, one teaspoon at a time, until spreadable. Spread frosting on top ⅓ for a hat and on bottom ⅓ for a beard, one cookie at a time. Sprinkle red sugar on hat and coconut on beard. Press on a marshmallow for tassel of hat, raisins for eyes and a cinnamon candy for nose. Makes 16 cookies.

Chocolatey Butterscotch Squares

Just as tasty with milk chocolate chips, too!

1½ c. graham cracker crumbs
14-oz. can sweetened condensed milk
1½ c. semi-sweet chocolate chips
1 c. butterscotch chips
1 c. chopped walnuts

Mix together all ingredients in a medium mixing bowl. Line a 9"x9" baking pan with aluminum foil and grease foil; press mixture in pan. Bake at 350 degrees for 30 to 35 minutes. Cool for 45 minutes, remove from pan and peel off foil. Cut into squares. Makes 2 dozen squares.

Orange Cream Cake in a Cup

Lemon cake with lemon pudding is just as yummy!

18½-oz. pkg. white cake mix
¾-oz. pkg. instant vanilla pudding mix
16 plastic zipping bags
2⅔ c. powdered sugar, divided
¼ c. orange drink mix, divided
8 12-oz. microwave-safe coffee mugs

Place cake mix and pudding mix in a large bowl and blend well with a wire whisk. Place ½ cup dry mix into 8 plastic zipping bags; smooth each bag to remove as much air as possible before sealing. Label each bag "Cake Mix." Place ⅓ cup powdered sugar and 1½ teaspoons drink mix in each remaining bag; label these bags "Glaze Mix." Place one of each mix into each mug. Attach a gift tag with instructions to each cup. Makes 8.

Instructions:

Generously coat inside of mug with non-stick vegetable spray. Empty Cake Mix into mug. Add one egg white, one tablespoon oil and one tablespoon water; stir well until combined. Microwave on high for 2 minutes. While cake is cooking, place Glaze Mix into a small bowl; add 1½ teaspoons water and mix well. Pour glaze over warm cake.

Holiday Eggnog Bread

This was one of the first things that I ever made at age 12. My family loves it during the holidays, and I make it as long as the grocery store sells eggnog in the dairy section!

2 eggs, beaten
1 c. sugar
1 c. eggnog
½ c. butter, melted
1 t. vanilla extract
2¼ c. all-purpose flour
2 t. baking powder
2¼ t. ground nutmeg

   Combine eggs, sugar, eggnog, melted butter and vanilla in a large bowl. Blend well. Add remaining ingredients; stir until moistened. Grease the bottom of a 9"x5" loaf pan; pour batter into pan. Bake at 350 degrees for 35 to 45 minutes, until a toothpick inserted near center comes out clean. Cool completely before slicing. Makes one loaf.

Summer Staib
Broomfield, CO

Holiday Gift Cakes

8-oz. pkg. cream cheese, softened
1 c. butter, softened
1½ c. sugar
1½ t. vanilla extract
4 eggs
2¼ c. cake flour, sifted and divided
1½ t. baking powder
8-oz. jar maraschino cherries, well-drained
   and chopped
1 c. pecans, finely chopped and divided
1½ c. powdered sugar, sifted
2 T. milk
Garnishes: red or green maraschino cherry halves,
   pecan halves

   Thoroughly blend cream cheese, butter, sugar and vanilla. Add eggs, one at a time, mixing well after each addition. Sift together 2 cups flour and baking powder. Gradually add sifted flour mixture to batter. Dredge cherries and ½ cup pecans in remaining flour; fold into batter. Grease four 3"x 5½" loaf pans; sprinkle with remaining pecans. Pour batter into pans. Bake at 325 degrees for 45 minutes, or until toothpick inserted near center comes out clean. Cool 5 minutes; remove from pans. To prepare glaze, combine powdered sugar and milk. Add more milk, if needed, for drizzling consistency. Drizzle glaze over top and sides of cake. Garnish with cherry and pecan halves, as desired. Makes 4 small loaves.

a brush of honey
To give your warm-from-the-oven bread a sweet, shiny glaze, brush it with honey... it also absorbs moisture, so your bread will stay fresh longer.

Holiday Gift Cakes

Lori's Rosemary Focaccia

I make this focaccia all the time. It's great by itself or on a sandwich.

3 c. bread flour
1 T. dried rosemary
1 T. sugar
1 t. salt
2¼ t. instant dry yeast
3 to 4 T. olive oil, divided
1 c. very warm water, 120 to 130 degrees
Optional: 1 c. shredded Cheddar cheese

Place all ingredients except one tablespoon oil and Cheddar cheese into a bread machine in the order listed. Set machine to dough cycle. When finished, divide dough in half. Form each half into a flattened 10-inch circle. Cover loosely with lightly greased plastic wrap. Let rise until double in size, about 30 minutes. Place on greased baking sheets. Brush tops with remaining oil; sprinkle with cheese, if desired. Bake at 400 degrees for 15 to 20 minutes, until golden. Makes 2 loaves.

Lori Peterson
Effingham, KS

Emma's Gingerbread Muffins

These muffins are moist, spicy and delicious. I received this recipe from a friend's mother.

1 c. sugar
½ c. butter or margarine, softened
½ c. shortening
3 eggs
½ c. molasses
½ c. light corn syrup
3 c. all-purpose flour
2 t. cinnamon
2 t. ground ginger
1 t. nutmeg
1¾ t. baking soda
1 c. buttermilk

Blend together sugar, butter or margarine and shortening. Beat in eggs, one at a time. Add molasses and corn syrup; set aside. Sift together flour and spices. Dissolve baking soda in buttermilk; add to batter alternately with flour mixture. Fill greased and floured muffin cups ⅔ full. Bake at 350 degrees for about 15 minutes. Makes 2 dozen.

Bernadette Dobias
Houston, TX

Mom's Chocolate Fondue

What fun to receive a fondue pot and all the fixin's to go with it! Keep fondue and fruit in the refrigerator until ready to serve.

6 1-oz. sqs. unsweetened baking chocolate
1½ c. sugar
1 c. half-and-half
½ c. butter or margarine
⅛ t. salt
Optional: 3 T. cocoa cream or orange-flavored liqueur
Items for dipping: marshmallows, pound cake, maraschino cherries, kiwi, strawberries and pineapple

Melt chocolate over low heat. Add sugar, half-and-half, butter or margarine and salt. Cook, stirring constantly, about 5 minutes, or until thickened. Stir in liqueur, if desired. Pour into a fondue pot and keep warm over heat source. Arrange dippers in individual bowls around fondue pot. Makes 2¾ cups.

Mom's Chocolate
Fondue

Patchwork Bean
Soup Mix

Cowboy Cornbread Mix

A great addition to breakfast, lunch or dinner!

1 c. all-purpose flour
1 c. cornmeal
¼ c. sugar
1 t. baking soda
1 T. baking powder
⅛ t. salt

Combine all ingredients; store in an airtight container. Attach instructions. Makes 2½ cups mix.

Instructions:
Place cornbread mix in a large mixing bowl; set aside. Whisk together 3 tablespoons melted and cooled butter and 1⅓ cup buttermilk in a separate bowl; mix in one egg. Pour into cornbread mix; stir until just combined. Spread into a greased 8"x8" baking pan; bake at 425 degrees for 30 minutes. Serves 6.

Patchwork Bean Soup Mix

This colorful soup mix would be great paired with crazy quilt potholders or oven mitts!

½ c. dried kidney beans
½ c. dried black-eyed peas
½ c. dried black beans
½ c. dried red beans
½ c. dried split green peas
½ c. dried Great Northern beans
½ c. dried kidney beans
½ c. dried lima beans
3 T. chicken bouillon
1 T. dried, minced onion
salt and pepper to taste
½ t. garlic powder
1 T. dried parsley flakes
1 t. celery seed
¼ c. brown sugar, packed

Layer beans in a one-quart, wide-mouth jar. Blend together seasonings in a plastic zipping bag. Attach instructions. Makes about 4 cups mix.

Instructions:
Add beans to a large stockpot; cover with hot water and soak overnight. Drain and add 2 quarts water. Bring to a boil; reduce heat and simmer, covered, one to 2 hours, until beans are almost tender. Stir in two 14½-oz. cans stewed tomatoes and seasoning mix. Simmer, uncovered, one to 1½ hours, until beans are tender. Makes 12 cups.

Quick & Easy Pancake Mix

Sprinkle fresh blueberries and strawberries on top of these moist, golden pancakes...so tasty!

10 c. all-purpose flour
2½ c. powdered milk
½ c. sugar
¼ c. baking powder
1½ T. salt

Combine all ingredients; blend well. Place in a large container or divide by 2-cup amounts into plastic zipping bags. Store in a cool, dry place for up to 8 months. Attach instructions. Makes 12 cups mix.

Instructions:
Combine 2 cups mix, one beaten egg and 1¼ cups water or milk until just moistened; drop by ¼ cupfuls onto a hot, greased griddle or skillet. Flip when bubbles form on the surface; cook until golden. Makes 12 to 14 pancakes.

homemade gift tags
Gather all your fun scrapbooking supplies and easily make the prettiest jar lables. Buttons, stickers, die-cuts, rick rack and decorative-edged scissors are all you need for whimsical, one-of-a-kind labels and tags!

Italian Soup Mix

Italian Soup Mix

Deliver a jar of soup mix with a loaf of freshly baked bread and all the ingredients (one onion, three carrots, three celery stalks and one can crushed tomatoes) to make the soup.

½ c. dried pinto beans
½ c. dried pink or red beans
½ c. dried kidney beans
1½ c. small bowtie pasta, uncooked
1 T. dried parsley
1 T. chicken bouillon granules
1 T. salt
1 t. dried oregano
1 t. dried basil
1 t. garlic salt
½ t. dried, minced garlic
¼ t. red pepper flakes

Layer beans in a 2-cup jar in order listed; secure lid. Place pasta in another 2-cup jar. Combine remaining ingredients; place in a small plastic zipping bag. Place bag on top of pasta; secure lid. Give with instructions for making soup.

Instructions:

Place beans into a bowl. Rinse with water; drain. Cover beans with water; let soak overnight. Drain, rinse and place in a 5-quart Dutch oven; add 8 cups water, one 28-ounce can crushed tomatoes, seasoning packet, one cup sliced carrots, one cup sliced celery and one cup chopped onion. Bring to a boil; reduce heat. Simmer, covered, for 2 hours; uncover and boil gently until thickened, about 35 minutes. Stir in pasta; cook until pasta is tender, about 20 minutes. Makes about 13 cups.

Mom's Best Marinade

When we went camping, we always marinated our steak or chicken with this recipe. So easy to follow... just place the meat in a bowl, pierce it slightly with a fork and then top with the marinade. Marinate meat in the refrigerator for two hours to two days, and grill using your favorite recipe.

½ c. soy sauce
⅛ t. garlic, minced
2 T. brown sugar, packed
1 t. ground ginger
2 T. vinegar

Mix together all ingredients. Makes about ¾ cup.

Lorna Petersen
Burbank, WA

Spicy Cajun Rub

I like to pack this spice blend in mini glass shaker-top jars, like those pizza parlors use for cheese!

¼ c. paprika
4 t. onion powder
4 t. garlic powder
4 t. cayenne pepper
4 t. salt
1 T. white pepper
1 t. pepper
2 t. dried thyme
2 t. dried oregano

Combine all ingredients in a bowl; mix well. Place in a small jar; attach instructions. Makes about ⅔ cup.

Instructions:

Sprinkle generously on pork chops or pork tenderloin before grilling or roasting. Excellent with fish, too...sprinkle over fillets before pan-frying.

Kerry Mayer
Denham Springs, LA

Vickie's Herb Seasoning

This all-purpose seasoning is super for grilling or roasting all kinds of meat.

¼ c. plus 2 t. dried parsley
2 T. pepper
2 T. onion powder
5 t. garlic powder
5 t. dried basil
1½ t. dried oregano
1½ t. dried thyme
Optional: 2 T. salt

Combine all ingredients; mix well and place in an airtight container. Makes about ¾ cup.

Vickie
Gooseberry Patch

Mom's Secret Spaghetti Seasoning Mix

This mix is a quick start to a delicious meal. (Pictured on page 314)

1 T. dried, minced onion
1 T. cornstarch
1 T. dried parsley
2 t. green pepper flakes
1½ t. salt
1 t. sugar
1 t. dried oregano
¾ t. Italian seasoning
¼ t. dried, minced garlic

Combine all ingredients; store in an airtight container. Attach Instructions. Makes about ⅓ cup.

Instructions:

To serve, brown one pound ground beef; drain. Add two 8-oz. cans tomato sauce, one 6-oz. can tomato paste, 2¾ cups tomato juice or water and seasoning mix to the beef; simmer sauce 30 minutes, stirring occasionally. Serve over cooked spaghetti. Serves 4 to 6.

Vickie
Gooseberry Patch

Hacienda Dressing Mix

I used to buy the little packets of ranch salad dressing mix all the time until I found this recipe! Now I keep a big jar of it handy.

3 T. dried, minced onion
1 T. dried parsley
2½ t. paprika
2 t. sugar
2 t. salt
2 t. pepper
1½ t. garlic powder

Combine all ingredients and store in an airtight container. Use 3 tablespoons mix when a one-ounce package of ranch salad dressing mix is called for. Attach instructions. Makes about ½ cup.

Instructions:

For Sour Cream Dip: Combine one tablespoon dressing mix with one cup sour cream. Chill for one hour before serving. Makes one cup.

For Buttermilk Ranch Dressing: Mix ½ cup mayonnaise with ½ cup buttermilk. Whisk in ½ tablespoon dressing mix. Chill for one hour before serving. Makes one cup.

Tonya Sheppard
Galveston, TX

Granny White's Barbecue Sauce

½ c. butter or margarine
¾ c. onion, chopped
¾ c. catsup
¾ c. water
⅓ c. lemon juice
3 T. sugar
3 T. mustard
3 T. Worcestershire sauce
2 t. salt
½ t. pepper

Melt butter or margarine in a skillet over medium heat; add onion. Cook until soft and translucent. Add remaining ingredients; simmer for 15 minutes. Makes about 3½ cups.

Vici Randolph
Gaffney, SC

"This recipe is one that my grandmother passed on to my mother and me...it's so good over chicken or pork. —Vici"

Granny White's BBQ Sauce

Dad's Sweet Mustard

This recipe has been in my dad's family for several generations. Dad loves to make it at Christmastime to go along with homemade pork sausage from a small hometown meat market. This mustard has a little zing to it…just the way we like it!

1 c. dry mustard
1 c. sugar
3 T. all-purpose flour
1 c. cider vinegar

Mix together mustard, sugar and flour in a bowl; set aside. Heat vinegar until hot, without boiling; add to dry ingredients. Pour into a blender; process until mixed. Store in a covered jar in the refrigerator. Makes about 3 cups.

Kathy Majeske
Denver, PA

Cranberry-Tomato Chutney

The tangy flavor of this quick-to-make chutney perfectly complements roast pork. For a delightful appetizer to serve with crackers, spoon some chutney over a block of cream cheese.

5 c. fresh cranberries
28-oz. can crushed tomatoes
1 c. golden raisins
¾ c. sugar
1 t. salt
¾ t. ground ginger

Combine all ingredients in a large heavy saucepan over medium heat. Bring to a boil. Reduce heat; cover and simmer for 20 to 25 minutes, stirring occasionally, until cranberries and raisins are tender. Transfer to a covered container; cool. Refrigerate for 2 to 3 days before serving. Keep refrigerated. Makes 6 cups.

Debi DeVore
Dover, OH

Backyard Barbecue Mango Chutney

Try this as an appetizer with cream cheese and crackers. It's also so tasty on chicken, pork chops and even fish!

3 c. white vinegar
6 c. sugar
6 c. brown sugar, packed
2 t. cinnamon
2 t. ground ginger
1½ T. allspice
1½ t. ground cloves
2 t. nutmeg
4 hot red chili peppers, seeded and chopped
1 t. kosher salt
2 onions, chopped
3 cloves garlic, chopped
1 c. golden raisins
1 c. raisins
16 c. mangoes, peeled, cored and sliced
½ c. sliced almonds
4 1-quart canning jars and lids, sterilized

Combine first 10 ingredients in a large saucepan; boil for 30 minutes. Add onions, garlic, golden raisins and raisins; boil for another 30 minutes. Reduce heat; stir in mangoes and almonds. Simmer for 30 minutes; pour into hot sterilized jars, leaving ½-inch headspace. Wipe rims and secure lids and rings. Process in a boiling-water bath for 10 minutes. Set jars on a towel to cool. Check for seals. Makes 4 jars.

a silver spoon

Silver-plated baby spoons are ideal for serving up dollops of mayonnaise, preserves, chutney and other condiments. Polish up Bobby and Janie's almost-forgotten little spoons or scoop up vintage finds at a tag sale.

Backyard Barbecue
Mango Chutney

Pike Family Jalapeño Jelly

*This is the best hot pepper jelly I have ever tried…
it's an essential treat around the holidays! Our family
serves it on whole-wheat crackers with a bit of cream
cheese. So pretty and so good!*

¾ c. green pepper, chopped
¼ c. jalapeño pepper, chopped
6 c. sugar
1½ c. cider vinegar
½ c. liquid fruit pectin
4 drops green food coloring
6 ½-pint canning jars and lids, sterilized

Add peppers to a food processor and pulse until
finely minced. Combine pepper mixture, sugar
and vinegar in a saucepan over medium-high heat;
bring to a rolling boil. Remove from heat; stir in
pectin and food coloring. Ladle jelly into hot sterilized jars, leaving ½-inch headspace. Wipe rims and
secure lids and rings. Process in a boiling-water
bath for 5 minutes. Set jars on a towel to cool.
Check for seals. Makes 6 jars.

Diana Pike
Mount Vernon, OH

Lazy-Day Apple Butter

*This slow-cooker recipe is great when made on a
rainy day. The house smells wonderful, and it's the
perfect afternoon snack.*

5½ lbs. cooking apples, cored, peeled
    and finely chopped
4 c. sugar
2 to 3 t. cinnamon
¼ t. ground cloves
¼ t. salt
4 1-pint freezer containers and lids,
    sterilized

Place apples in a 6-quart slow cooker; set aside.
Combine sugar, spices and salt; sprinkle over apples
and mix well. Cover and cook on high setting for

one hour. Reduce heat to low setting; cook for 7 to
10 hours, stirring occasionally, until thickened and
dark brown. Uncover; continue to cook on low
setting for one additional hour. Spoon apple butter
into containers, leaving ½-inch headspace. Cool
to room temperature, about one hour. Secure lids.
Refrigerate apple butter up to 3 weeks, or freeze
up to one year. Makes 4 containers.

Pam Littel
Pleasant View, TN

Lemon Curd

*The sweet-tart flavor of homemade lemon curd is
delicious on fresh-baked scones.*

½ c. butter
1⅔ c. sugar
juice of 4 lemons
4 eggs, beaten
zest of 4 lemons
2 ½-pint canning jars and lids, sterilized

Melt butter in a double boiler over hot water.
Add sugar, lemon juice and eggs; mix well. Stir in
lemon zest. Cook, stirring constantly, until thickened, about 15 minutes. Remove top of double
boiler from heat; cool slightly. Pour curd into hot
sterilized jars, leaving ¼-inch headspace. Wipe
rims and secure lids and rings. Keep refrigerated
for up to one week. Makes 2 jars.

Jennifer Niemi
Nova Scotia, Canada

great gift!
Tuck a jar of Lemon Curd into a gift basket
of extra-special scones. Stir up a favorite
scone recipe or mix, pat out the
dough and cut out with a heart-
shaped cookie cutter.

Lemon Curd

Tamara's Pickled Beets

This is my version of my family's favorite recipe at summer camp.

⅓ c. red wine vinegar
⅓ c. sugar
⅓ c. water
½ t. cinnamon
¼ t. salt
¼ t. ground cloves
5 whole peppercorns
2 c. beets, peeled, cooked and sliced, or
    16-oz. can sliced beets, drained

Combine all ingredients except beets in a saucepan over medium-high heat. Bring to a boil, stirring constantly. Add beets and return to a boil. Reduce heat and simmer, covered, 5 minutes. Let cool and chill in the liquid for 4 hours to overnight. Store in refrigerator up to 2 weeks. Serves 4 to 6.

Tamara Ahrens
Sparta, MI

Marinated Greek Olives

A few simple ingredients can do wonders for ordinary canned olives! (Pictured on page 314)

2 c. green olives, drained
1 to 2 cloves garlic, slivered
3 thin slices lemon
1 t. whole peppercorns
3 bay leaves
¼ c. wine vinegar
¼ to ½ c. olive oil

Combine all ingredients except oil in a wide-mouth jar with a lid. Add enough oil to cover ingredients. Secure lid. Refrigerate at least 24 hours to blend flavors before serving. Makes 2 cups.

Sharon Velenosi
Stanton, CA

Dilly Green Beans

I remember my grandmother preparing this recipe each harvest season. Her pantry shelves would be lined with jars of these beans, along with tomatoes, bread & butter pickles and hot peppers.

3½ c. white vinegar
3 c. water
3 T. kosher salt
¼ c. sugar
6 1-pint canning jars and lids, sterilized
1 onion, cut into six ¼-inch slices
36 whole black peppercorns
18 whole green peppercorns
¼ t. mustard seed
¼ t. dill seed
6 bay leaves
4 lbs. green beans, trimmed and cut into
    4-inch pieces
6 small serrano chiles, rinsed and stems
    removed
6 baby carrots, halved lengthwise
6 cloves garlic, peeled and halved
3 bunches fresh dill, stemmed
1 lemon, cut into six ⅛-inch slices and seeded

Combine vinegar, water, salt and sugar in a large saucepan; bring to a boil over high heat. Reduce heat and simmer while packing jars. Place an onion slice, spices and one bay leaf in the bottom of each jar. Pack green beans, chiles, carrots and garlic tightly into jars. Place fresh dill on top, tucking in so none touches the rim. Top each jar with a lemon slice to hold down dill. Spoon boiling vinegar mixture into jars, leaving ¼-inch headspace. Make sure all of the dill is tucked in. Wipe rims and secure lids and rings. Process in a boiling-water bath for 10 minutes. Set jars on a towel to cool. Check for seals. Allow to set for at least 3 weeks before using. Makes 6 jars.

Kerry Mayer
Denham Springs, LA

Bread & Butter Pickles

When I was growing up, we canned everything we grew in our family garden. Canning pickles was such fun! I liked slicing the cucumbers, so that was my job. Now my daughter, Erika, and I can pickles every summer for my parents.

4 lbs. pickling cucumbers, sliced
3 to 4 onions, sliced
2 green peppers, sliced into strips
½ c. canning salt
3 c. cider vinegar
5 c. sugar
1½ t. turmeric
1½ t. celery seed
2 T. mustard seed
6 1-quart canning jars and lids, sterilized

Combine cucumbers, onions, green peppers and salt in a large bowl or crock. Add ice water and ice to cover; let stand for 3 hours. Drain; place in a large kettle and set aside. Combine vinegar, sugar and spices; stir well and pour over cucumber mixture. Bring to a boil over medium-high heat. Reduce heat and continue cooking until cucumbers turn a deep yellow color. Remove from heat and fill hot sterilized jars, leaving ½-inch headspace. Wipe rims and secure lids and rings. Process for 20 minutes in a boiling-water bath. Set jars on a towel to cool. Check for seals. Makes 6 jars.

Rhonda Hauenstein
Tell City, IN

Bread & Butter Pickes

menus for all occasions

Fright Night Fun
Serves 6

Halloween Party Mix (page 268)

Parmesan Cheesy Twists (page 279)

Trick-or-Treaters' Taco Soup (page 283)

Black Kitty Kat Cupcakes (page 305)

Caramel Apples (page 312)

Easter Tea
Serves 8

Minty Orange Iced Tea (page 64)

Egg Salad Minis (page 86)

Cucumber Tea Sandwiches (page 293)

Watercress & Cream Cheese Sandwiches (page 86)

Grand Ma-Ma's Deviled Eggs (page 64)

Yummy Carrot Cake (page 206)

Supper for your Sweetie

Serves 4

Filet Mignon with Mushrooms (page 238)

Savory Mashed Potatoes (page 88)

steamed green beans

Hot Fudge Brownie Sundaes (page 160)

Star-Spangled Supper

Serves 8

Mother's Fried Chicken (page 129)

Smoky Grilled Corn (page 144)

Tomato Pie (page 143)

Tangy Watermelon Salad (page 155)

Patriotic Cupcakes (page 305)

Snacks for Game Day

Serves 12

Claudia's Famous Wing Dip (page 165)

Patricia's Super Nachos (page 166)

Mom's Summer Salsa (page 112)

Incredible Mini Burger Bites (page 62)

Cookie Dough Brownies (page 334)

Home Run Hits

Serves 8

Old-Fashioned Ginger Beer (page 170)

Bacon-Stuffed Burgers (page 134)

Buffalo Potato Wedges (page 147)

Grandma Dumeney's Baked Beans
(page 141)

Down-South Creamy Coleslaw (page 303)

*double recipe

Bridal Luncheon

Serves 8

Creamy Asparagus Soup (page 283)

Stuffed Strawberries (page 60)

Rosemary-Dijon Chicken Croissants (page 87)

Michele's Fruit Sticks (page 93)

Aunt Elaine's Pink Lemonade Pie (page 106)

Kid's Christmas Party

Serves 8

Homemade Root Beer (page 116)

Cheesy Pizza Fondue (page 11)

Chili Crescent Cheese Dogs (page 139)

Spicy Carrot French Fries (page 45)

Santa Claus Cookie Pops (page 339)

Homestyle Festive Feast

Serves 12

Ham with Bourbon, Cola & Cherry Glaze (page 289)

*Loaded Baked Potato Casserole (page 49)

*Green Beans Supreme (page 147)

Homemade Butter Rolls (page 227)

Oma's Lemon Cheesecake (page 98)

Holiday Treats Swap

Serves 16

Tiffani's Hot Spiced Cider (page 219)

Cheese Straws (page 318)

Comet's White Chocolate Crunch (page 317)

Sunflower Seed Brittle (page 324)

White Chocolate Cranberry Cookies (page 260)

Crunchy Biscotti (page 312)

* double recipe

Hearty Weekend Breakfast

Serves 4

Multi-Grain Waffles (page 171)

Honey-Baked Bananas (page 171)

Brown Sugar-Glazed Bacon (page 21)

White Cheddar Cheese Grits (page 18)

Simple Weeknight Supper

Serves 4

Simple Chicken Tetrazzini (page 30)

Spring Spinach Sauté (page 93)

Cornmeal-Cheddar Biscuits (page 175)

METRIC EQUIVALENTS

The recipes that appear in this cookbook use the standard U.S. method for measuring liquid and dry or solid ingredients (teaspoons, tablespoons, and cups). The information in the following charts is provided to help cooks outside the United States successfully use these recipes. All equivalents are approximate.

METRIC EQUIVALENTS FOR DIFFERENT TYPES OF INGREDIENTS

A standard cup measure of a dry or solid ingredient will vary in weight depending on the type of ingredient.
A standard cup of liquid is the same volume for any type of liquid. Use the following chart when converting standard cup measures to grams (weight) or milliliters (volume).

Standard Cup	Fine Powder (ex. flour)	Grain (ex. rice)	Granular (ex. sugar)	Liquid Solids (ex. butter)	Liquid (ex. milk)
1	140 g	150 g	190 g	200 g	240 ml
¾	105 g	113 g	143 g	150 g	180 ml
⅔	93 g	100 g	125 g	133 g	160 ml
½	70 g	75 g	95 g	100 g	120 ml
⅓	47 g	50 g	63 g	67 g	80 ml
¼	35 g	38 g	48 g	50 g	60 ml
⅛	18 g	19 g	24 g	25 g	30 ml

USEFUL EQUIVALENTS FOR LIQUID INGREDIENTS BY VOLUME

¼ tsp	=				1 ml
½ tsp	=				2 ml
1 tsp	=				5 ml
3 tsp	= 1 Tbsp		= ½ fl oz	=	15 ml
	2 Tbsp	= ⅛ c	= 1 fl oz	=	30 ml
	4 Tbsp	= ¼ c	= 2 fl oz	=	60 ml
	5⅓ Tbsp	= ⅓ c	= 3 fl oz	=	80 ml
	8 Tbsp	= ½ c	= 4 fl oz	=	120 ml
	10⅔ Tbsp	= ⅔ c	= 5 fl oz	=	160 ml
	12 Tbsp	= ¾ c	= 6 fl oz	=	180 ml
	16 Tbsp	= 1 c	= 8 fl oz	=	240 ml
	1 pt	= 2 c	= 16 fl oz	=	480 ml
	1 qt	= 4 c	= 32 fl oz	=	960 ml
			33 fl oz	=	1000 ml = 1 liter

USEFUL EQUIVALENTS FOR DRY INGREDIENTS BY WEIGHT

(To convert ounces to grams, multiply the number of ounces by 30.)

1 oz	=	1/16 lb	=	30 g
4 oz	=	¼ lb	=	120 g
8 oz	=	½ lb	=	240 g
12 oz	=	¾ lb	=	360 g
16 oz	=	1 lb	=	480 g

USEFUL EQUIVALENTS FOR LENGTH

(To convert inches to centimeters, multiply the number of inches by 2.5.)

1 in			= 2.5 cm		
6 in	= ½ ft		= 15 cm		
12 in	= 1 ft		= 30 cm		
36 in	= 3 ft	= 1 yd	= 90 cm		
40 in			= 100 cm	= 1 meter	

USEFUL EQUIVALENTS FOR COOKING/OVEN TEMPERATURES

	Fahrenheit	Celsius	Gas Mark
Freeze Water	32° F	0° C	
Room Temperature	68° F	20° C	
Boil Water	212° F	100° C	
Bake	325° F	160° C	3
	350° F	180° C	4
	375° F	190° C	5
	400° F	200° C	6
	425° F	220° C	7
	450° F	230° C	8
Broil			Grill

index

Baked Jalapeño Poppers (page 13)

breakfast

Grandma
McKindley's
Waffles (page 67)

cakes & cupcakes

candies

condiments, sauces & seasonings

cookies & bars

desserts

frostings, fillings & toppings

main dishes

Easy Southern-Style
Pork Barbecue
(page 130)

Pumpkin Pie Ice
Cream Fantasy
(page 207)

sandwiches

side dishes

soups & stews

Our Story

Back in 1984, we were next-door neighbors raising our families in the little town of Delaware, Ohio. Two moms with small children, we were looking for a way to do what we loved and stay home with the kids, too. We had always shared a love of home cooking and making memories with family & friends and so, after many a conversation over the backyard fence, **Gooseberry Patch** was born.

We put together our first catalog at our kitchen tables, enlisting the help of our loved ones wherever we could. From that very first mailing, we found an immediate connection with many of our customers and it wasn't long before we began receiving letters, photos and recipes from these new friends. In 1992, we put together our very first cookbook, compiled from hundreds of these recipes and, the rest, as they say, is history.

Hard to believe it's been over 25 years since those kitchen-table days! From that original little Gooseberry Patch family, we've grown to include an amazing group of creative folks who love cooking, decorating and creating as much as we do. Today, we're best known for our homestyle, family-friendly cookbooks, now recognized as national bestsellers.

One thing's for sure, we couldn't have done it without our friends all across the country. Each year, we're honored to turn thousands of your recipes into our collectible cookbooks. Our hope is that each book captures the stories and heart of all of you who have shared with us. Whether you've been with us since the beginning or are just discovering us, welcome to the **Gooseberry Patch** family!

Your friends at Gooseberry Patch

We couldn't make our best-selling cookbooks without YOU!

Each of our books is filled with recipes from cooks just like you, gathered from kitchens all across the country.

Share your tried & true recipes with us on our website and you could be selected for an upcoming cookbook. If your recipe is included, you'll receive a FREE copy of the cookbook when it's published!

www.gooseberrypatch.com

We'd love to add YOU to our Circle of Friends!

Get free recipes, crafts, giveaways and so much more when you join our email club...join us online at all the spots below for even more goodies!